Elba
and the
Tuscan Archipelago

Travellers' Guide

Elba
and the
Tuscan Archipelago

by Christopher and Jean Serpell

with 16 photographs by Alfred Lammer

Jonathan Cape London 1977

First published 1977
Text and maps © Copyright Helga Greene 1977
Photographs © Copyright Alfred Lammer 1977
Maps by Janet Landau
General Editors: Judith Greene and June Gordon-Walker

Jonathan Cape Ltd
30 Bedford Square, London WC1

British Library Cataloguing in Publication Data

Serpell, Christopher
   Elba and the Tuscan Archipelago. – (Travellers' guide).
   Bibl. – Index.
   ISBN 0-224-01352-1
   1. Title 2. Serpell, Jean 3. Lammer, Alfred 4. Series
   914.5'56
   914.5'57   DG975.G/
   Giglio – Description and travel – Guide-books

Typeset by Computacomp (UK) Ltd,
Fort William, Scotland,
and printed in Great Britain
by R. and R. Clark, Edinburgh

CONTENTS

Page 28 **Introduction**

34 **Getting to Elba**
34 Air
35 Sea
35 Rail
36 Road
36 Travel documents

37 **Travel on Elba**
37 Buses
38 Guided tours
38 Taxis
38 Car and motor-scooter hire
39 Motoring
40 Petrol
40 Maps
40 Excursions by sea

42 **Hotels and restaurants**
42 Categories and prices
44 Hotels and pensions
54 Rooms, flats and bungalows to rent
56 Camping
58 Restaurants
59 Nightlife

59 **Practical information**
59 Tourist information
60 Climate and clothes
63 Health and drinking water
65 Money changing and banks
66 Shopping
68 Souvenirs
68 Tipping
69 Cinemas and dancing
70 Sport
72 Holidays and feast days
73 Postal information
75 Weights and measures

77   **Geography and geology**

80   **Minerals**

83   **Flora**

84   **Fauna**

96   **History**
96   Prehistory
97   Classical period
100   Dark and Middle Ages
104   Fourteenth and fifteenth centuries
105   Sixteenth century
111   Seventeenth century
113   Eighteenth century
117   Napoleon and Elba
128   Nineteenth and twentieth centuries

131   **Archaeology**

138   **Population**

139   **Economy**

141   **Government and administration**

141   **Religion**

142   **Language**

143   **Customs and folklore**

144   **Food and drink**

148   **Introduction to routes**
148   Walking

150   **Portoferraio**

170   **Excursions from Portoferraio**
170   Villa San Martino
173   Viticcio and Capo d'Enfola
175   Biodola Bay
176   Portoferraio Bay and Bagnaia
181   Monte Orello, Colle Reciso and Marmi

183   **Route I: Portoferraio to Porto Azzurro**

184 **Porto Azzurro**

186 **Excursions from Porto Azzurro**
186 Sanctuary of Monserrato
189 Naregno and Fort Focardo
189 Rio nell'Elba, Rio Marina and Cavo
194 Capoliveri and Monte Calamita
197 Monte Castello and Cima del Monte

198 **Route 2: Porto Azzurro to Marina di Campo**

203 **Marina di Campo**

205 **Excursions from Marina di Campo**
205 Sant'Ilario, Monte Perone and San Piero
209 Cavoli, Seccheto, Fetovaia and Pomonte

212 **Route 3: Marina di Campo to Marciana Marina**
214 Marciana Alta

216 **Marciana Marina**

217 **Excursions from Marciana Marina**
217 Sanctuary of the Madonna del Monte and Monte Capanne
221 Monte Capanne (by cable-car), Poggio and Monte Perone
224 West coast towards Sant'Andrea

225 **Route 4: Marciana Marina to Portoferraio**

228 **Giglio**

228 **Getting to Giglio**
228 Road
228 Rail
229 Sea

230 **Travel on Giglio**

230 Roads
230 Buses
230 Taxis and car hire

231 **Hotels and restaurants**
231 Hotels and pensions
232 Bungalows and camping sites
233 Restaurants

234 **Practical information**
234 Tourist information
234 Health and drinking water
234 Bank
234 Shopping and souvenirs
234 Dancing
234 Holidays and feast days
234 Post Office

235 **Geography**

236 **Fauna and flora**

236 **History**

239 **Archaeology and architecture**

241 **Population and economy**

242 **Government and administration**

242 **Religion**

242 **People, language and customs**

243 **Wine**

243 **Routes**
245 Excursions from Giglio Porto
246 Excursions from Giglio Castello

249 **Selected bibliography**

250 **Index**

MAPS AND CHARTS

page 26 Chart of excursions
87 Historical chart
126 Napoleon on Elba
146 Diagram of routes, excursions and walks for Elba
152 Portoferraio
244 Diagram of excursions and walks for Giglio

Madonna del Monte

right   Madonna di Monserrato

below   Votive offerings in the vestry of Madonna del Monte

right Market, Portoferraio

below Elban peasant and donkey near San Piero in Campo

right Terraced field on the Sant'Andrea-Chiessi coast road

below Spiaggia delle Ghiaie (beach of pebbles)

right Lighthouse on Forte Stella, Portoferraio

below Torre di San Giovanni

Golfo Stella (nearest), Golfo della Lacona, and Golfo di Campo. Monte Capanne in the background. View from the Capoliveri-Calamita road

Fortress of Volterraio

Porto Azzurro: fishing nets and harbour

Portoferraio harbour: view from Forte Falcone

right   View from the Monte Perone road towards Marina di Campo
below   Mulini Gardens, Portoferraio

Poggio: view from Marciana Alta

Acknowledgments
Our thanks are due above all to Helga and Stuart Connolly who inspired this book and encouraged our researches with their kindness and hospitality. We also owe much to John Greenwood of the London office of the Italian State Tourist Organization who took an active interest in our work and, with his colleagues in the Rome office of his organization and in the provincial offices of Livorno and Grosseto, was able to assist us at various times with transport and accommodation. We are also grateful for the help given to us by British Airways and Alitalia.

In Elba itself we were always able to depend on the advice and information provided by Dr Gentini, of the Ente per la Valorizzazione dell'Isola d'Elba, and his colleague, Signora Pirras. Dr Ettore Galletti kindly gave us access to the historical records of the Biblioteca Foresiana at Portoferraio, and Professor Alfonso Preziosi, president of the Scuola Media 'Raffaello Foresi', supplied us with much valuable information on local folk-lore. Other expert information on the geology of the island came from our friends and fellow-explorers of Elba, Sandy and Ruth Freir, of Dornoch.

Finally we should like to pay a tribute to the ordinary people of Elba who bore our curiosity with courtesy and patience and invariably showed themselves friendly and helpful.

Chart of Excursions

TOWN SIGHTS

	Major	**Minor**
Portoferraio	*Old Town* Medicean Harbour and Fortifications Porta a Mare Forte Stella Palazzina dei Mulini Galeazze (covered market) Church of the Holy Sacrament Church of the Misericordia *New Town* Le Ghiaie beach	Piazza della Repubblica Cathedral Piazza Cavour Roman Altar at Town Hall Porta a Terra Forte Falcone (exterior) Le Viste beach Salita Napoleone Teatro dei Vigilanti
Porto Azzurro	Waterfront Porto Longone prison-fortress	Church and Oratory of San Giacomo
Marina di Campo		Watchtower in old port
Marciana Alta and Marciana Marina	*Marciana Alta* Old Town Fortress Antiquarium museum	*Marciana Alta* City wall and gateway Parish church *Marciana Marina* Watchtower and breakwater Promenade

OUT OF TOWN

Major

Excursion A
Villa San Martino (6km.) p. 170
Excursion D
Roman Villa at Le Grotte (6km.) p. 177
Volterraio Fortress (11km.) p. 179

Minor

Excursion B
Viticcio (6km.) Capo d'Enfola (6·6km)
p. 173
Excursion C
Biodola Bay (10km.) p. 175
Excursion D
Church of Santo Stefano (10km.) p. 178
Bagnaia (12·5km.) p. 179
Nisporto (15km.) Nisportino (18·5km.)
p. 179
Excursion E
Monte Orello, Colle Reciso (26km.)
p. 181

Excursion 1A
Sanctuary of Monserrato (2·5km.) p. 187
Excursion 1C
Rio nell'Elba (10km.) p. 191
Grassera site (13·3km.) p. 191
Rio Marina (12km.) p. 192
(Mineral museum and iron mines)
Excursion 1D
Capoliveri (5·3km.) p. 194
Calamita Peninsula (15km.) p. 196
Excursion 1E
Monte Castello (8km.) p. 197

Excursion 1A
Barbarossa beach (1·5km.) Reale beach
(2·5km.) p. 188
Excursion 1B
Naregno beach (3·8km.) p. 189
Fort Focardo (4·3km.) p. 189
Excursion 1C
Cavo (19·5km.) Ortano (15km.) p. 193
Excursion 1D
Madonna delle Grazie (8km.) p. 196

Excursion 2A
Sant'Ilario (5·7km.) and San Piero (church &
belvedere) (8km.) p. 205
San Giovanni (ruined church and watchtower)
(8km.) p. 206

Route 2
Madonna di Lacona (12km.) p. 200
The Monument (12km.) (Walks from
this point) p. 201
Excursion 2B
Seccheto (7·5km.) p. 209
Pomonte (13·8km.) p. 211

Excursion 3A
Sanctuary of Madonna del Monte (11km.)
p. 217
Shrine of San Cerbone (11·5km.) p. 219
Excursion 3B
Monte Capanne (9·6km.) p. 221
Poggio (7·6km.) (Church of San Niccolo and
Church of San Difendente) p. 223

Route 3
Chiessi (12·6km.) p. 212
Sant'Andrea (21·2km.) p. 213
Church of San Lorenzo (26·2km.)
p. 216
Excursion 3B
Fonte Napoleone (6km.) p. 222
Monte Perone (8·8km.) p. 224
Route 4
Procchio (7·4km.) p. 226

INTRODUCTION

The Tuscan Archipelago consists of seven Italian islands, together with a few islets and shoals, all of them but one lying between the west coast of the mainland of Italy, in the region of Tuscany, and the northern half of the French island of Corsica. The one exception is the small island of Gorgona, lying slightly farther north. The archipelago falls naturally into two sections; a northern group of islands – including Elba, Pianosa, Capraia and Gorgona – which forms part of the administrative Province of Livorno, and a southern group – Giglio, Giannutri and Montecristo. The two former are part of the Province of Grosseto; Montecristo comes under the communal administration of Portoferraio in Elba.

The two largest islands, Elba and Giglio, are the only ones capable of accommodating a large influx of visitors, and it is with them that this Guide is principally concerned. Of the other islands, three – Pianosa, Capraia and Gorgona – are the sites of Italian penal colonies; in Pianosa and Gorgona visitors are not allowed to land without a permit (see p. 41). Although part of the territory of Capraia lies outside the prison precincts, no attempt has been made to encourage tourists to visit there. In the southern group, Montecristo, which has been private property in the past, is now a national nature reserve and virtually uninhabited; day excursions can be made to it from Giglio during the summer season but permits for individuals to land or camp there are rarely given and must be obtained from the State Property Office (*Demanio dello Stato*) in Rome. Giannutri was also until recently the private property of a single family; it has now been divided among several privately-owned summer villas and also contains a small camping-site mainly used by skin-divers; during the summer ferries call there from Giglio and the mainland harbour of Porto Santo Stefano.

Elba, the largest island of the archipelago and the main subject of this book, has been said to offer three surprises to those who visit it for the first time: it is less remote, less diminutive, and less lonely than people imagine. (Indeed some people, with its Napoleonic associations in mind, are apt to confuse it with St Helena.) In fact, it is barely eleven kilometres from the Italian mainland at the port of Piombino, and connected with it by frequent car and passenger ferries. Its area, 224·6 square kilometres, is roughly half that of the Isle of Wight or twice that of the island of Jersey. Since the early 1950s it has made tourism its main industry; it now has nearly 200 hotels of various categories, numerous *pensioni* or private hotels, several motels and camping sites. Recently developers have added holiday villas and blocks of apartments to the available accommodation. It has an adequate network of motor-roads, and the island is large enough to absorb all this development without being seriously disfigured except in a few restricted areas. Its many beaches, crowded as they are during the height of the summer season, are still relatively empty during the so-called 'low seasons' of spring and late summer.

The shape of Elba on the map could be compared with that of an archaic and many-finned fish, a coelacanth perhaps, with its blunt head pointing westwards towards Corsica and its wide, fluked tail towards the Italian mainland. Its greatest dimension as the crow flies – from nose to tail, as it were – is just over 30km. (19 miles); its breadth, from north to south, varies from 21km. (13 miles) at the widest to less than 5km. (3 miles) at the narrowest; and these variations are due to the many promontories or 'fins' which give it a coastline some 147km. (92 miles) long.

This irregular coastline provides a succession of bays and beaches, some sandy, some shingly, and some just rocky coves; it reflects also the essentially mountainous character of the island. The surface of Elba is crumpled into an extraordinary variety of peaks and valleys which give it one of the most romantically beautiful landscapes of Southern Europe and, incidentally, make all local distances by road much greater than they might appear on the map. Relief maps show more than twenty named *monti,* or mountains, in Elba; they are none of them very high – Monte Capanne, at the western end of the island, dominates it at 3,308 feet – but they are all the outcome of geological disturbances which have tilted the rock strata in all directions and given the hills an impressively dramatic appearance. The highest slopes are bare rock and boulders; below them there are either forests of sweet chestnut and other trees, or stretches of the richly aromatic *macchia* (or, as the French call it, *maquis*), a dense vegetation of Mediterrean shrubs and flowering plants. Wherever a hillside offers the slightest opportunity for cultivation, the Elbans have terraced it for the vines which produce the island's excellent wine, though nowadays some of the highest terracing has been abandoned and allowed to revert to *macchia*. Only in the eastern fringe of the island, on the mountain slopes facing the mainland, does the ancient Elban industry of iron-ore mining continue on a modest scale; it is mainly open-cast mining which has scooped the hillside into a series of semicircular shelves. As an industry it is curiously unobtrusive, partly because it is screened from the rest of Elba by the eastern mountain range and partly because it involves very little industrial plant or processing; the ore is now all shipped to foundries on the mainland.

The Elban climate resembles that of mainland Tuscany, modified and mitigated by the surrounding sea. Winters are milder and summers more temperate than on the mainland. Bad weather for the Elbans tends to be windy weather, particularly during the winter months. In summer the breezes off the sea provide a welcome ventilation, and even in the cooler days of spring and autumn the hilly landscape can usually provide shelter from the wind if needed. As might be expected, there is abundant sunshine.

Elba offers scope for more than one kind of holiday, and it is small enough too for the visitor to sample more than one kind during the same stay and from the same centre. For the sea-lover there is every kind of beach and every kind of diversion. The broad, sandy 'plages', like those of Procchio or Biodola on the north coast or Lacona and Marina di Campo in the south, are ideal for sun-bathers and families with young children. Generally speaking, bathing is safe except in rough weather all round the island, although the bottom shelves steeply in the rocky inlets at the western end of Elba and along the little-frequented eastern coast of the Calamita promontory. These rocky stretches of coast, with their deep and clear waters, are much favoured by skin-divers. There are sailing-dinghy clubs in the Bay of Portoferraio, at Cavo on the east coast, and elsewhere. Many visitors bring their own inflatable rubber dinghies with outboard-motors, so that in calm weather they can explore the coastline from one cove to the next.

Inland there are the mountains offering a quite different world, although it is only a mile or two from the beaches. Motorists making a hurried visit can sample the mountain scenery without leaving their cars; a new and finely engineered road climbs across the western massif from Marina di Campo and Sant'Ilario on the south side to Poggio and Marciana on the northern slopes and then down to the coast road along the north shoreline. The eastern range of limestone hills is crossed by a rougher but still quite practicable road which links Magazzini, on the Bay of Portoferraio, with Rio nell'Elba and Rio Marina on the east coast. There are also the rough-surfaced and often pot-holed secondary roads which penetrate more deeply into the hills; these are quite passable for the small car driven slowly and with due regard to the suspension. And finally there are many mule-tracks and footpaths which once formed Elba's only network of communications and still take the walker into lonely and enchanting places (see Diagram of Routes, p. 146); it is paths like these which make the island a unique place for the traveller with specialized interests – for the rock-climber and hill-walker, for the geologist and 'rock-hunter', for the botanist, bird-watcher, and naturalist.

The 'sights' of Elba are modest and limited in number. There is the walled city of old Portoferraio, constructed as a single architectural unit for Cosimo de' Medici in the sixteenth century and, in spite of war damage and rebuilding, still a pleasant place in which to spend a morning exploring, shopping, photographing or sketching. There are the places associated with Napoleon, notably the Palazzina dei Mulini in old Portoferraio and the country residence, Villa San Martino, just outside the capital. It is perhaps worth making the point here that Napoleon, during the ten months he spent in Elba, was still nominally a reigning sovereign; the island was allocated to him as his 'principality' and in it he held his court and maintained his miniature army. The restraints on his liberty were largely formal and, as the event proved, easily evaded; it was not until after he had escaped and had been defeated at Waterloo that he became the lonely prisoner-exile of St Helena.

Other 'sights' exist in Elba but more as an excuse for an outing through lovely scenery than for their intrinsic importance. There are the remains of a vast Roman villa, mainly foundations and underground store-rooms, overlooking Portoferraio Bay (see p. 177). There are the relics of the Pisan occupation of the island in the eleventh and twelfth centuries – watch-towers set up to give warning of the North African corsairs, severe little romanesque churches, abandoned, mostly roofless and sited usually in solitary places, and the magnificent eagle's-nest of a stronghold, Volterraio, perched on a crag high above Portoferraio Bay. There are a number of sanctuaries of the Madonna, plain edifices frequented once or twice a year by pilgrims on the appropriate feast day, but otherwise left deserted in remote corners of the woods and mountains; outstanding among them are the sanctuary of the Madonna del Monte in the mountains above Marciana, and that of the Madonna di Monserrato in a nightingale-haunted limestone gorge, north of Porto Azzurro. And there are the picturesque hill-villages of Monte Capanne, on the north side Poggio and Marciana, to the south San Piero and Sant'Ilario. They all have the remains of fortifications which in the end failed to protect them against raiders from the sea; today they are all subjects for the artist or photographer.

In an island as small and as well served with roads as Elba, recommendations on where to stay are perhaps less necessary than usual. Generally speaking, people who want to stay in lively centres of population, with a choice of restaurants, a cinema or two, and a variety of souvenir shops, should look for accommodation in Portoferraio itself, in Porto Azzurro, Marciana Marina, or Marina di Campo. The best *sandy* beaches, as already mentioned, are to be found at Biodola, Procchio, Lacona and Marina di Campo. Campers will find a number of sites mentioned in this guide (p. 56); on the whole, Lacona Bay offers the greatest choice. People who want to get away from the crowd and are willing to put up with simple (but always clean) accommodation should consider some of the smaller villages and resorts; for example, Morcone on the west coast of the Calamita promontory, Seccheto and Fetovaia at the western end of the south coast, Sant'Andrea and Viticcio on the north coast. But these are only a few names among many and much will depend on individual preferences. The saving clause is that, even if you are disappointed in the locality where you have booked accommodation, a car or a moped or even the local bus will open up the rest of the island for your daily excursions.

It is, however, important to offer one warning to intending visitors to Elba. In spite of their rapid and continuing development, the island's tourist facilities are fully stretched during the 'high season', that is, from the second half of June to mid-September. The island's main roads carry a lot of traffic during this season; and even the normally adequate water supply is over-taxed and has to be supplemented by tanker-vessels. On the other hand the Italians, who form the majority of the high-season visitors, leave Elba comparatively alone during the two 'low seasons' – from Easter to mid-June, and from mid-September to the end of October. The casual visitor will then find plenty of accommodation of all kinds at short notice and at lower prices, even though some of the larger establishments will have begun to close down for the winter before the end of October. The roads will be much less crowded and there will be surprisingly few people on the beaches. And yet, apart from the occasional showery or windy day, the weather of either low season is as warm and sunny as that of an exceptionally good English summer; sea-bathing, especially in September and October, is not merely possible but thoroughly enjoyable.

This general consideration applies also to the smaller island of Giglio which, because it is not only smaller but nearer to Rome, tends to be even more overcrowded during the high season, but equally welcoming before and after it.

Only 9km. (5½ miles) long and 5km. (3 miles) wide, Giglio is the dry-land summit of a single submarine mountain. It is primarily a resort for those who enjoy boating, bathing from the rocks, and skin-diving. It has one fair-sized sandy beach at Giglio Campese but, along most of its coastline, its slopes plunge steeply into a wonderfully clear sea; and wherever they are furrowed by a watercourse, they open into little rocky coves at sea-level, many of them only accessible by sea. Inland, it is a place of vineyards, *macchia,* and bare rock; the only 'sight' is the ancient walled town of Giglio Castello on the mountain crest, a picturesque huddle of old tenements, narrow streets, and flights of steps within the enclosing ramparts. Hotels, *pensioni,* and rooms to let are to be found mainly in the neighbourhood of Giglio Porto, the harbour for the ferry services which connect the island with the mainland terminal, Porto Santo Stefano, and at the little resort of Giglio Campese on the island's west coast.

This Guide deals first with Elba, describing how to get there and how to use the communications of the island itself, listing hotels, *pensioni,* and restaurants and offering practical advice on how to get the best out of a holiday there. A section on its geography, geology, history and natural history is followed by another listing the routes that may be followed by those exploring the island. The second part of the Guide deals similarly but more briefly with Giglio. The Chart of Excursions (p. 26–7) is designed to give help in planning expeditions and lists the main sights in each area.

GETTING TO ELBA

For the latest information on fares and timetables consult the Italian State Tourist Office (E.N.I.T. for short), 201 Regent Street, London W1R 8AY.

AIR

The international airport nearest to Elba is at Pisa, some 106km. to the north of Piombino, which is the mainland terminus for ferries to the island. British Airways and Alitalia combine to provide a daily scheduled service between London and Pisa; the flight time is approximately two hours. The flights normally leave Heathrow during the morning, arriving at Pisa in time for lunch; return flights are usually in the afternoon. Charter flights also operate between British airports and Pisa, and some travel firms which offer package tours to Elba provide transport by bus from Pisa to the ferries.

Although Elba has no full-scale airport, it does have a single-runway grass airstrip, suitable for light aircraft only. During the summer a private airline, Aerelba, runs a service between Pisa and Elba, operating only once a day on Mondays, Wednesdays and Fridays; the flight time is 30 minutes, and take-off from Pisa is at 13.45. Travellers to Elba using this service should arrange beforehand with their hotels for transport to meet them at the island airstrip.

Both British Airways and Alitalia offer 'fly-drive' schemes which enable passengers to pick up a rented car on arrival and use it for their holiday in Italy; this is particularly convenient for visitors to Elba who will thus be able to drive immediately from Pisa airport to Piombino, and will also find it a great advantage to have their own transport on the island itself. It is advisable to allow two hours for the journey by road from Pisa to the car-ferry terminal at Piombino.

The Italian tourist agency, CIT, also offers a 'fly-drive' scheme involving a two weeks, go-as-you-please tour in a hired car. As far as Elba is concerned, this scheme is based on Sunday charter flights between Gatwick Airport and Pisa; it has the added advantage that CIT supplies free 2nd class railway tickets to London from anywhere on the British mainland for travellers booking one of their package holidays. The prices vary according to the number of persons planning to share the car for a two week holiday.

SEA

From Piombino, two shipping lines, TO.RE.MAR. and NAV.AR.MA., run regular car-ferry services to Portoferraio in Elba; some of these services also stop en route at Cavo, the Elban harbour nearest to the mainland. During the high season — from the end of June to the middle of September — each line runs ten services a day; in the two low seasons — from April 22nd to June 27th, and from September 18th to 30th — they each run eight services; out of season each runs five services. The trip to Portoferraio takes about one hour; cars are driven directly on and off the ship at either end; the ferries are commodious vessels with bars and restaurants. During the high season it is advisable to book car-passages in advance, otherwise you may have to queue for the first available space. Bookings can be made through travel agencies in London or by telephoning the shipping line branch offices on the quayside at Piombino. The telephone number for TO.RE.MAR. is Piombino 32508 or 31100; for NAV.AR.MA. 33031 (Telex 50293). TO.RE.MAR. also run a daily ferry service to Rio Marina and Porto Azzuro

Between Piombino and Portoferraio hydrofoil services, for foot-passengers only, are run by Società Alilauro Aliscafi S.N.A.V. During the summer the hydrofoils run roughly twice an hour and take a half-hour for the trip.

One car-ferry service a day is run to Portoferraio from Livorno between mid-April and the end of September. The ship, *Capo Bianco,* belongs to TO.RE.MAR. and leaves Livorno at 08.30, except on Wednesdays when it sails at 13.00. The trip takes about three hours.

RAIL

Access by rail to Piombino is by a branch line connecting the port with Campiglia Marittima, a station on the main line which runs down the west coast between the Italian border and Rome. Passengers on international trains should make sure they are due to stop at Campiglia; otherwise it is necessary to change on to a locally stopping train at Pisa Central. The Italian railway system maintains two timetables, one for the summer months from the last Sunday in May to the last Saturday in September, the other for the rest of the year. During the summer, there are seventeen trains a day, from 06.29 to 21.10, from Campiglia Marittima to Piombino Marittima, the quayside terminus of the line; passengers should be careful not to leave the train at two earlier stops in the *town* of Piombino. With more than one service an hour, passengers do not often have to wait long to make the connection at Campiglia. Typical journeys, based on the summer timetables, are:

Pisa	Campiglia	Campiglia	Piombino M.
	11.50		13.21		13.39		14.06
dep.	14.20	arr.	15.27	dep.	15.32	arr.	15.57
	15.44		16.45		17.16		17.42

ROAD

Motorists in a hurry to reach Elba from points beyond the Italian border will find the *autostrada* (motorway) network useful. One *autostrada* can be joined at Ventimiglia, on the Riviera frontier with France, and followed along the coast past Genoa, La Spezia and Pisa to a point a few kilometres north of Livorno. Here it joins National Route 1 which should be followed south through Cecina to a small town called San Vincenzo, some 80km. south of Pisa. Here a sign-posted road forking off to the right covers the remaining 22km. to Piombino. For motorists entering Italy through the Alps there are other *autostrada* links with the route from Ventimiglia; one such link joins Turin with Savona on the coast route; another runs from Milan to Genoa; a third runs from Florence and joins the coast route just north of Pisa.

Motorists heading for Elba from Rome can either take the Rome–Florence autostrada and then the Florence–Pisa link, or they can proceed more directly northwards along National Route 1 up the coastline. At Venturina, 63km. north of Grosseto, they will find a branch road off to the left to Piombino.

TRAVEL DOCUMENTS

A British passport-holder requires no visa for travel to Italy.

For motorists, whether they are driving their own car or picking up a hired vehicle in Italy, a British driving licence meets official requirements but should be accompanied by an Italian translation (obtainable, free, from the A.A. or the R.A.C. or from E.N.I.T. (p. 59)); an international driving licence is an acceptable alternative and does not require a translation. The 'green card' or international insurance certificate is no longer strictly necessary for motorists inside countries which, like Italy, are members of the European Economic

Community; but it is still strongly recommended by motoring organizations and travel agents. It has the effect of increasing third-party coverage to comprehensive and sometimes reassures local authorities that insurance requirements have been met.

There are usually Italian tourist petrol concessions – 26 per cent reduction – for cars entering the country from the U.K. and elsewhere; for details apply to E.N.I.T. (p. 59), or to one of the British motoring organizations. Such concessions do not apply to cars hired by tourists inside Italy.

TRAVEL ON ELBA

BUSES

Regular scheduled bus services (*autolinee*) radiate from Portoferraio to the rest of the island; they all start from Calata Matteotti in the old harbour, and they all make a second stop five minutes later on Calata Italia in the modern harbour.

There are three main bus routes. The first goes from Portoferraio to Porto Azzurro with interconnecting services to Cavo and other points along the east coast, and a subsidiary service to Capoliveri and Pareti. The second route runs along the north coast to Procchio and then turns south across the island to Marina di Campo; from there it follows the coast road westwards as far as Pomonte. (Two services a day on this route turn back from Fetovaia to call at the hill-villages of San Piero and Sant'Ilario.) The third route also goes to Procchio but then continues along the north coast as far as Marciana Marina where it turns inland and uphill to Poggio and Marciana Alta, with an occasional extension on to Pomonte from the north. There is also a twice-a-day service between Portoferraio and the neighbouring bay of Biodola. For roads traversed by bus services see the front end-paper.

The Elban bus system is not unnaturally designed to meet the requirements of the inhabitants of the island rather than those of visitors; the services start at an unearthly hour in the morning and their frequency – never very great – is reduced on Sundays and holidays (*giorni festivi*). Even on weekdays (*giorni feriali*) some services are cancelled when the schools are closed for the holidays. The bus timetable is therefore extremely complicated and visitors who plan to use public transport, especially cross-country walkers, are advised to go as soon as possible to the headquarters of the bus company (*Società Autolinee Elbane*), on the ground floor of the skyscraper (*grattacielo*) in modern Portoferraio, and ask for a copy of the current timetable (*Orario in vigore*); the entrance to the company's offices is in Viale Elba, just round the corner from Calata Italia. With the help of this timetable, visitors may be able to adjust their itineraries to avoid long and frustrating waits at the bus-stop (*fermata*). There are plenty of such stops along the main roads but the buses do not pick up or set down passengers between them. The timetable is usually *not* displayed at these wayside stops.

GUIDED TOURS

A number of half-day and whole-day guided bus-tours are available for those who wish to see the outstanding features of Elba in a hurry. They are organized by the travel agencies, and details of them may be obtained in Portoferraio from Agenzia Viaggi Aethaltours in Viale Elba, or from Agenzia Viaggi Intourelba, Via Carducci.

TAXIS

The main taxi-rank is in Portoferraio at the landward end of the main jetty, Molo Massimo, ready to provide transport for foot-passengers leaving the ferries. From here the taxi-drivers are prepared to take you anywhere in the island, including places which are far from the bus-routes. But the fares are not cheap, and during the high season are apt to be exaggerated. There is an agreed tariff, but it is not on show and the taxis do not carry meters; it is therefore necessary to ask a driver, before you hire him, how much he will charge to take you to your destination — '*Quanto per andare a ...* ?' Inflation makes it difficult to quote sample taxi-fares, but a visitor wanting to be driven from the jetty to one of the more distant points of Elba, such as Pomonte on the west coast, should reckon on paying at least 10,000 lire (between £6.00 and £7.00).

Some hotels and pensions will meet ferries with their own transport; it may be worth asking about this when making your booking.

CAR AND MOTOR-SCOOTER HIRE

If you wish to hire a car with driver during your stay in Elba for a particular excursion, this too can probably be arranged most cheaply and conveniently through the management of your hotel or pension.

If however you prefer to make your own arrangements, the names and telephone numbers of suitable firms and garages can be found in a booklet, *Notizie utili per il Turista*, issued by the local tourist organization, E.V.E., from its offices in the Portoferraio skyscraper (Calata Italia 26).

If you wish to rent your own self-drive transport, you can arrange for it either by applying in advance to the London office of the Italian Tourist Agency (CIT (England) Ltd, 10 Charles II Street, London SW1Y 4AB), or by going to one of the numerous garages and agencies on the spot. Both Hertz and Avis have branch offices in Portoferraio, the former in Calata Matteotti and the latter in Calata Italia; names and addresses of other agencies will be found in the E.V.E. booklet. As a rough guide to the cost, the rental for a small car, the Fiat 126, in 1976 was 92,000 lire (119 U.S. dollars) a week with unlimited mileage.

If you are so inclined, there is a good deal to be said for touring Elba on a motor-scooter. The lowest powered mopeds will probably not be able to tackle the steeper gradients, but a medium-powered motor-scooter, such as the Vespa 150SV or the Gilera 125SV, will give the rider and a pillion passenger considerable mobility at low cost. The E.V.E. booklet recommends that you rent motor-cycles or scooters from Moto Club Elba, in Via Puccini, Portoferraio.

The driver of a hired car must be at least 21 years old and under 70. For small mopeds under 50c.c., such as the Vespa 50 or the Gilera 50 Trial, no licence is required and the minimum age is 14; for more powerful motor-cycles or scooters, requiring a licence, the minimum age is 18. For driving licence requirements see p. 36.

Although hired cars and scooters are usually insured against third-party risks, it is usually necessary when renting them to pay a small sum over and above the hiring charge to cover damage to the vehicle; the alternative is to put down a returnable deposit which may be as much as £50 for a car.

MOTORING

Driving in Italy is of course on the right-hand side of the road. Unless road signs indicate that side roads are subordinate to the main road, traffic entering the main road from the right has priority; this rule entails the need for caution, especially in towns and built-up areas. It is obligatory for all cars to carry a red warning triangle which, in the event of a break-down, accident, or unforeseen stoppage on the highway, must be set up in the road at least 30 yards behind the car.

The main roads in Elba present no problem except for the large number of blind corners and sharp bends dictated by the geography of the island; these often make passing difficult, especially for British vehicles with right-hand drive. The Italian word for a bend in the road is *curva*, and a common Elban road sign says *curve continue per x kilometri*. The word *tornanti*, also seen on road signs, means hairpin bends of the kind that may require a gear change.

The Elban secondary roads, sometimes misleadingly described on local maps as *strade a macadam*, are rough by British standards; their metalling consists often of loose stones scattered on a sandy road-bed, and there are pot-holes and wash-outs resulting from the winter storms. But most of these roads can be negotiated without much difficulty by the enterprising motorist who is prepared to take them slowly and with due regard for the car's suspension; it goes without saying that they are not suitable for the large American-type car. Such roads are worth exploring because they will often conduct the motorist into unfrequented parts of the island, including some of the finest mountain scenery.

PETROL

There are filling stations in and around all the inhabited centres of Elba. Petrol is expensive, especially the 'super' grade recommended for private cars, but in Elba at least mileages are apt to be short. Italian cars are generally designed to be economical in fuel consumption.

MAPS

The Touring Club Italiano (CTI) series (scale 1:200,000) of road maps of Italy covers Elba and the southern islands of the archipelago on sheet 15; however this is rather a small-scale map for anyone wishing to explore the islands thoroughly. This and a larger-scale map of Elba (1:50,000) published by Litografia Artistica Cartografica, Florence, can be obtained in England from Edward Stanford Ltd, 12–14 Long Acre, London WC2, or from The Map House, 54 Beauchamp Place, London SW3.

For information about large-scale maps for walkers see p. 149.

EXCURSIONS BY SEA

The circuit of the Elban coastline by motor-launch is recommended as offering a series of fine views and also a good general idea of the variety of the island's scenery and geology. Regular trips are run from Portoferraio throughout the summer; inquiries about timetable and bookings should be made to Umberto Giulianetti at the *Bagni Elba* establishment on Le Ghiaie beach, or to local tourist agencies. Motor-launch excursions are also arranged from Porto Azzurro. Small motorboats and craft with outboard motors may be hired at Porto Azzurro and Marina di Campo.

The sheltered waters of Portoferraio Bay are ideal for small sailing craft; a number of sailing clubs and sailing schools exist along its shores, most of them catering for beginners and some of them attached to hotels (see p. 71).

Travellers who want to get a close view of the other islands in the northern sector of the Tuscan Archipelago – Gorgona and Capraia to the north of Elba, and Pianosa to the south – may do so by taking one of the regular ferries operated by TO.RE.MAR. Because there are penal colonies on all three islands, landings on Gorgona and Pianosa are not allowed without a special permit issued by the Italian Ministry of Justice, granted normally only to relatives visiting the inmates, and part of Capraia is also closed to those without such permits. In the unrestricted area of Capraia there is reported to be 'limited accommodation in inns and private houses', but the local inhabitants have done little to encourage tourism.

To visit at least the harbours of Capraia and Gorgona, the determined traveller must take the ferry service which leaves Portoferraio on Mondays only at 13.00, and after calling at Marciana Marina goes, by way of the two islands, to Livorno where it arrives at 18.00. It is not possible to return the same day, but a boat leaving Livorno at 8.00 on Tuesdays makes the direct trip back to Portoferraio in just under three hours. There are services to Pianosa on Wednesdays and Saturdays; starting from Piombino the Wednesday boat calls at Rio Marina and Porto Azzurro, the Saturday boat also at Marina di Campo. Travellers without permits must stay on board until the boat returns. It is risky even to approach the coastline of Pianosa in private craft; not long ago the guards of the penal colony, who were expecting an escape attempt, opened fire on three young Germans in a rubber dinghy who ignored their signals and came in too close; one of them was killed.

HOTELS AND RESTAURANTS

There are, normally speaking, three ways of finding accommodation for a stay in Elba.

(1) Join a package tour in which all arrangements will be made by the organizers.

(2) Select your own accommodation by writing, in the first instance and early in the year, to the local tourist organization (Ente Valorizzazione Elba, 57037 Portoferraio, Calata Italia 26, Isola d'Elba, Provincia Livorno, Italy), and asking for their current list of 'Hotels, pensions and inns', with their respective prices for the current year. (You *may* be able to obtain this list from E.N.I.T. in London). Having selected two or three establishments, ask a competent travel agent to make the bookings for you; he may ask you to put down a deposit. Prices are quoted as indicating the maximum and minimum cost of a single room, a double room, and *pensione completa* (i.e. full board); it is usually possible also to arrange for *demi-pensione*, i.e. for bed, breakfast, and one full meal. Most hotels quote two prices under each heading; the second and higher price is for the high season from June 15th to September 15th, the lower being for other periods and especially for the two low seasons, from Easter to June 14th and from September 16th to the end of October.

(3) If you are travelling in Italy, and particularly if you are travelling by car, you may prefer to go directly to Elba and find your own accommodation on the spot. The island is small enough for you to visit and inspect five or six hotels and pensions in a day. But it is *only* worth doing this during one or other of the low seasons: in the high season, virtually all accommodation is fully booked and the chances of finding a last-minute vacancy are small.

CATEGORIES AND PRICES

Italian hotels fall into five classes – *Di Lusso* (i.e. Luxury), and 1st, 2nd, 3rd, and 4th class; there are no luxury hotels in Elba but all the other classes are represented. This classification is based mainly on the amenities and the scale of accommodation provided, and it is arranged by the provincial tourist boards (for Elba, the tourist board of Livorno). The list is published officially and is valid for two years, after which it may be revised. It is not uncommon in Elba or elsewhere in Italy to find a hotel which seems to qualify for a class higher than that under which it is listed; this is either because it has been developed and improved during the two years since it was listed, or because the management sees some tax advantages in remaining in a class lower than that to which the hotel is entitled.

Hotel prices, which are revised every year, have no direct connection with the classification, although obviously the higher you go in the scale of amenities the more you will be expected to pay. But within each class prices may vary from one hotel to another; they are fixed by the hoteliers with regard to local competition and to what they think the market will bear. The hotelier will then pass his tariff to the provincial tourist board which will register it for the current year; during that period they must not exceed the published maxima.

The official description of the amenities required from each class of hotel is misleading, being based on out-of-date minimum requirements. For example, the official definition of a luxury hotel stipulates that at least 50 per cent of its bedrooms must have private bathrooms; in practice every guest booking into a luxury hotel and paying its prices would expect a private bathroom. In Elba all three 1st Class hotels, most of those in the 2nd Class and many in lower categories offer bathrooms with every double room; in the lower categories the bathroom may provide a shower rather than a bath. Perhaps the clearest distinction between classes of hotel lies in the number of bedrooms and the extent of the public rooms at the disposal of the guests. Fourth class hotels must have at least nine bedrooms; third class hotels a mimimum of 30 bedrooms. Both these classes must also have a 'hall' and a dining-room, according to the official definitions, as well as service-bells, a toilet on every floor, and 'a qualified person always on duty'. In practice, they are likely to have running water in every bedroom and perhaps a private shower and toilet for at least half the bedrooms. Hotels of the first and second classes must have at least 40 bedrooms and a much greater range of public rooms. One of the disadvantages of hotels in the lower categories is that, unless you retreat to your bedroom, you cannot escape the television, usually installed in the only available lounge and almost invariably turned up to maximum volume. Outdoor amenities, such as swimming pools and tennis courts, are not mentioned in the official descriptions of the five categories; in practice they are almost invariably provided by Luxury and 1st Class hotels, and often appear in the lower categories as well. In Elba there are 2nd and 3rd class hotels with tennis courts, and at least two 3rd class pensions with swimming pools.

Pensioni are sometimes misleadingly equated with boarding-houses; in fact the English term does not convey the character or atmosphere of an Italian *pensione* which is much more like a small private hotel, providing a restaurant with separate tables, often a bar, and sometimes a garden or open-air terrace. Officially 1st, 2nd, and 3rd class pensions must offer the same amenities as 2nd, 3rd, and 4th class hotels; in practice a 3rd class pension may have more bedrooms, and indeed more bedrooms with bathrooms, than a 4th class hotel. For the visitor the important diference is that the rates charged by a pension will usually be lower than those of the equivalent class of hotel; the number of staff will be smaller; and frequently the management will consist of the owner's family plus some outside assistance during the high season. Below the 3rd class pension, there is one other category, the *locanda*, usually translated as 'inn' or 'lodging-house', where the accommodation is of the simplest variety and there may not even be a telephone. But here, as in all the higher categories of accommodation, the visitor to Elba can be sure of finding absolute cleanliness; this is ensured not only by the inpsections of the tourist board but also by the naturally high standards of the Elban people.

HOTELS AND PENSIONS

The following list of hotels, pensions, and lodging-houses is not necessarily exhaustive, although it is based on official lists available at the time of writing, for the tourist industry in Elba is still expanding. The list is intended as a general guide to the types of accommodation available in the various parts of the island with some indication of where the various establishments may be found. Telephone numbers are given in brackets.

Portoferraio and District
HOTELS
First Class   *Hermitage*, La Biodola (93932).
                       Above broad sandy beach of secluded Biodola Bay, ten minutes' drive from capital; accommodation includes independent bungalow suites, skilfully located on wooded slope.

Second Class

Acquabona, Acquabona (98212).

Out-of-town and inland, on road to Porto Azzurro; owning and adjoining Elba's only (nine-hole) golf course.

Adriana, Padulella (92057).

Just outside Portoferraio, on north coast of promontory; pleasant, family-run establishment with bedrooms opening on to terraces overlooking small, shingly cove.

Darsena, Calata Mazzini 11 (92661).

Modern building incorporated into harbour-wall of old, walled city.

Fabricia, Magazzini (966181).

Out-of-town, near fishing-village on Portoferraio Bay, looking across at old city.

Garden, Schiopparello (966043).

Out-of-town, overlooking bay; suites with separate entrances; pine-shaded grounds; own sand and gravel beach.

La Biodola, La Biodola (93966).

Same locality as Hermitage (see above).

Massimo, Calata Italia 23 (92766).

New building on harbour-front of modern Portoferraio, near ferry-jetty.

Picchiaie Residence, Picchiaie (966072).

Out-of-town and inland; modern bungalow-style accommodation sited on hilltop with fine views.

Touring, Via Roma 13 (93851).

Inside old city, small but well-appointed.

Villa Ottone, Ottone (966042).

Out-of-town, on Portoferraio Bay; recently modernized with new annexes and also separate bungalow-style accommodation.

Third Class

Ape Elbana, Salita C. de'Medici (92245).

Inside old city, Elba's oldest hotel.

Emi, Via G. Carducci 32 (92370).

On main thoroughfare through modern city.

Falconetta, Via Ninci 5 (92130).

On quiet street below old city fortifications.

Nobel, Via Manganaro 72 (93217).

In modern Portoferraio.

Villa Fonteviva, Acquaviva (93392).
Out-of-town, on road to Viticcio along north coast.

Fourth Class   *Il Faro*, Le Ghiaie (92364).
On northern edge of town.
Mare, Magazzini (966069).
Out-of-town, on Portoferraio Bay.
Santo Stefano, Santo Stefano (966161).
Out-of-town, inland, in secluded valley.

PENSIONS
Second Class   *Nuova Padulella*, Padulella (93506).
Just outside town, on northern coastline.
Villa Ombrosa, Viale De Gasperi 3 (92363).
On northern edge of town.

Third Class   *Al Tramonto*, Viticcio (93382).
Out-of-town, in seaside village on north coast.
Casa Rosa, La Biodola (93931).
Out-of-town, overlooking Biodola Bay.
Danila, Scaglieri (93915).
Out-of-town, in village on Biodola Bay.
Clara, Bagnaia (966279).
Out of town, on west of Portoferraio bay.
Grotte del Paradiso, Le Grotte (966057).
Out-of-town, on Portoferraio Bay, near remains of
Roman villa.
Nuova Padulella annexe (92742).
Just outside town, on northern coastline.
Soggiorno Paradiso, Viticcio (93385).
Out-of-town, in seaside village on north coast.
Tirrena, Schioparello (966002).
Out-of-town, on Portoferraio Bay.
Villino Marte, Bagnaia (966055).
Out-of-town, in village on Portoferraio Bay.

LODGING-HOUSES
Le Ghiaie, Ghiaie (93178).
North edge of town.
Marinella, San Giovanni (93676).
Out-of-town, near spa.
Scoglio Bianco, Viticcio (93394).
Out-of-town, in seaside village on north coast.
Stella del Mare, Acquaviva (91352).

Porto Azzurro and District

HOTELS

Second Class	*Hotel Cala di Mola*, Mola (95225).
	Overlooking estuary, outside Porto Azzurro harbour.
	Plaza, Punta Fanaletto (95010).
	Above level of main road on 'Lighthouse Point' just outside Porto Azzurro harbour.
Third Class	*Arrighi*, Porto Azzurro, Via V. Veneto (95315).
	On main road into town.
	Due Torri, Porto Azzurro, Via XXV Aprile (95132).
	Gavila's, Sassi Turchini (95328).
	About 1½ km. out of town, beside the road to Rio Marina.
	Khair Ed Din, Barbarossa (95418).
	Rocco, Porto Azzurro, Via Kennedy (95129).
	Vecchia Elba, Mola (95272).
	On estuary, outside harbour.
	Villa Italia, Porto Azzurro, Vle. Italia (95119).

PENSIONS

Second Class	*Belmare*, Porto Azzurro, Banchina IV Novembre. (95012).
	On main square overlooking harbour.
	Lido, Lido (95767).
	Near Lido beach, out of town.
Third Class	*Barbarossa*, Barbarossa (95087).
	Near Barbarossa beach, just north of Porto Azzurro.
	Virgili, Barbarossa (95429).

LODGING-HOUSES

Villa Bocchetto, Bocchetto (95214).
Villa Wanda, Lido (95733).

Rio Marina and District

HOTEL

Second Class	*Hotel Rio*, Rio Marina, Via Palestro (962016).
	Overlooking harbour.

Rio nell' Elba and District

HOTEL

Third Class	*La Feluca*, Bagnaia (966184).
	Across mountains from Rio, overlooking Portoferraio Bay, 90 metres from beach.

PENSIONS
Third Class   *La Ginestra*, La Ginestra (94181).
                 Above main road to Rio and Rio Marina; swimming
                 pool.

LODGING-HOUSE
                 Idaly, Bagnaia (94712).

Cavo and District
HOTELS
Third Class   *Cristallo*, Cavo (949898).
                 With dining-terrace overlooking sea-front.
                 Ginevra, Cavo (949845).
                 Marelba, Cavo (949920).
                 45 metres from beach.
                 Maristella, Cavo (949859).
                 Pierolli, Cavo (949812).

PENSIONS
Third Class   *Belvedere*, Cavo (949841).
                 La Pineta, Cavo (949808).

Capoliveri District

HOTELS
Second Class   *Alfio*, Lacona (964052).
                 Antares, Lido (95731).
                 Overlooking Stella Bay on south coast, with access to
                 Lido beach.
                 Elba International, Naregno (968611).
                 Large modern establishment high on wooded
                 promontory, Capo della Tavola, across the bay from
                 Porto Azzurro; nearest beach at Naregno.
                 Hotel della Lacona, Lacona (960450).
                 Large and recently built; about ·90 metres back from
                 sea in Lacona Bay; own stretch of beach.
Third Class   *Drago*, Morcone (968429).
                 On beach below Capoliveri, looking west from
                 Calamita peninsula.
                 Frank's, Naregno (968427).
                 Overlooking beach on north-east side of Calamita
                 peninsula, across bay from Porto Azzurro.

Le Acacie, Naregno (968526).

Overlooking same beach as Frank's (above).

Fourth Class   *Baia del Sole*, Lido (95700).

At Lido beach on Stella Bay.

Dino, Pareti (968518).

In sheltered cove, with sandy beach, on west side of Calamita peninsula.

Elba Residence, Naregno (968548).

Overlooking beach on north-east side of Calamita peninsula.

Mini Hotel, Lacona (960441).

On plain of Lacona, easy access to sea.

Romana, Naregno (968572).

(See 'Frank's' above)

Stella Maris, Pareti (968425).

(See 'Dino' above)

Villa Maria Carla, Colle Lido (968416).

On rising ground above Lido beach.

PENSIONS
First Class   *Capo Sud*, Lacona (964021).

Overlooking Stella Bay, with private beach.

Second Class   *Piccolo Hotel*, Lacona (964027).

Third Class   *Anfora*, Naregno (968573).

Casanova, Lido (95705).

Ferretti, Lido (95707).

Giardino, Lacona (964059).

La Scogliera, Morcone (968424).

La Voce del Mare, Naregno (968455).

L'Etrusca, Lacona (964036).

Excellent restaurant on shore. Friendly, English-speaking management.

Villa Miramare, Pareti (968673).

Villa Rodriguez, Naregno (968423).

LODGING-HOUSES

Baia Morcone, Morcone (968558).

Casino del Bosco, Straccoligno (968537).

In wooded country south of Naregno.

Da Pilade, Mola (968635).

On estuary, south of Porto Azzurro harbour.

Villa Angelica, Le Calanchiole (95761).

Villa Obrull, Morcone (968558).

Marina di Campo and District
HOTELS
First Class   *Iselba*, Pineta (97096).
                     Most modern of Elba's 1st Class hotels; spacious
                     stone buildings set among umbrella-pines behind
                     broad, sandy beach, east of M. di Campo.
Second Class   *Bahia*, Cavoli (987055).
                     Constructed in terraces down cliff above good sandy
                     beach; Cavoli is cove west of M. di Campo.
                     Club Hotel Marina 2, La Foce (97332).
                     In hamlet at extreme eastern end of beach from M. di
                     Campo.
                     Hotel dei Coralli, Via Pineta, M di Campo (97336).
                     Set in the pine belt behind beach to east of town.
                     La Barcarola 2, M. di Campo (97255).
                     Lo Scirocco, Fetovaia (987031).
                     Meridiana, M. di Campo, Viale Etruschi (97308).
                     On edge of town, close to beach and pine belt; owned
                     by La Barcarola pension.
                     Riva, M. di Campo, Viale degli Eroi (97316).
                     S. Caterina, M. di Campo, Via Pineta (97452).
                     Select, M. di Campo, Via Roma (97272).
Third Class   *Barracuda*, M. di Campo, Viale Elba (97147).
                     Eden Park, Piana di Mezzo (97285).
                     Inland, in foothills overlooking M. di Campo.
                     Galli, Fetovaia (987065).
                     In coastal village, west of Cavoli and M. di Campo,
                     set back from sandy beach.
                     Il Rustichello, Alzi (97584).
                     Motel Lido, M. di Campo, Via Mascagni (97040).
                     Tre Colonne, M. di Campo, Via Fattori (97320).
                     Near the middle of town. ·
                     Villa Cristina, La Pila (97483).
                     Near airstrip, on road between Procchio and M. di
                     Campo.
Fourth Class   *Orsa Minore*, M. di Campo, Viale degli Etruschi
                     (97027).

PENSIONS

Second Class	*Lilly*, M. di Campo, Viale degli Etruschi (97026).
	Villa Nettuno, M. di Campo, Vle. degli Etruschi (97028)
Third Class	*Da Fine*, Seccheto (987017).

Along coast to west of M. di Campo.

Da Italo, Seccheto (987012).

Elba, M. di Campo (97224).

In S. Mamiliano at east end of town.

La Barcarola, M. di Campo, Piazza del Municipio (97043).

Friendly, with excellent restaurant.

La Conchiglia, Cavoli (987010).

Lorenza, Cavoli (987054).

Montemerlo, Fetovaia (987061).

Stella, Seccheto (987013).

Thomas, M. di Campo, Vle. degli Etruschi (97286). With annexe.

Villa Etrusca, Vle. degli Etruschi (97363).

LODGING-HOUSES

Anna, Fetovaia (987037).

Dell'Amicizia, Vallebuia (987051).

Attractive situation up mountain valley above Seccheto.

Vilaggio Eden, La Foce (97453).

Marciana and District

HOTELS

First Class	*Hotel del Golfo*, Procchio (907565).

At western end of longest sandy beach on north coast; gardens and front on beach; special arrangements with Acquabona golf course; ferries met with own transport.

Second Class	*Desirée*, Procchio (907502).

On Spartaia cove, just west of Procchio Bay, with own sandy beach and sheltered harbour; bedrooms with private terraces; secluded and very comfortable.

Fontaleccio, Procchio (907431).

Slightly inland.

Hotel di Procchio, Procchio (907477).
On edge of village.
La Perla, Procchio (907401).
On main road leading into Procchio from east.
Monna Lisa, Procchio (907519).
Set back from sea but with private beach.
Renée, Procchio (907559).
On main road, slightly east of village.
Valle Verde, Procchio (907545).
In Spartaia cove, west of Procchio village; raised slightly above sea-level but with own section of beach.

Third Class
Arcobaleno, Redinoce (907510).
Just above main road between Procchio and Marciana Marina; path down to rocky beach.
Brigantino, Procchio (907543).
In the Campo All'Aia resort, east of Procchio, overlooking Procchio Bay with own gardens and section of beach, equipped with bathing cabins.
Delfino, Procchio (907455).

Fourth Class
Hotel delle Coste, Marciana, Via le Coste 12 (99924).
Only hotel in Marciana Alta; small but well situated for mountain walks.

PENSIONS
Second Class
La Pergola, Procchio (907506).
Quiet, in own gardens and about 70 metres from beach. Offers wood-pigeon and thrush-shooting in October.
Tre Api, Procchio (907560).

Third Class
Bambu, S. Andrea (99812).
This pension, like the nine following, is situated in the little fishing-village of Sant'Andrea, at the foot of a steep hill down from the western coast-road at Zanca; although somewhat cut off from the rest of Elba, Sant'Andrea is very popular, with its small beach and rocky shore, for family holidays.
Da Giacomino, S. Andrea (99810).
Bellavista, S. Andrea (99815).
Da Ilio, S. Andrea (99818).

Gallo Nero, S. Andrea (99817).
Il Veliero, S. Andrea (99829).
La Cernia, S. Andrea (99871).
Piccola Pineta, S. Andrea (99822).
Piccolo Hotel Barsalini, S. Andrea (99813).
Bel Tramonto, Patresi-Mortaio (99827).
On hillside above coast-road, looking north-west; two swimming pools and road down to rather distant free beach.
Da Renzo, Procchio (907505).
Da Sardi, Pomonte (99845).
In Elba's westernmost village, on coast-road.
L'Edera, Procchio (907525).
Monte Capanne, Poggio, Via dei Pini (99083).
In hill-village; start of ascent of Monte Capanne.
Villa Rita, Patresi (99895).

LODGING-HOUSES

Belmare, Patresi-Mortaio (99867).
Da Giuseppino, Pomonte (99842).
Il Perseo, Chiessi (99800).
Monte Capanne annexe, Poggio.
Oleandro, S. Andrea (99825).
Rifugio Santuario Madonna del Monte (99941).
Tre Stelle, Procchio.
Villa Mare, Pomonte (99843).

Marciana Marina District

HOTELS

First Class   *La Primula*, Marciana M., Viale Cerboni (99010).
In town centre, short distance from sea-front.

Second Class   *Gabbiano Azzurro*, Marciana M., Viale Amedeo (99226).
Inland at edge of town, on road up to Marciana Alta.

Third Class   *Imperia*, Viale Amedeo (99082).
Inland, on road to Marciana Alta.
La Conchiglia, Marciana M., Via XX Settembre (99016).
On main street through town.

Marinella, Marciana M., Viale Margherita (99018).
On sea-front.
Villa Maria, Marciana M., Viale Amedeo (99020).
Inland, on road to Marciana Alta.

Fourth Class   *Anselmi*, Marciana M., Viale Amedeo (99078).
J. Marie, Bagno (99201).
At seashore hamlet between Marciana M. and Spartaia.
La Pace, Marciana M., Piazza della Vittoria (99049).
Mimosa, Le Sprizze (99076).
On coast towards Procchio, near Bagno.

PENSIONS
Third Class   *Andreina*, La Cala (99937).
Secluded, reached by footpath, overlooking sea between Marciana M. and S. Andrea.
Le Bricide, Redinoce (907538).

LODGING-HOUSES
Casa Brignetti, Marciana M. (99339).
Casa Lupi, Marciana M. (99143).
Tagliaferro, Marciana M. (99029).

ROOMS, FLATS AND BUNGALOWS TO RENT

As well as hotels, pensions, and lodging-houses, Elba offers a number of establishments where visitors can rent furnished accommodation but provide their own meals, either going out to local restaurants or, where a kitchenette forms part of the accommodation, cooking for themselves. There are *hotels meublés* and *residences* which offer single, furnished rooms or complete self-contained apartments; and there are groups of *bungali* or *villette*, where each visiting party occupies an entire and separate bungalow, generally with kitchenette, living-room and bathroom as well as beds. Sometimes there is a central restaurant or snack-bar. The following list, not necessarily exhaustive, groups these establishments according to districts and briefly describes their character. (Telephone numbers in brackets where available.)

Portoferraio and District

Fil.Ce.	Flatlets in houses on Padulella Beach, 2 – 6 beds: apply Portoferraio, Piazza Cavour 6 (92238).
I Bungali	On Biodola Bay, bungalows with 2 – 8 beds, kitchenette and bathroom; private beach (93916).
Residence S. Michele	In valley near Bagnaia, block of 60 apartments, each with living and dining-room, 3 – 4 beds, kitchen and bathroom; swimming pool and tennis (966119).
Bungalows La Valdana	In Valdana valley beside Porto Azzurro road, about $^1/_2$km. from Lido beach; flatlets in country bungalows, each with one room, kitchen and bathroom (968519/966141).
Camping Levante Rosselba	Near Ottone on Portoferraio Bay, wooden cabins with 2 – 4 beds (966101).
Camping La Grande Baia	At Nisporto, facing westwards, across mountains from Rio, wooden cabins with 2 – 4 beds.

Porto Azzurro and District

Residence del Sole	Block of flatlets containing one room, kitchen and bathroom, facing sea (95105).
Miniappartamenti Bizzarri	At Barbarossa Beach, apartments with 2 – 4 beds (95108).
Miniappartamenti G. Carmignani	On rise overlooking Barbarossa Beach, terraced bungalows, 2 – 4 people, with bedroom, living-room and kitchenette and separate terraces.
Residenza Reale	At Reale, on coast north of Porto Azzurro, flatlets with room, kitchen and bathroom, 90 metres from beach (95231).
Gavila's	At Sassi Turchini, above Porto Azzurro – Rio Marina road, apartments for 2 – 6 people (95328).

Capoliveri and District

Villa Le Grazie	Capoliveri, Via Soprana; flatlets with one room, kitchen and bathroom, near sea (968553).
Elba Residence	Near Naregno beach, 20 bungalows, each with living-room, bedroom, kitchenette and bathroom and own terrace; 270 metres from sea (968548/95132).

Minihotel	On Lacona plain, 360 metres from sea, one-room flatlets in villa, each with kitchen and bathroom (964041).
Villa Maria Carla	On rising ground above Lido beach, one-room flatlets in villa, each with kitchen and bathroom, 200 metres from sea (968416).
Villa Angelica	At Le Calanchiole on Calamita peninsula, apartments with 2 – 3 – 4 beds near beach; adjoining camping area (95761).
Villa dell'Innamorata	On Calamita peninsula, south of Pareti, flatlets with 2–3–4 beds, on edge of sea (968568).

Marina di Campo and District

Residence Elite	Apartments with 2 – 5 beds, kitchenette and bathroom, fully furnished in modern block; garden, swimming pool, tennis, miniature golf and bar (97374/97248).
Hotel Meridiana	'Hotel Meublé', 2nd class; 27 bedrooms with bath or shower and separate W.C.; 2 public rooms, bar and T.V. (97308/97352).
Ville degli Ulivi	In La Foce hamlet at east end of Marina di Campo beach, apartments in villa comprising 1 room (2 – 3 beds), kitchenette and bathroom (97048).
Villaggio Eden	In La Foce hamlet, apartments for 2 – 4 people in bungalows, 135 metres from beach (97453).

CAMPING

At the last count there were 23 camping sites officially recognized in Elba; application should be made to the Ente Valorizzazione Elba (p. 59)for a leaflet, complete with map, giving full details of their ratings and facilities. The following list is intended only as a rough guide to their localities.

Portoferraio District

Camping Acquaviva	At foot of Acquaviva valley on seashore, below road from Portoferraio to Viticcio.
Camping La Sorgente	Adjoining the above.

Camping Enfola	Farther along same road, overlooking Capo d'Enfola.
Star Camping	Biodola Bay, behind village of Scaglieri.
Camping Levante Rosselba	At Ottone, on Portoferraio Bay, between Magazzini and Bagnaia.

There are also camping sites on the shore at Nisporto and Nisportino which, although in the communal territory of Rio nell'Elba, are in fact on the other side of the eastern mountain range, looking westwards out to sea; they are reached by very rough country roads and are largely patronized by skin-divers.

Porto Azzurro District

Camping da Mario
Camping Arrighi
Camping Barbarossa   Barbarossa Bay.
Camping Sassi Turchini
Camping Reale   At southern end of Reale beach, just north of Barbarossa Bay.

Capoliveri District

Camping Laconella Punta Contessa	Lacona Bay, at point dividing sandy from shingle beach.
Camping Tallinucci *Camping Valle S. Maria* *Camping Lacona* *Camping Stella Mare*	Lacona Bay.
Camping Lido	On rising ground above Lido beach.
Camping Le Calanchiole	Near Lido beach.
Camping Europa	Near Lido beach.
Camping Croce del Sud	On slopes above Morcone and Pareti.

Marina di Campo District

Camping La Foce	Along with two following sites, at hamlet of La Foce, just beyond eastern end of Campo beach.
Camping del Mare	La Foce.
Camping dell'Isola, Ville degli Ulivi	La Foce.

RESTAURANTS

Apart from the hotel-restaurants there is such an abundance of *ristoranti* and *trattorie* in Elba that particular recommendations may be invidious; there is room for everyone to make their own discoveries. By tradition, the *trattoria* is cheaper and less ambitious in menu than the *ristorante*, but nowadays the distinction is blurred, and you can often eat better in a good *trattoria* than in a more expensive but less well-managed *ristorante*. Restaurants which have the special cooking equipment for making the *pizza* are apt to announce the fact in their titles, e.g. *ristorante-pizzeria*, but strictly speaking the *pizzeria*, as such, is primarily a snack-bar where *pizza* and other hot snacks are served. Those sampled in Elba were neither outstanding nor particularly cheap. *Tavola calda* is a self-service establishment where a restricted range of hot and cold dishes are served from a counter to customers who may either take them out or eat them at a table provided. *Osteria* used to mean an inn or eating house of lower grade than *trattoria*, but it has now become a self-consciously 'quaint' title, like the Anglo-American 'tavern'.

Eating out in Italy is no longer as cheap by British standards as it used to be; in a good but not luxurious establishment, a meal of two or three courses, with carafe wine, a half-bottle of mineral water, and coffee, is likely to cost the equivalent of between £4.00 and £5.50. Doing without the wine will not save you more than around 30 — 40 p

While not attempting to offer a comprehensive or exhaustive gastronomic guide, it is perhaps worth mentioning by name a few Elban restaurants where the authors have enjoyed their meals. In the old city of Portoferraio, there is a convenient row of restaurants along the lower side of the Piazza della Repubblica; of these, *Bologna* can be recommended, in spite of the noisy traffic outside. In the main street of the modern city, Via Carducci, *Elbana* is good, though not cheap. In Porto Azzurro, there are four fair restaurants in Via Vitaliani – *La Tavernetta*, *La Caravella*, *Il Delfino Verde*, and *La Lanterna*. At Rio Marina, *Da Alfonso* has good food and a pleasant outdoor terrace. At Marina di Campo, there are several restaurants specialising in sea-food, among them, *Ristorante da Mario* and *Trattoria Il Cacciucco*; the authors are particularly fond of *La Barcarola* in the Piazza del Municipio, where the proprietor presides over the kitchen and a cordial, family atmosphere prevails. On the northern side of Elba, it is worth climbing to the village of Poggio for a meal at *Ristorante-*

Pizzeria Publius, a modern restaurant with an excellent menu and friendly service.

NIGHT LIFE

Night life in Elba is confined to a few cinemas (see p. 69), night-clubs, generally with free admission, dance-halls, and discotheques, which are to be found all over the island during the high season; most of them close down early in September.

PRACTICAL INFORMATION

TOURIST INFORMATION

Elba has its own official tourist organization called the Ente Valorizzazione Elba (E.V.E. for short), with offices on the second floor of the multi-storey block opposite the ferry-pier in the modern harbour of Portoferraio; its address is 57037 Portoferraio, Calata Italia 26, Isola d'Elba, Provincia Livorno, Italy, and its Elban telephone numbers are 92671 and 92672. If calling from other parts of Italy or abroad, these numbers must be preceded by the group 0565. The staff of E.V.E., some of whom speak English, will give advice on hotels and other accommodation; they will make bookings; and they will also give friendly advice on other tourist problems. E.V.E. is affiliated to the Italian national tourist organization (E.N.I.T.) which has its London office at 201, Regent Street, W1R 8AY, and its New York office at 630, Fifth Avenue, New York 10020, N.Y.

On the ground floor of the same building as the E.V.E. the Associazione Albergatori Elbani (Elban Hotel-keepers' Association) has its offices with a window on the promenade; it will supply publicity literature about the hotels which belong to the association and will make bookings. Its address is Calata Italia 21/A, Isola d'Elba; its telephone number 92754.

There are also a number of commercial tourist agencies which will supply railway, air, and ferry tickets and arrange car hire. These include the Agenzia Viaggi Tesi, Calata Italia (tel. 92386) and the Ufficio Turistico Caprai, Calata Matteotti (tel. 92275). Guided bus tours of the island can be arranged through Agenzia Viaggi Aethaltours, Viale Elba (tel. 92391) or Agenzia Viaggi Intourelba, Via Carducci 162, (tels. 91034 and 91155). Baggage and larger consignments can be forwarded by Bagaglio e Spedizioni, Via Carducci (tel. 92192). The Automobile Club Italiano (A.C.I.), which has reciprocal arrangements with the British motoring organizations is in Viale Elba (tel. 93081). The headquarters of the firm running the Elban bus services (Autolinee Elbane SAE) is on the ground floor of the *grattacielo*, with its entrance on the Viale Elba.

The two companies running car-carrying ferry services between Elba and the mainland are TO.RE.MAR., Calata Italia (tel. 92022) 92022) and NAV.AR.MA., Calata Italia (tel. 92133). They run other services through the islands of the Tuscan Archipelago and will supply timetables and make bookings. There are also two companies running the faster passenger services by hydrofoil to the mainland; these are S.N.A.V., Molo Massimo (tel. 93885) and Alilauro, Calata Italia 2, (tel. 92133).

Outside Portoferraio, the following tourist agencies are available:

Porto Azzurro	Ufficio Turistico Arrighi, Banchina IV Novembre, (tels. 95000 and 95150).
	Agenzia TO.RE.MAR. Banchina IV Novembre, (tel. 95004).
Marciana Marina	Agenzia Immobiliare G. Venci, Piazza Vittoria 18, (tel. 99279).
Capoliveri	Ufficio Turistico Della Lucia, Via Mellini 9, (tel. 968417).
Marina di Campo	Ufficio Turistico C.I.P.A.T., Via Roma 86, (tel. 97414).

CLIMATE AND CLOTHES

Elba has what might be called a Riviera climate modified by its more southern latitude and the surrounding presence of the sea. That is to say, it enjoys a great deal of sunshine and a moderate rainfall confined mainly to the winter months. As an island, it is more temperate than the mainland in both hot and cold weather; as an island, it is also exposed to the winds which may vary from a welcome breeze on hot summer days to furious gales in late autumn and winter. But since it compresses a complex mountain system into a relatively small surface area, the Elban landscape can usually provide shelter from whatever wind may be blowing. In Elba, the *rosa dei venti* (rose of the winds), as Italian mariners call the points of the compass, still preserves the traditional proper names for the winds from each quarter: from the north, *tramontana*; from the north-east, *grecale*; from the east, *levante*; from the south-east, *scirocco*; from the south, *mezzogiorno*; from the south-west, *libeccio*; from the west, *ponente*; from the north-west, *maestrale*; while a dead calm is called, with the characteristic Italian modification, *bonaccia*, with the connotation 'tiresomely good weather'.

Average seasonal temperatures for Elba are:

	°C	°F
Winter	9·7	49·6
Spring	13·9	57·0
Summer	22·7	72·8
Autumn	16·6	61·9

Monthly minimum and maximum temperatures are:

Month	Minimum		Maximum	
	°C	°F	°C	°F
January	1	32·8	16	60·8
February	1	32·8	17	62·6
March	6	42·8	18	64·4
April	8	46·4	22	71·5
May	12	53·5	25	77·0
June	14	57·2	31	87·8
July	18	64·4	30	86·0
August	18	64·4	32	89·6
Sept	15	59·0	28	82·4
October	10	50·0	28	82·4
Nov	10	50·0	22	71·6
Dec	6	42·8	18	64·4

The average temperature of the sea off the Elban beaches is recorded for the island's 'season' as follows:

	°C	°F
April	19·0	66·0
May	20·2	68·3
June	24·1	75·3
July	24·3	75·7
August	27·3	79·1
Sept	25·5	77·9
October	23·1	73·5

Observations taken at Portoferraio show that, on an average, Elba experiences 167 days a year of unclouded sunshine; 87 days of mixed sun and cloud; and 111 days are overcast. Rainfall varies according to the altitude; annual figures for three selected points are:

Portoferraio (sea-level, N. coast) – under 28 in.
Capoliveri (540 ft, S.E. coast) – 34 in.
Marciana (1,326 ft, northern mountain slopes) – 42 in.

These figures are comparable with those of the eastern counties of England but with one important difference: in a Mediterranean climate with wet westerly winds in winter, most of the rain falls in late December and the first three months of the year. In normal summers rain falls only in occasional thunderstorms. Snow is so rare in Elba as to be regarded as an extraordinary phenomenon; and over a recorded period of 22 years, the temperature fell below freezing-point only four times.

During the May to October tourist season, visitors to Elba should bring clothing considerably lighter than that suitable for a summer holiday in the British Isles; for example, the average British tweed sports jacket is too warm a daytime garment even during October in Elba. Normal daytime wear for both sexes can be thin slacks and an open-necked shirt, or for women summer frocks from June to September. On the other hand, the sharp changes in altitude make it advisable to carry a light woollen over-garment, such as a sweater, for protection in high or windy places; it will also be welcome in the evenings. A light mackintosh is useful for the occasional rainy weather early in the season or for summer thunderstorms.

Footwear is largely a matter of personal taste; sandals or espadrilles are obviously suitable for the beaches and are sold in the local shops. But, as we have indicated in this guide, Elba is also a place for walkers, and anyone who intends to take advantage of its system of mountain tracks and bridle-paths should bring a pair of stout comfortable shoes, preferably with rubber soles which will not slip on rocks or steep, grassy slopes.

Mosquitoes exist in Elba, as in all Mediterranean resorts, but they are noticeable only in the lower-lying areas and especially after dark. Elban hotel-keepers tend to keep their rooms well sprayed with insecticides, but it is as well to bring or buy one's own aerosol spray, as well as some sort of application to relieve the irritation of insect bites, especially if you are camping or renting furnished apartments. The important rule, in coping with mosquitoes, is to keep windows and shutters closed after nightfall, as long as the lights which attract insects are on.

HEALTH AND DRINKING WATER

The two principal health hazards for visitors to Elba are over-exposure to sunlight, resulting in painful sunburn or headaches, and an unfamiliar diet, including foods cooked in oil, which may produce stomach upsets and mild diarrhoea. Obvious precautions against the former are to go slow on sun-bathing until you are acclimatized, to keep legs and arms lightly covered, and to wear sun-glasses. Your own doctor or chemist will be able to recommend suitable proprietary remedies for stomach trouble; they are worth including in your suitcase if only as insurance. The traditional Italian diet for an upset stomach is plain boiled rice (*riso al bianco*), and lemon juice (*spremuta di limone*), taken with as litle sugar as possible.

For more serious problems, it may be necessary to consult the local municipal doctor (*medico condotto*), who works for the commune in which you are staying. Normally he holds daily clinics in an office adjoining the town-hall (*municipio*), or elsewhere; your hotel-keeper or a local café proprietor will be able to tell you where to find him. You may expect him to be serious and sympathetic; he may or may not be able to speak English – many Italian doctors do – but unless you yourself speak Italian, it would be sensible to take an interpreter with you for your first consultation. The doctor's charges for a simple prescription or injection will be about 2,000 lire.

As a citizen of a member country of the European Economic Community, you are entitled to free medical treatment on presenting the special form known as E 111; this can be obtained by getting from your local Health and Social Security Office another form, called CM1, and filling it in well in advance of your departure. But bureaucratic procedures in Italy for dealing with the E 111 are complicated and involve visiting a sickness insurance office and exchanging the form for yet another document before visiting the doctor. For the ordinary holiday in Elba, you will find it far more convenient to pay the small premium for the comprehensive insurance offered by travel agents or package tour operators.

For emergencies requiring first aid (*pronto soccorso*) or an ambulance (*autoambulanza*), contact one of the following:

Pronto Soccorso Reverenda Misericordia, Piazza della Republica, Portoferraio (tel. 92009).
Pronto Soccorso SS Sacramento, Via Camerini, Portoferraio (tel. 92010).
Pronto Soccorso Croce Verde, Calata Buccari, Portoferraio (tel. 92796).
Pronto Soccorso, Porto Azzurro (tels. 95053/4 and 95005).

There is a Civil Hospital (*Ospedale Civile Elbano*) in the old city of Portoferraio which will treat casualties on an emergency basis. If you are taking a casualty to it in your own car, enter Piazza Cavour in the old city from the sea-front, and turn left into Via Guerrazzi at the left-hand end of the piazza. Follow this street to its end and then turn sharp right uphill, bearing left at the first fork. You are then in Via Carmine which you will follow as far as a small piazza called Piazza Victor Hugo. Via Victor Hugo leaves this piazza on the opposite side, and the hospital is immediately on the left.

SPAS
Elba, like so many Italian resorts, boasts its own spa for sufferers from certain chronic diseases. This is a commercial establishment called the *Terme* (Baths) *San Giovanni*; it is situated on the edge of Portoferraio Bay in the area where the old salt-pans used to exist, about 1 km. from the city centre. It specializes in the treatment of cellulitis, arthritic diseases, and acne; and it employs for this purpose a deposit of marine mud rich in organic sulphur and iodine, which is said to resemble

the 'Liman' of the Black Sea. It is a modern establishment, clean and pleasant in appearance and staffed by professionals, some of whom speak English. The direction recommends that persons desiring treatment should bring with them a letter from their own physician describing the nature of their complaint. To reach the Terme San Giovanni, take the Porto Azzurro road to the left from the road junction known as Bivio Boni, just outside Portoferraio. On the left, about 180 metres from the junction, an avenue of poplars leads down to the Terme on the shore.

With the rare exception of taps marked *Non Potabile* (Not Drinkable), Elban water is safe for human consumption. In some hotels, but by no means all, it may taste flat or slightly brackish but can still be used for washing and teeth cleaning. For drinking purposes in such cases, ask the hotel-service for a bottle of mineral water (*una bottiglia di acqua minerale*) for drinking in your room, and see that the waiter leaves a stopper (*un tappo*) for sealing it after it is open. Italian mineral-water is normally tasteless and pure, bottled at controlled and medically inspected natural springs; it is often slightly alkaline and a useful antidote to over-indulgence. It may be sparkling (*frizzante*) or still (*non frizzante*) according to requirement, and the sparkling varieties will often serve as a substitute for sodawater.

MONEY CHANGING AND BANKS

At the time of publication the official rate of exchange fluctuates around 1,500 Italian lire to the pound sterling, and 651 lire to one U.S. dollar. The lira can be purchased more cheaply outside Italy, but present regulations forbid tourists to bring into the country more than 35,000 lire (roughly equivalent to £23.50) per head. The enforcement of this rule is left to foreign banks which, in Britain at least, decline to supply more than the regulation amount in currency. British travellers can take up to £300 each in travellers' cheques.

Probably the commonest coin is the attractive silver-coloured 100 lire piece which resembles our own 10p. in size but is worth rather less; it is a convenient tip for small services.

The leading Italian banks all have branches in Portoferraio either along the sea-front or in Piazza Cavour, the main square of the old city. Typical names are Banco di Roma, Banca Commerciale, Monte dei Paschi di Siena, Cassa di Risparmio. Banking hours are 8.30 to 13.30, Mondays to Fridays inclusive, except on public holidays (p. 72) when they are closed. There are also a few money-changing establishments (Ufficio Cambio) where the opening hours may be more elastic than those of the banks. Both banks and money-changers usually exhibit a board showing the day's rates of exchange; and at periods when the exchange rate is fluctuating widely, it is sometimes worth shopping around to see where you can obtain the best rate for your travellers' cheques. All banks and money-changers expect to see your passport when cashing travellers' cheques.

At weekends and in emergencies, hotel-keepers and sometimes also restaurant-keepers will change travellers' cheques, but almost always at a lower rate than that obtainable from the banks. In Elba it is also possible to cash cheques at the head office of the bus company (Autolinee Elbane SAE) at Portoferraio.

SHOPPING

Normal Italian shopping hours are from 8.30 or 9.00 to 13.00 and again from 15.30 or 16.00 to 19.30 or 20.00. Like the banks, the shops are closed on national holidays and local feast days (*feste*), (p. 72) although for the latter some food shops may be open during the morning.

For buying food for picnicking or camping, the best place in Elba, if you are within reach of Portoferraio, is the covered market in the Old City, open every shopping day in what used to be the Galeazze, or naval arsenal. As you enter it from the Via Galeazze (leading out of the eastern end of the Piazza Cavour), a row of stalls on your right supplies anything you are likely to need: loaves (*pani*), bread rolls (*panini*), butter (*burro*), cheese (*formaggio*), packaged cheese (*formaggini*), boiled ham (*prosciutto cotto*), smoked parma ham (*prosciutto crudo*), several varieties of salami, and luncheon sausage (*mortadella*); there is also a smoked pork-meat resembling parma ham but rather fatter and cheaper, called *coppa*, which is excellent for sandwiches. All these meats will be sold sliced (*affettato*) unless you ask for an uncut piece (*un pezzo*). For quantities see Weights and Measures (p. 75); the smallest quantity, suitable for one or two people, is usually *un mezz'etto* (50 grammes, or just under 2 oz.). Some of these stalls supply sugar (*zucchero*), jam (*conserva*) or the delicious local honey (*miele*); and at least one of them sells table wine (*vino da tavola*) in litre bottles, for about 500 lire, as well as mineral water (*acqua minerale*). The basic local wine, Elbano, is red (*rosso*) or white (*bianco*); the problem with white wine is to keep it chilled.

Across the aisle, other stalls are laden with seasonal fruit and vegetables which they will sell in suitable small quantities; the vendors are used to foreigners pointing to what they require, and they will always scrupulously write the bill on a piece of scrap paper. At one end of the market, up a steep staircase, there is Upimelba, a large, serve-yourself hardware store where you can buy crockery or glassware, as well as paper plates and plastic utensils suitable for picnics.

Outside Portoferraio bread and rolls can be bought at the local bakery (*panificio*), and most other foodstuffs and drinks at a general food-store (*alimentari*). For baby-foods, go to the chemist (*farmacia*). Salt (*sale*) is a government monopoly, and is sold at tobacconists.

Articles of clothing, some of them extremely elegant, are offered to the Elban holiday maker at inflated prices, especially in the smart little boutiques to be found in Portoferraio, Marina di Campo, and Porto Azzurro; woollen goods are particularly expensive. Better bargains are to be had at the weekly open-air markets held in all the main centres. They have stalls offering clothing, footwear, textiles, and fancy goods, as well as those for produce. At these markets, good buys to take home are leather goods – gloves, shoes, belts, hand-bags and purses – most of them cheaper than in the U.K. Useful words for would-be purchasers are *Quanto*? (How much?) and *Troppo!* (Too much!), but unless you have fluent Italian, it is not much use trying to bargain: the vendors have too much business to waste time with the hovering foreigner. However, if a reasonably large purchase is being made, it is sometimes worth asking for *un piccolo sconto* (a small discount); this is something which every Italian housewife will demand and it may result in a few lire being knocked off the price.

Elban market-days are:

Portoferraio (Piazza della Repubblica, Old City).	Friday
Porto Azzurro	Saturday
Marciana	Sunday
Marciana Marina (during the season)	Sunday
Pomonte	Sunday
San Piero	Sunday
Rio Marina	Monday
Poggio (and Marciana Marina out of season)	Tuesday
Marina di Campo	Wednesday
Capoliveri (Piazza Garibaldi)	Thursday

Procchio   Thursday
Rio nell'Elba   Tuesday
Sant'Ilario and La Pila   Saturday

SOUVENIRS

There are now no authentic Elban handicrafts except those produced
by the prisoners in Porto Longone gaol and sold in a small shop inside
the main gateway. The most characteristic souvenir of the island is
perhaps a sample of the various semi-precious gemstones (*pietre dure*)
which are found in the mines and quarries as well as on some of the
pebble beaches. They are to be found on sale all over the island,
sometimes in the rough, sometimes polished but unmounted,
sometimes made up as jewelry or knick-knacks. Prices vary according
to size, rarity, and the workmanship involved: a ring or bracelet of
silver-alloy, set with the chunky crystals of iron pyrites (or 'fool's
gold') may cost no more than about 1,000 lire. For large specimen-
minerals there is a well-stocked shop in the main piazza of Rio
nell'Elba. In Rio Marina, in addition to the mineral museum, there is
a commercial establishment where gemstones are polished and
mounted, and are also sold in parcels for home jewellers.

Another characteristic Elban product is the local wines (See Food
and Drink p. 144). They are sold ready packaged in assortments of
different varieties. The dessert wines, Moscato and Aleatico, are also
sold in fancy souvenir bottles, made by glass-blowers to resemble
horse-pistols, human figures etc. and adorned with imitation leather
trappings. Both these and the normal bottles of table wines are on
offer in bars and cafes, but perhaps the best place to buy them is one of
the Elban wine-bottling establishments (*cantine*), which are usually
open to the public. There is one to the left of the main road about
1·5km. before entering Porto Azzurro from Portoferraio. Another is
situated in the beautiful mountain valley inland from Seccheto, and
this sells not only wine but also several varieties of Elban honey,
harvested from the row of bee-hives outside the building.

TIPPING

Most Italian hotels and restaurants automatically add a service charge
of from 10 to 15 per cent to their bills; if you are in any doubt about
this, ask whether service has been included (*E compreso il servizio?*) It
is not necessary to add a tip over and above this but most people do

leave an extra 200 or 300 lire if they are satisfied that they have received value for their money. Never allow waiters to assume that they can automatically pocket the change (*Il resto*); insist on seeing it (*Il resto, per favore*) before deciding to give all or part of it back.

For ordinary small services, such as having your bag carried to your room or being guided round a church by the verger, 100 or 200 lire is an adequate tip. After staying a week at a hotel, you will find the room-maid hopes for something in addition to the *servizio* which appears on the bill but may not reach her wagepacket; 1,000 lire is suitable for a week's stay. Porters at railway stations and airports make a fixed charge, based on the number of pieces of baggage; taxi-drivers and boatmen are satisfied with 10 per cent of the fare.

CINEMAS AND DANCING

There are three cinemas which are open all the year round, the *Astra*, Piazza Cavour, Old City and *Pietri*, Viale Elba, in Portoferraio, and in Porto Azzurro, the *Italia*, Via Cavalotti. In summer there are cinemas in Capoliveri (*Elba*) and in Marina di Campo (*Verdi*), and open-air cinemas at Rio Marina and Cavo. The films shown are Italian or dubbed into Italian.

The Italian love of dancing to loud music is catered for by a number of small clubs and dance halls in Elba; most of them are only open for the high season, and they range from relatively sophisticated night-clubs to simple open-air dance floors. The best known are *Norman's Club* and *Club 64*, on the main road between Portoferraio and Procchio not far from the turn-off to La Biodola, *Club Rodeo* on the road between Procchio and Marina di Campo, and *Club Bahia*, attached to the Bahia hotel at Cavoli on the south coast beyond Marina di Campo. Others are the *Nido del Falco*, romantically situated on the Belvedere of the hill-village, San Piero, and in Portoferraio itself the *Salonai* in Via Pietro Gori or *La Stalla* just outside the town in the hamlet called Le Foci, reached by turning off the Procchio road just after Bivio Boni. There are summer dance-floors in Marina di Campo called *Capriccio* and *Kon Tiki*. Lacona has *Elbolanda*, an establishment which combines dancing with 'mini-golf' and Italian bowls or *bocce*. There is dancing at the *Hobby Club* in Porto Azzurro, at the *Mandelbar* at Morcone, at *La Botte* on the Lido beach, and at *Pierolli's* in Cavo; no doubt other 'dancings' will advertise themselves each season.

SPORT

BEACHES

Elba offers every variety of bathing from sandy beaches, *relatively* safe for children, to rocks and shoals from which you can dive into deep water. Wherever there are special facilities, such as changing cubicles, deck-chairs etc., the concession for that stretch of beach belongs to a hotel or bathing establishment and a small charge is payable by the day or half-day; but one section of every beach is officially reserved for the public, and it is usually recognizable because nobody clears up the mess of paper and plastic utensils which accumulate on it. Some hotels go to the length of depositing loads of sand for the season on stretches of beach which are normally gravel or pebbles.

Sandy beaches in Elba are:

North Coast	Scaglieri and La Biodola; Spartaia; Procchio and Campo all'Aia.
South Coast	Stella Bay (Lido and Margidore); Lacona; Marina di Campo; Cavoli; Fetovaia; Seccheto (sand and rock).
East Coast	Barbarossa; Reale; Cavo (sand and rock).
Calamita Penin-sula	Naregno; Pareti; Morcone; Straccoligno.

SKIN DIVING

Elban waters are said to be ideal for skin-diving especially along the rocky west and north-west coast, and also along the east coast of the Calamita Peninsula, south of Porto Azzurró, which is only accessible from the sea. At Portoferraio there is the 'Teseo Tesei' Underwater Club which admits visitors as associate members and will advise on equipment and locations; skin-diving clubs with equipment for re-charging air cylinders exist at Morcone, near Capoliveri, and at Barbarossa Beach, north of Porto Azzurro.

BOATING AND FISHING

Small boats, usually with outboard motors, are for hire with or without boatmen at Portoferraio, Porto Azzurro, Marina di Campo, Rio Marina, and other seaside places. The best way of finding what is available is to consult the management of your hotel or of the principal bar on the water-front; They can usually make the necessary arrangements.

Sea-fishing, whether from boats or under water, is free except in an area between Le Ghiaie pebble beach at Portoferraio and Capo Bianco, where the offshore waters are protected as a submarine nature reserve.

SAILING

Elba is also a yachting centre for large and small craft with sheltered moorings at Portoferraio, Porto Azzurro, Rio Marina and Marina di Campo. Portoferraio provides mooring facilities along the water-front for vessels up to medium tonnage, while there is anchorage in the bay for vessels of all kinds. There are watering, provisioning, refuelling and sanitation services in the port and several ship-building and repairing yards. For details of these and for the service charges apply to the *Capitaneria del Porto* (Port Authority) at its offices in the skyscraper on Calata Italia, overlooking the ferry-pier. Porto Azzurro, Rio Marina and Marina di Campo, have facilities for vessels of smaller tonnage and pleasure-craft.

There are a number of sailing clubs and schools in Elba, membership of which includes the use of small craft. In the Portoferraio area there is the Scuola Velica (Sailing School), c/o Bagni Elba at the Ghiaie Beach; also the Casa della Vela in the Schioparello area of Portoferraio Bay. Schools attached to hotels include the Hotel Garden in Schioparello, the Hotel Villa Ottone, and the Pensione Grotte del Paradiso, their Germanic names indicating their principal patrons. At Rio Marina, on the east coast, there is the Centro Velico Elbano which offers courses in sailing to learners; at Campo all'Aia the Sea Club 'Paola'.

TENNIS

Apart from the hotels with tennis courts (see p. 44), there is at Portoferraio a Tennis Club with courts adjoining the Napoleonic Villa at San Martino.

GOLF

Elba has one nine-hole golf course at Acquabona, on the main road between Portoferraio and Porto Azzurro and about halfway between them. The course, which is attached to the Acquabona Golf Hotel, admits associate members on a seasonal subscription. It is beautifully situated and carefully maintained, and it includes a driving-range, a practice putting-green, a professional, and a bar and restaurant.

Riding

Although no one yet has organized pony trekking over the Elban country roads and mule-tracks, there is a riding school near Porto Azzurro, in the neighbourhood of Barbarossa Bay.

Shooting

Tourists wishing to shoot in Italy during the autumn season, which begins in the last week of August and continues until November, must obtain a special permit from the Italian consulate in their own country. The permit costs £3.34p and allows the holder to bring with him to Italy either a rifle with 200 cartridges or two shotguns with 100 cartridges each. The Italian Ministry for Agriculture and Forestry publishes an annual booklet giving detailed information about the hunting season, restrictions on game etc.. Game in Elba includes red partridge, quail, hares, and wild pig, as well as the migrant thrushes which are shot down by local sportsmen during October and November.

HOLIDAYS AND FEAST DAYS

Public Holidays

January 1st	New Year's Day
January 6th	Epiphany
February 11th	Half-holiday in honour of the Concordat
March 19th	St Joseph's Day
Movable	Easter Monday
April 25th	Liberation Day
May 1st	Labour Day
Movable	Ascension Day (6th Thursday after Easter Sunday)
Movable	Corpus Domini (9th Thursday after Easter Sunday)
June 2nd	Anniversary of Proclamation of Republic
June 29th	St Peter and St Paul
August 15th	Ferragosto; Feast of Assumption of Virgin Mary
October 4th	St Francis; half-holiday
November 1st	All Saints' Day
November 4th	Victory Day
December 8th	Conception of Virgin Mary
December 25th and 26th	Christmas Day and Boxing Day

Feast Days

April 29th	*San Cristino*, patron saint of Portoferraio

May 1st-3rd	Minor pilgrimages to *Madonna del Monte* above Marciana
May 5th	Service to commemorate death of Napoleon at Church of Misericordia, Portoferraio
July 15th	SS Giacomo and Quirico, patron saints of Rio nell'Elba
August 7th	*San Gaetano*, patron saint of Campo
August 12th	*Santa Chiara*, patron saint of Marciana Marina
August 15th	Major pilgrimage to *Madonna del Monte* above Marciana
August 16th	*San Rocco*, patron saint of Rio Marina
August 29th	Traditional procession of Misericordia Brotherhood to San Rocco church, Portoferraio
September 8th	*Nativity of Virgin Mary*, patron of Porto Azzurro
September 8th-15th	Pilgrimages to *Madonna di Monserrato*
November 25th	*Santa Caterina*, patron saint of Marciana Alta
December 8th	*Immaculate Conception of Virgin Mary*: feast at Capoliveri in honour of the *Madonna delle Grazie*

MOVABLE FEASTS

Easter Monday	Pilgrimage to the *Shrine of the Madonna del Monte* above Marciana
Ascension Day	Pilgrimage to the *Shrine of Santa Lucia*, outside Portoferraio

POSTAL INFORMATION

The central Post Office is in Piazza Repubblica, Portoferraio (Old City); there are also branch offices in Marina di Campo (Via Marconi), Marciana, Procchio, Marciana Marina (Via Principe Amedeo), Porto Azzurro (Via Roma), Rio Marina (Via Magenta), and Rio nell'Elba.

Stamps may be bought either from post offices or from tobacconists. A post-box (*cassetta postale*), usually painted yellow or pale blue, will generally be found near the tobacconist's shop. Some basic postal rates are:

	Internal	*To the U.K.*
Letters (up to 20g)	150 lire	180 lire

Postcards	100 lire	5 words only	100 lire
		fully written	150 lire
Express letters	400 lire		530 lire
Registered letters	400 lire		750 lire

The Italian word for 'Express' is *Expresso*; for 'Registered' *Raccomandato*.

Correspondence can be sent to Italy *poste restante* by addressing it to the Post Office (*Ufficio Postale*) of the locality and adding the words *Fermo Posta*. Delivery will be made at the Post Office concerned upon identification by passport and payment of 50 lire.

TELEGRAMS
Telegrams to places inside Italy may be sent from any of the post offices listed above. The charges, for up to 16 words, are: ordinary: 1,500 lire; urgent: 3,000 lire. Every extra word costs 40 lire (ordinary) or 100 lire (urgent). Telegrams to places outside Italy are sent by the commercial organization ITALCABLE which in Elba operates from the Central Post Office at Portoferraio. Its rates for telegrams to the U.K. are: up to 16 words, approx. 2,000 lire.

TELEPHONES
Although the Italian telephone system does not come under the post office, its service is described here. The most efficient and convenient way for a British visitor to place international calls from Elba is to go to the central telephone exchange in Portoferraio where a helpful operator at the reception desk will arrange the call and indicate a booth from which to make it. The exchange is on Viale Manzoni, the broad tree-lined avenue which runs north from Piazza del Ponticello (Piazza Citi); to reach it, turn up an alley on the left, about 45 metres from the corner with Via Carducci. A three-minute call to the U.K. costs from 1,850 to 2,500 lire, according to the distance.

Local calls may be made from public telephones which are located in post offices, tobacconists, bars and news-stands; to operate them, you must purchase from the cash desk a special counter (*gettone*) which costs 50 lire. Long-distance calls to other places in Italy will often be placed by hotel managements, adding the charge to the bill. Some hotels will place international calls.

WEIGHTS AND MEASURES

The metric system is used in Italy. Here is a table of equivalents:

14 grammes	$\frac{1}{2}$ oz.	Pound	2/5th kilo
Etto (hectogram)	$3\frac{1}{2}$ oz.	Quarter	$12\frac{1}{2}$ kilos
Kilo (kilogram)	2lb. 3 oz.	Cwt	51 kilos
Quintale	$220\frac{1}{2}$ lb.	Ton	1,017 kilos
Tonellata	$19\frac{3}{4}$ cwt	Pint	3/5th litre
Litro	$1\frac{3}{4}$ pints	Quart	1 1/10th litres
Ettolitro	22 gallons	Gallon	$4\frac{1}{2}$ litres
Centimetre	2/5th inch	Inch	$2\frac{1}{2}$ centimetres
Metre	39 inches	Foot	$30\frac{1}{2}$ centimetres
Kilometre	3/5th mile	Yard	9/10th metre
Ettaro (hectare)	$2\frac{1}{2}$ acres	Mile	1 2/3ds km.
Km. quadrato	2/5th sq. mile	Acre	4,050 sq. metres
		Sq. mile	2·6 sq. kms.

CLOTHING AND SIZES

Women's dresses and suits

British	34	36	38	40	42	44
Continental	40	42	44	46	48	50

Women's shoes

British	3	4	5	6	7	8
Continental	35	36	37	38	39	40

Men's suits and overcoats

British	36	38	40	42	44	46
Continental	46	48	50	52	54	56

Shirts and collars

British	14	$14\frac{1}{2}$	15	$15\frac{1}{2}$	16	$16\frac{1}{2}$	17	$17\frac{1}{2}$
Continental	36	37	38	39	40	41	42	43

Men's shoes

British	7	8	9	10	11	12
Continental	41	42	43	44	45	46

Hats

British	$5^1/_2$	6	$6^2/_3$	7	$7^1/_8$	$7^1/_4$	$7^3/_8$	$7^1/_2$
Continental	53	54	55	56	57	58	59	61

The sizes for socks, stockings and gloves are the same.

TEMPERATURE

Italians measure temperatures on the Centigrade (Celsius) scale. To convert Centigrade temperatures to Fahrenheit, multiply the given temperature by nine, divide by five, and add 32. To convert Fahrenheit temperatures to Centigrade, subtract 32 from the given temperature, multiply the result by 5, and divide by 9.

ELECTRICITY

Italian voltages vary according to locality, but that of Elba is 220 (50 cycles). Although some hotels have universal outlets for all types of plugs fitted in the bathrooms, it is wiser to play safe and purchase an adaptor-plug for your appliances with the wider Continental spacing of the prongs; this will go into any Italian outlet.

TIME

Normal Italian time is GMT plus 1 hour. Italian Summer Time (*Ora Legale*) is GMT plus 2 (British Summer Time plus 1). Unfortunately Summer Time in the two countries does not always coincide, and there may by intervals in the spring or autumn when either the clocks in the two countries coincide or the Italian clocks are two hours later than those in the U.K.

GEOGRAPHY AND GEOLOGY

Elba is naturally divided into three easily distinguished regions, the eastern sector, the middle sector, and the western sector. Each of them has a different character, and the landscape of each is governed by a different underlying tectonic structure.

The eastern sector consists of a range of mountains running from north to south but interrupted by the Gulf of Porto Azzurro and the alluvial valley that lies behind it. They are not really high mountains – they reach a maximum of 1677 feet – but, north of Porto Azzurro, they rise very steeply from sea-level to a crown of limestone crags and violently distorted strata, while south of Porto Azzurro, there is the more rounded but still imposing mass of Monte Calamita which plunges very steeply to the sea all round its coastline. These eastern mountains contain the iron-mines which have given Elba its own strategic importance throughout its history. They are largely open-cast workings, making a characteristic scar on the landscape, as seen from the air. But from ground level, they are not obtrusive.

The inhabited centres of the eastern sector are Cavo, a residential resort in the extreme north; Rio nell'Elba, the ancient mining town perched halfway up the slope of the mountainside, and its busy little port on the coast, Rio Marina; Porto Azzurro, formerly Porto Longone, on the deep inlet of the sea which divides the eastern coastline; and Capoliveri, a typical Elban hill-town on the shoulder of Monte Calamita.

The central sector of Elba, divided from the eastern mountains by the linked valleys which run down to Porto Azzurro in one direction and to the Bay of Portoferraio in the other, has as its backbone a range of lower, rounded hills, formed of ancient volcanic rock and running from east to west. They are thickly wooded with *macchia*, the dense Mediterranean scrub composed of a special assortment of low trees and bushes, some of them evergreen and many of them aromatic. To the north of these hills, the coastline consists of two large bays divided by a hammer-shaped promontory. The eastern bay is that named after the island's capital, Portoferraio, which overlooks it from the west side of its entrance; it is a beautiful semi-land-locked anchorage fringed mainly by gravel beaches, with the eastern mountains as its majestic background. The western Bay of Procchio is divided by minor promontories into three separate coves, two of them – Biodola and Procchio itself – with excellent sandy beaches. The south coastline of the central sector has three beautiful bays, divided from each other by bold headlands and each offering its own excellent sandy beaches: the easternmost is Stella Bay; the next is Lacona Bay; and the third is the Bay of Campo with the town and port of Marina di Campo.

The principal town of the central sector is Portoferraio, the island's administrative and economic centre, with a population of over 10,000. Marina di Campo, the second largest town on Elba, is a holiday resort with fine beaches as well as a port. Procchio, another resort, is also situated on an important junction of the island's road network.

A second belt of lower-lying alluvial land, running from north to south between Procchio and Marina di Campo, separates central Elba from the western sector, the great granite massif of Monte Capanne (3,306 feet) and its subsidiary peaks. Once again the landscape changes completely; instead of looking outward towards the sea, the eye is constantly turning inland towards the towering mountains. Their lower slopes, on the northern side, are covered with forests of chestnut and oak; on the barer slopes to the west and south terraced vineyards are pushed up the narrow torrent-valleys, and the ridges between them are thick with *macchia*. Higher up, there is little but bare rock-screes, sheep-cropped grass, and enormous weathered boulders, some of which have taken on fantastic shapes.

The principal town in this sector is Marciana, an ancient mountain-town built high up among the chestnut trees of the northern slopes, a town by virtue of its antiquity and its role as centre of a commune but with a population of only just over 2,000. Below it, on the northern seashore, is the resort-town of Marciana Marina, built along an open bay with a pebble beach. The cliffs round the western end of Elba are broken by a series of small coves, each with its fishing village. Some of these, notably Sant'Andrea to the north and Cavoli, Seccheto, and Fetovaia to the south, have been developed into holiday resorts; the southern group have good, small, sandy beaches.

According to the most generally accepted theory Elba, like most of the other islands of the Tuscan Archipelago, originally was part of a landmass which, during the Miocene Period, some 30 million years ago, linked the Western Alps with Corsica and Sardinia. A subsidence occurring between the Miocene and Pliocene Periods broke up this mass into islands and promontories; a second post-Pliocene subsidence reduced the surface area of the islands and changed the Tuscan coastline; it may have been this subsidence, rather than the rising sea-level, which eventually cut off Elba from the mainland. Finally an elevation of the whole area gave the coast and islands the general shape they have today.

Evidence to support the theory of subsidence is found in the fact that, apart from the paradoxical island of Pianosa, no part of the Tuscan Archipelago shows any Miocene or Pliocene formations. In Elba the landscape above the 650 foot contour is typical of land which has been above sea-level from a very remote period; below that contour, among softer sedimentary rocks, such as sandstone and marls, there are both marine deposits laid down during a period of submersion and alluvial deposits formed after that land had risen again. There is also some evidence to show that, either because of continued elevation or because of alluvial deposits, the coastline of Elba has continued to change. A chapel built on the water's edge some 500 years ago, to mark the point where Pope Gregory XI disembarked during his voyage from Avignon to Rome, is now 1km. inland.

The three sectors into which Elba is divided topographically are also distinguished by their geological structure. In the mountains of the eastern sector, the entire series of Elban rock formations can be seen in continuous stratification although the strata have been violently disturbed. The sandstones, limestones, schists and argillaceous schists laid down during the Eocene Period are penetrated by eruptive serpentine formations and intrusions of metalliferous rocks such as the iron-ore deposits. In the middle sector of Elba, separated from the eastern block by alluvial valleys, the underlying rocks are eruptive porphyries, overlaid in many places by Eocene sandstone and calcareous clays. In the western sector, separated again by a low-lying tract, a basis of sedimentary rocks with serpentine and porphyritic intrusions has been covered by an enormous granite cap, the massif of Monte Capanne. The date of this granite has been much disputed but it is generally supposed to be post-Eocene. A comparison with certain formations in the Maremma, on the Tuscan mainland, suggests that the Elban granite may date from a period between the Upper Eocene and the Middle Miocene when a vast upheaval was giving birth to the Alps and the Appennines.

MINERALS

About 150 different minerals have been found in Elba, and the island has been described as a natural museum. As such, it is of interest not only to the academic student of geology but also to the amateur mineralogist or 'rock-hunter', and particularly to those who collect semi-precious gemstones for polishing and mounting. To those who take up mineralogy for the first time on arrival in Elba, the purchase of one of the numerous specimen-cards, on sale in many Elban shops, which exhibit small samples of twenty or more of the island's minerals, will be of considerable help in identifying further specimens.

One of the Elban localities favoured by mineralogists is on the lower slopes of Monte Capanne, to the south and south-east, near the villages of San Piero and Sant'Ilario in Campo. Here there is an area of pegmatite, a coarse-grained crystalline rock related to granite, which is rich in tourmalines, rock crystals, feldspar, garnet and beryls. Certain spots on these slopes, with names like Grotta d'Oggi and Fonte del Prete, are said to be particularly happy hunting-grounds but they do not appear on any map and are hard to trace without a local guide. However a British gemmologist reports that if you follow the road to the cemetery, due south of the village of San Piero, and branch off it to the left down a short path which descends the hillside to the main road below, it is possible to find on and around this path some fine black tourmalines spectacularly embedded in white quartz. In the same area he has found rock crystal and common white opal; opal, that is, which is without fire or colour but can still be polished *en cabochon* to produce lustrous and semi-translucent stones. Lumps of this white opal, often marred by impurities, are also to be found embedded in patches of grey clay along the embankment of the road at the foot of this path.

It should be noted that while Elbans are accustomed to the mineral-collector and do not mind him wandering about their countryside, they do not expect him to start digging up the ground or seriously disturbing walls or embankments, and will view such activities with disfavour.

Further along the southern slopes of Monte Capanne, the hillside between San Piero and the two coastal villages of Cavoli and Seccheto is intersected by a number of mule-tracks and footpaths. Provided the weather is clear and you stick to the path, you are in little danger of getting lost. Some of these tracks lead past small quarries where workmen cut the local granite into building blocks, kerb-stones, and vineyard-posts, and where they occasionally find geodes, hollow concretions of rock with amethyst or other crystals inside them. If you can find a quarry which is not being worked, you should look there for amethyst, smoky quartz, and, if you are lucky, beryl. Further to the west, in the long mountain valley leading inland from the coastal village of Pomonte, copper pyrites have been found some 2·5km. up the track from the coast.

While the northern slopes of Monte Capanne are not of great interest to the mineralogist, the eastern slopes between Sant'Ilario and the shrine of the Madonna del Buonconsiglio might repay study. Much of the land is overgrown with *macchia* or cultivated, but the course of the Forcione stream is said to have been a fruitful source of mineral finds.

The volcanic rocks of the central sector of Elba – porphyries and quartz – do not seem to provide gem-stones but can be satisfactorily polished to produce ornamental book-ends, etc. Along the coast between Capo d'Enfola and Portoferraio, there is aplite, a milky-coloured rock liberally spotted with small dark-grey or brown incipient tourmalines which often look like stains; this gave rise to the legend that the stains were oil splashes left on the beaches by ancient Greek mariners after anointing themselves. The beach of Le Ghiaie at Portoferraio is formed of such pebbles.

The eastern sector of Elba is, of course, the site of the iron mines operated by the big Italian state concern called Italsider. The open-cast workings may be visited by special permission on Saturdays, when work stops; application should be made to the Italsider offices in Rio Marina. The exposed soil is ruddy with haematite and studded like a plum cake with the opaque gold-coloured crystals of iron pyrites, the commonest gemstone of Elba. There are also mines to the south, in the promontory of Monte Calamita, where one of the principal ores is magnetite, giving rise to the name Calamita which means 'lodestone'. These mines are not open to visitors although they are particularly rich in minerals. But the keen rock-hunter has nevertheless an opportunity to sample their resources.

He should take the road which runs south from Capoliveri towards Punta Calamita high above the sea. After a few hundred metres of tar macadam, its surface is metalled only with the small stones that have come from the screening, dressing, and cleaning plants of the Calamita mines. The whole road is in effect a mine's waste tip where a great variety of minerals can be identified and collected. The most conspicuous are malachite and azurite, because of their brilliant green and blue colours, but a British expert has made the following list of minerals identified on this road:

Magnetite	Pyrites
Ilvaite	Copper Pyrites
Heidenbergite	Blende
Epidote	Malachite
Feldspar	Azurite
Limonite	Erythrite
Aragonite	Galena

Because some of these substances are soluble in water, the road surface is more rewarding in the summer, after the dry season, than in the spring after the winter rains. One of the rarest of these minerals is aragonite which ranges in colour from milky white to a strong Cambridge blue, but, in spite of its rarity, great blocks of it are used as door-stops in some of the Capoliveri houses.

Great care should, however, be exercised on this road as it zig-zags round a series of blind bends, and apart from the danger of the occasional Italian motorist driving with undue exuberance, there are also the heavy Italsider lorries which travel at considerable speed; the zealous rock-hunter should not become so immersed in his search as to forget them. Care should also be taken in parking your own car; lay-bys are infrequent and on its seaward side, the road-shoulder is narrow, and often overhangs a drop amounting virtually to a cliff.

Apart from minerals associated with the mines, the northern mountains in the eastern sector also contain serpentine of a rather brittle and shaley variety, and red jasper, which is to be found round Monte Grosso although it is somewhat difficult of access.

For those who do not want to do their own mineral-hunting, there are shops in all the major centres which sell gems and geological specimens, some worked and some unworked; one of the best-stocked is in the main piazza of Rio nell'Elba, although some of the specimens on offer there have been imported from Brazil or Portugal. Travellers are also likely to see small boys offering examples of haematite and pyrites, either holding them out at the roadside or taking them round café tables in the towns; about half the asking-price should be paid unless the specimen is of exceptionally good quality.

FLORA

In Elba, in spite of its small area, a great variety of typical Mediterranean plants may be found. Among them are a number of the so-called 'old' trees, such as the Carob, Myrtle, Plane, Judas tree, Olive, Vine, and Lentisk, surviving from Tertiary times because the last Ice Age did not overwhelm the Mediterranean basin; many of these plants have few or no close relatives, which shows they diverged from the main stock a long time ago, all closely related species having become extinct. Other typical Elban trees and shrubs – the Palms, Loquats, Eucalyptus, Mimosa, Oranges and Lemons, as well as Agaves and Cacti – have all been imported into the region from elsewhere.

Because of the marked geological difference between the granite at the western end of Elba and the limestone and other calcareous rocks of the eastern and central sections, there is a contrast in vegetation. The lower slopes of Monte Capanne in the west are covered with deciduous forest, while the worn-down hills of the centre and the slopes below the limestone crags in the east are dense with that most characteristic of Mediterranean plant communities, the *macchia*.

The forests on the northern slopes of Monte Capanne, round Marciana and Poggio, are predominantly sweet chestnut, mixed with acacia and holm oak. They have an undergrowth of herbaceous, tuberous and bulbous annuals, such as cyclamen (both spring-flowering and autumn-flowering varieties), iris, daphne, anemone, hellebore, orchids, gladiolus and periwinkle; there are also climbing plants such as clematis, honeysuckle, smilax, black briony, and jasmine.

The *macchia* is formed of dense, and sometimes impenetrable thickets of shrubs. According to botanists, it may be either primary *macchia* which is the highest development of vegetation under particular local conditions, or secondary *macchia* which is the result of man's operations against an original evergreen forest. In Elba where wood was cut from prehistoric times to fuel the ore kilns, it is almost certainly secondary. The island offers examples of both 'high *macchia*' and 'low *macchia*'. The former is characterized by the presence of trees, some of which may grow as high as 12–15 feet; they include Holm and Kermes oak, Juniper, Strawberry Tree (Arbutus unedo), Judas Tree, Aleppo Pine and a number of larger shrubs such as Myrtle, Spanish Broom, and Tree Heather. The 'low *macchia*' is without trees and its bushes tend to be 4–6 feet high; they include Lentisk, *Phyllerea media*, Rosemary, Jerusalem Sage, Butcher's Broom, Christ's Thorn and various heathers. There is of course no hard and fast distinction between 'high' and 'low' *macchia* which merge into one another.

Elba is notable for a particular sub-variety of this vegetation, the Cistus *macchia*, in which various species of Rock-rose are conspicuous, including *Cistus Albidus, Cistus Villosus*, and *Cistus Monspeliensis* The Cistus exudes a fragrant resinous gum called *ladanum* which may be the biblical myrrh; it is used today in perfumery and medicine. The odour of *ladanum* is only one ingredient in the aromatic breath of the *macchia*; the various herbs – sage, thyme and rosemary for example – all contribute their characteristic perfumes and the heat of the summer sun draws off the resinous oils of many other plants.

The plants of Elba flower in the spring and the autumn; during the high summer, the dark evergreens of the *macchia* stand out against the grey of the rocks and the brown of dried-up pastures. The flowers are particularly magnificent in May and early June when the various forms of broom are in full butter-coloured bloom and the rock-roses, pink, pale mauve, and white, are seen everywhere along the roadside and the tracks through the *macchia*. With the first rains of the autumn from October onwards *Cyclamen Neapolitanum* and *Cyclamen Graecum* come into flower along with several varieties of Autumn Crocus.

FAUNA

MAMMALS

The largest wild animal known to exist in Elba is the roe-deer; it has been re-introduced for the benefit of Italian sportsmen who enjoy shooting it in the autumn hunting season, but there is enough dense cover to favour its survival. The authors watched a doe and two half-grown fawns walk calmly out of the woods on to the motor-road across Monte Perone, retreating unhurriedly when they realized they were under observation. Local guides report the reintroduction also of the wild boar (*cinghiale*) which frequents the hills beyond the Maremma on the Tuscan mainland, but there is no evidence to suggest that it has survived the annual onslaught of the hunting season.

Among smaller mammals, hares and rabbits are now very scarce, and a species of marten which once inhabited the woodlands is said to have been hunted to extinction. Rodents include the fat, or squirrel dormouse, said to be common in the chestnut woods round Marciana, and several members of the mouse family, including *Mus sylvaticus* and *Mus decumanus*. Hedgehogs are common. Two varieties of bat have been seen, *Vesperugo noctula* and, more rarely, the horseshoe bat.

Offshore fishermen have occasionally captured the monk seal (*Pelagius monachus*) which used to play havoc with the nets of the tunny fisheries while that industry survived; this seal is said to be commoner along the lonely shores of Capraia. Cetaceans sighted off the Elban coastline include two varieties of dolphin, *Delphinus delphis* and *Delphinus tursio*.

BIRDS

Elba has a rich bird life in spite of the fact that edible species are also threatened during the hunting season. British visitors should remember that in Italy the song-thrush (*Tordo*) is regarded as a game-bird, and regularly appears on restaurant menus. The island has been called 'the Heligoland of the Mediterranean' because of the great variety of migrants which use it as a way-station: some 230 different species have been sighted. But there are also more than 40 resident species, most of them protected by the dense cover of the *macchia*. The list includes:

Buzzard, peregrine falcon, kestrel, tawny and little owls, raven, red-legged partridge, rock dove, cormorant, Cory's shearwater and sooty shearwater, little grebe, Audouin's gull, black-headed and lesser black-backed gulls, blue, long-tailed, and great tits, nuthatch, wallcreeper, Alpine accentor, cirl bunting, blue rock thrush, black-winged pratincole, white and pied wagtails, crested and wood larks, Italian house sparrow and tree sparrow, several finches, and a variety of warblers.

Two birds which are likely to catch the attention of the casual observer are the nightingale, regarded as a migrant, which sings all day long on the wooded flanks of the eastern range of hills, and the Sardinian warbler, a small black-capped bird with a flash of white in its tail which flutters along the roads through the chestnut woods in the western part of the island.

REPTILES

Two venomous snakes belonging to the Viper family are to be found in Elba, the asp and the adder. They tend to be small and timid, and are certainly no more common than the adders to be found in various southern English counties; the authors saw one unusually large adder, about 2 feet long, sunning itself on a sandy track on the southern slopes of Monte Capanne.

More common than either of them is the non-venomous *Coluber viridiflavus* which belongs to the whipsnake family; it has a latticed skin pattern of dark brown, pale yellow, and olive-green, and can grow to a length of $4^{1}/_{2}$ feet though such specimens are rare. A darker variant, *carbonarius*, without the yellow in its skin pattern, is also found.

There is an abundance of lizards, the commonest being the green and wall lizards; there is also the three-toed sand skink, with four rudimentary legs, which is popularly and quite erroneously supposed to be poisonous; it is not often seen because it normally buries itself in sand. Among the lizards must also be included the snake-like but quite harmless slow worm. Two species of gecko are to be found, *Platydactylus mauritanicus* and *Hemidactylus turcicus*; since the former hails from North Africa and the latter from Asia Minor, it is tempting to suppose that they were carried to Elba in the ships of the Moorish and Turkish pirates who so often descended on its shores. The edible frog and the common toad are widespread in the island.

The Greek tortoise and another variety called *Testudo lutea* are occasionally seen on Elba; the authors had to stop their car one evening near Magazzini while an unusually large specimen majestically crossed the road. The loggerhead sea turtle is occasionally seen offshore.

HISTORICAL CHART

PERIOD	DATE	EVENTS	EVIDENCE
Palaeolithic (Elba linked with mainland)	approx, 48,000 B.C.	Mousterian culture (Neanderthal) 1st wave.	Chipped and flaked implements in association with bones of large mammals.
	approx. 38,000 B.C.	Mousterian culture, 2nd wave.	
	approx. 18,000 B.C.	Arrival in Elba of *Homo sapiens*.	Slightly more sophisticated implements.
Neolithic (Elba an island)	approx. 5–4,000 B.C.	Seafaring migrants from east reach Elba and Giglio.	Polished stone implements; pottery with impressed ornament.
Bronze Age	approx. 3–2,000 B.C.	Rinaldonian culture in Elba.	Arrow and spear heads, flat axes, copper daggers.
	approx. 2,000 to 700 B.C.	Sub-Apennine culture in Elba (? Ilvates).	Pottery milk-boilers, querns, spindles, loom-weights, razor-shell scrapers.
Iron Age	700–300 B.C.	Greek colonial expansion into W. Mediterranean. Growth of Etruscan power in N. Italy.	Remains of copper and iron-ore kilns; Aristotle's mention of 'Aethalia', as source first of copper, then of iron. Unconfirmed reports of Etruscan tombs in Elba.
	540 B.C.	Battle of Sardinian Sea, in which Etruscans defeated Greeks.	

PERIOD	DATE	EVENTS	EVIDENCE
Roman Republic approx. 300 B.C. to 30 B.C.	approx. 300 B.C.	Rome takes Elba from Etruscans of Populonia. Elban mines main source of iron for Republic's armies. Romans exploit Elban granite quarries.	Roman tombs in Elba. Virgil's reference to Elba's mines of steel. Island capital called Fabricia. Elban granite used in Pantheon.
Roman Empire 30 B.C.– A.D. 410	30 B.C.– A.D. 14	Augustus, first Emperor, bans mining from Italian soil. Elban iron industry halted. During later Empire, Tuscan islands become places of retirement for wealthy or of exile for banished courtiers.	Large Roman villas at Le Grotte and Cavo in Elba, and on Giglio and Giannutri.
Dark Ages	410–850	Islands offer refuge to religious fugitives.	In early fifth century Rutilius Namazianus refers to monks on Capraia.
	approx. 450	St Mamilian, bishop of Palermo, fleeing Vandals, reaches Elba and then Montecristo.	
	approx. 550	St Cerbone, bishop of Populonia, fleeing Lombards, hides in Elba	

PERIOD	DATE	EVENTS	EVIDENCE
	755	Following Arabs' conquest of N. Africa and Spain, their forces occupy Corsica and Sardinia. First raids on Elba follow.	
Rise and fall of Pisan Republic	850–1398		
	850 onwards	Pisa becomes interested in Elban iron mines.	Pisan fortresses (Volterraio and Marciana) in Elba as well as watch-towers and fortified churches.
	1004–16	Pisan wars with 'Saracens' led by Musetto; Elba sacked by Arabs.	
	1138	Pisa exercising full sovereignty over Elba.	
	1293 onwards	Genoa competing with Pisa for possession of Elban iron-mines.	
Appiano Lordship	1398–1548		
	1398	Gherardo d'Appiano sells Pisa to Milan but retains lordship of Piombino, Elba, Pianosa and Montecristo.	Appiano family takes over fortress of Marciana and builds 'Casa degli Appiani', in town.
	1402	Appiano family yield Elban iron-mines to Genoa.	Shrine to S. Cerbone built by Appiano family.

PERIOD	DATE	EVENTS	EVIDENCE
	1442	Elba attacked by Tunisian corsairs.	
	1501–3	Cesare Borgia, Duke of Valentino, briefly possess Elba and Piombino but is expelled after death of Pope Alexander VI.	
	1504	Aroodje Barbarossa commanding Tunisian fleet, captures papal galleys off Elba.	
	1543	Khair-ed-Din Barbarossa, chief admiral of Turkish forces, raids Rio in Elba.	Permanent destruction of Elban town, Grassera.
	1544	Khair-ed-Din Barbarossa ravages Elba as reprisal against Jacobo d'Appiano for failing to release hostage.	
Partitioning of Elba	1548–1650		
	1548	With agreement of Emperor Charles V, Duke Cosimo de'Medici of Florence establishes fortified harbour and city at Portoferraio, on pretext of defending bay against Turkish fleets	Old city and harbour of Portoferraio.

PERIOD	DATE	EVENTS	EVIDENCE
	1553–5	Two massive attacks on Elba by Dragut, now in command of Turkish navy.	Destruction of walls of Marciana.
	1560 onwards	Jacobo VI d'Appiano squeezed out of Piombino by Spanish garrison, takes up residence in Elba.	
	1603	Spanish viceroy of Naples sends force to Elba to construct fort overlooking Porto Longone.	Inner walls of Porto Longone fortress.
'Promis- cuity of Powers'	1603–1794		
	1603	Last direct male heir of Appiano family, Jacobo VII, dies.	
	1646	French capture and re-fortify Porto Longone.	Outer walls of fortress.
	1650	Spanish, aided by Italians recapture Porto Longone.	
	1678	After brief revival of African corsair operations Spaniards strengthen defences of Porto Longone.	Forte Focardo.

PERIOD	DATE	EVENTS	EVIDENCE
	1708	Austrian invasion of Spanish-held Elba, as an operation in War of the Spanish Succession. Invasion withstood and defeated by Spanish governor, Pinel.	'Sassi Tedeschi' named after defeat of Austrians.
	1738	Grand Duchy of Tuscany passes after death of last de' Medici to Austria and is assumed by Lorraine family. So Austrian governors take over Portoferraio while Spanish governors, appointed by Bourbons of Naples, are in Porto Longone.	
	1786	Abortive British attempt to purchase Portoferraio as naval base.	
	1794	French royalists, fleeing from Revolution, are landed in Elba.	

PERIOD	DATE	EVENTS	EVIDENCE
French Elba		1794–1815	
	1796	British garrison placed in Elba as defence against French holding Livorno, but withdrawn after nine months.	'Forte Inglese' at Portoferraio.
	1799	After invading Tuscany French make landing in Elba. They are expelled by Elbans under Bourbon leadership after 4 months.	Memorial at Shrine of Madonna del Monte.
	1801–2	Second French landing in Elba and 13 month siege of Portoferraio. Island ceded to France under Treaty of Amiens, becomes French territory.	
	1814	The Emperor Napoleon Bonaparte, having surrendered to Allies under Treaty of Fontainebleau is granted sovereignty over the 'principality of Elba'.	Palazzina dei Mulini, Villa di S. Martino etc.
	1815	After stay of nine months and 22 days Napoleon escapes from Elba to France.	

PERIOD	DATE	EVENTS	EVIDENCE
Risorgi-mento	1815–60		
	1815	Island reverts to patrimony of Austrian Grand Dukes of Tuscany.	
	1848	Popular demonstra-tion in Portoferraio in support of Garibaldi.	
	1860	Elba, like rest of Tuscany, incor-porated in new Kingdom of Italy.	
Modern	1860–1950		
	1900	Commercial blast-furnaces built at Portoferraio.	
	1916	Portoferraio bom-barded by Austrian submarine.	
	1920–21	Industrial unrest at Portoferraio steel works.	
	1943	After collapse of fascist regime during World War II, Elba is occupied by Germans after bomb-ing Portoferraio.	Inscription outside town hall in Portoferraio.
	1944	After many Allied air-raids on Porto-ferraio, Free French expeditionary force lands on south coast and gains control of Elba.	'Il Monumento' and small war cemetery.

PERIOD	DATE	EVENTS	EVIDENCE
	1945	After war's end, company owning steelworks decides to dismantle plants as uneconomic.	
	1950	Elban authorities decide to develop tourist industry.	

HISTORY

PRE-HISTORY

The chipped and flaked stone implements of Palaeolithic Man have been found in Elba and other islands of the northern sector of the Tuscan Archipelago, the earliest of them being attributed to the Mousterian culture of Neanderthal Man and dating from perhaps 50,000 years ago. A second wave, also Mousterian, is believed to have entered the area 10,000 years later; and rather more advanced implements of the Upper Palaeolithic period suggest that *homo sapiens* arrived there about 20,000 years ago. However all these palaeolithic remains were found in association with the bones of large mammals, cave bear, rhinoceros and hippopotamus during the earlier period, and bears, wild goats, stags and roe-deer later on. This association indicates that, with the exception of Giglio and Giannutri (which were already islands), the archipelago did not then exist but was merely the higher levels of a great promontory stretching westwards from the mainland towards Corsica (and perhaps including it), a territory still accessible to migratory animals and the human hunters who followed them.

The pre-history of Elba as an island begins much later, with the arrival there of a neolithic people some five-thousand years after a progressive rise of the Mediterranean sea-level had cut it off from the other islands and eventually from the mainland. Between 5,000 and 4,000 B.C., sea-faring migrants who had moved gradually westwards and perhaps hailed originally from Asia Minor made landfalls in what they found to be uninhabited islands. Their polished stone implements, found in Elba, Pianosa and Giglio, include not only the famous axes set in bone or wooden hafts but also flint sickles and other artefacts which suggest an agricultural community. There are also fragments of pottery with impressed decoration, dating from this period.

With the beginning of the Bronze Age came the first exploitation of those mineral resources which have played such an important part in Elban history ever since. The first miners, in search of Elban copper ore, are believed to have arrived there between 3,000 and 2,000 B.C. They belonged to the so-called 'Rinaldonian Culture', (named after a site on the mainland near Bolsena), and have left abundant evidence of their active occupation of the island in the form of arrow-heads, spear-heads, flat axes and copper daggers. These weapons have been found at burial sites which were either man-made pits or natural holes and crannies in the rocks. They have also been found in the neighbourhood of copper-bearing deposits (as at Colle Reciso and Pomonte), together with slag and remains of the crude, cone-shaped kilns in which they smelted the ore. No trace of permanent settlements has been found, a fact which suggests that the miners may have lived in temporary encampments, transporting the raw copper to the mainland for further working.

The latest of the pre-historic peoples to leave evidence of their existence in Elba was the so-called 'Sub-Apennine' culture, an offshoot of the pastoral Apennine culture which flourished on the mainland during the Bronze Age between 2,000 and 1,000 B.C. The Sub-Apennine people seem to have combined the maintenance of flocks and herds with some degree of agriculture. Their settlements have been found in Elba near water-springs in the high places of the island and particularly in the group of peaks surrounding Monte Capanne. Here they constructed habitations among the boulders, supplementing the natural shelter of the rocks with hide and brushwood coverings and making floors of clay. These Sub-Apennine mountain shelters represent the last strongholds of a people driven from the more fertile lowlands by sea-raiders, like so many Elban populations after them. The remains found on these sites include grind-stones, querns, spindles and loom-weights, razor-shells collected from the seashore and used as knives or scrapers, as well as an abundance of rather specialized pottery. One utensil peculiar to this culture was a milk-boiler with a perforated lid designed to prevent the contents from boiling over. These people seem to have lived in Elba undisturbed from about 1,000 to 700 B.C. when they were overtaken by the Iron Age and the first stirrings of recorded history.

CLASSICAL PERIOD

The significance of Elba during the transition from the Bronze to the Iron Age was summarized by Aristotle, some five hundred years after the event. He wrote, 'They say that in Etruscan territory there is an island, to this day called Aethalia, in which there is a mine of copper, the metal from which they make the bronze which is used even nowadays in the manufacture of bronze vessels. But one day the mine gave out and produced no more copper. So after that they stopped mining for copper and mined instead for iron, as they still do today.'

The Greeks' name for Elba was derived from their word *aithalos*, meaning 'a smoky flame' or 'the thick smoke of a fire', so that Aethalia meant something like 'Smoke Island' or 'Fire Island'. This name was also applied to the Greek island of Lemnos, sacred to Hephaestus, the god of fire and blacksmiths. The fires of Lemnos were volcanic but there seems no doubt that the Tuscan island earned its name from the tall columns of smoke which Greek sea-farers saw rising along its shores from numerous primitive iron-kilns; their traces are still to be found today in lumps of slag and half-smelted ore. But although the Greeks had this word for it, Elba's true name from an early period was 'Ilva'. The ancient Romans knew of a tribe in the Ligurian Alps which they called the 'Ilvates'; and, if it is true, as some archaeologists believe, that the Sub-Apennine people of Elba came from Liguria, they may have been the first to name it. Ilva it was to the Romans; by the Middle Ages it had become modified to Ilba; succeeding centuries, possibly combined with Spanish influence, made it Elba.

Aristotle's reference to 'Etruscan territory' is also significant. During the period of Greek colonial expansion – from 750–550 B.C. – their colonists had no serious difficulty in gaining a footing in Sicily and southern Italy. But further north they clashed with the Etruscan Confederacy which was itself going through an expansive phase. Elba, then one of the very few sources of iron in the Mediterranean world, must have been contested between them. Which of them arrived there first is uncertain, but the Greeks knew a port in Elba which they called Argoos, doubtfully identified with the modern Portoferraio. Later, classical historians claimed that Jason, returning from the adventure of the Golden Fleece, had beached his ship, the Argo, there for overhaul; but since the Golden Fleece story commemorates a Greek raid or trading venture into the Black Sea, the presence of the Argo in the Western Mediterranean is, to say the least, improbable. The name Argoos could be derived from the Greek root *arg-*, meaning 'bright' or 'shining': it might then be taken to refer to the dazzling shingle and the white cliffs along the northern shore of the promontory on which Portoferraio is situated. Even so, the myth-makers have the last word: the dark spots of tourmaline which dapple the white pebbles of that coast are said to have been caused by the oil with which the Greek mariners anointed themselves.

Greek expansion in this area was eventually repulsed after an Etruscan victory in the Battle of the Sardinian Sea in 540 B.C. But although the Etruscans then exploited the iron-mines, they do not seem ever to have settled in large numbers on Elba. No Etruscan city sites have been found and there are no recognizable Etruscan place names, with the possible exception of the mountain-fortress, Volterraio, sometimes associated with Volterra in Tuscany.

Some Etruscan artefacts have been found in Elba but unfortunately only by those enthusiastic private excavators and treasure-seekers who preceded scientific archaeology. Their finds included a mirror, a necklace and earrings of gold, a small bronze figurine, and some black *bucchero* pottery. But these objects were all removed, like most of Elba's antiquities, to museums on the mainland where they are given the *provenance* 'Elba' without any indication of site. An Etruscan cemetery is reported to have been found and plundered on Capo Stella during the nineteenth century. The Etruscans, like their copper-seeking predecessors, the pre-historic 'Rinaldonians', seem to have visited Elba for the purpose of mining iron-ore and smelting it but then carried the crude metal back to the mainland, most probably to their city of Populonia, which lies on the coast just north of Piombino and still shows the slag and other by-products of a thriving iron trade.

The Etruscan Confederacy gave way to the expanding power of the Roman Republic and it is legitimate to deduce that Elba, as a source of iron, was an early Roman objective. The Roman Republic is thought to have taken over control of the island from the Etruscan rulers of Populonia about 300 B.C. Once again the archaeologist is frustrated by the treasure-seekers of past centuries; Roman tombs are known to have been found and plundered in the neighbourhood of Rio in the iron-mining area of Elba, and from contemporary descriptions of what was found in them, it is believed that they dated from the second century B.C.. Roman smelting techniques seem at that period to have been almost as unsophisticated as those of their predecessors in the island; the ore was heated in underground furnaces between layers of wood or charcoal without the addition of any flux-agent; the production rate was only 30 per cent of what might have been extracted, and the crude metal was of a spongy consistency.

Nevertheless it may be true that Elban iron carved out the foundations of the Roman Empire even if it ceased to be used after that Empire had been established. The poet, Virgil, wrote of 'Ilva, the island rich in unexhausted mines of steel', but Virgil's emperor,

Augustus, issued a decree forbidding the extraction of minerals, including iron, from the Italian sub-soil. Pliny, who records this decree in his *Natural History* indicates that metal of a superior quality was by then coming in from the iron-mines of Bilbao in Spain and Noricum (modern Austria). Evidence of Elba's previous importance to the Roman state is to be found in the Latin name for its capital on the site of the modern Portoferraio: it was called Fabricia i.e. 'the place of smiths'. Other Roman settlements known to have existed in Elba were Pomonte ('Post Montem'), Caput Liberum (now Capoliveri), Faleria (near Cavo), and Marciana.

During the Roman imperial period the islands of the Tuscan archipelago dropped out of history except as occasional places of exile for distinguished people who had incurred the emperor's displeasure, perhaps chosen for that purpose because they were also regarded as attractive retreats for the well-to-do. The remains of large and luxurious villas have been found on several of the islands. In Elba the ruins at Le Grotte, looking across the Bay towards Portoferraio are so elaborate and extensive in ground-plan as to give rise to the theory that they are the remains of the palace of the Roman governor of the island. Owing to the depredation of sea-raiders and perhaps also of the local population looking for building material, little now remains of them above ground. There are only foundations and underground store-rooms, but it is still possible to see that the villa once occupied an entire headland. Elba still had one industry under the Empire: its granite-quarries round Monte Capanne catered for the Roman passion for public monuments. Some of the pillars of the Pantheon in Rome are made of Elban granite, and one almost complete pillar survives unused in a quarry near Seccheto at the western end of Elba.

DARK AND MIDDLE AGES

As the Western Roman Empire approached its decline, the Tuscan islands, like many other parts of Italy, are believed to have become increasingly deserted. They were, however, places of refuge for fugitives from the fire and slaughter on the mainland; and as the spirit of Christian monasticism spread westwards from Egypt and Syria, they became retreats to which hermits and ascetic communities fled from the spiritual as well as the physical dangers of a wicked world.

St Mamilian, bishop of Palermo, was banished from his see by

Genseric, king of the invading Vandals, and sent off to imprisonment in North Africa. Escaping in a small boat, he took up the hermit life, first in Sardinia and then in Elba where a small hamlet is named after him just outside Marina di Campo. From Elba on clear days he could see the conical outline of Montecristo, then called *Mons Jovis* (Mount of Jupiter) after the pagan temple on its summit; and thither about A.D. 450 he eventually retired. Legend says that he defeated a monstrous serpent and made the island 'Mons Christi', living out the rest of his days in a cave in the mountainside. He let it be known that when he died, a cloud would appear on the mountain top; and when this signal was duly sighted the people of Giglio hastened to Montecristo and removed the saint's body to their own island where it was entombed for 600 years. Then his bones were transported to Pisa but the men of Giglio were allowed to retain his right arm. There it survives, encased in silver and hung with votive offerings, with the reputation of having repelled a raid of Turkish pirates.

Just over a century later, Italy was invaded and conquered by another barbarian horde, the Teutonic 'Long Beards' or Lombards. Like the Vandals before them, the Lombards subscribed to the Arian heresy which subordinated God the Son to God the Father, a fact which perhaps encouraged them to persecute the Church in Italy with special savagery. As one of their leaders, Gummarith, approached Populonia the bishop of that place, St Cerbone, fled with some of his clergy to Elba, and set up a hermitage in the chestnut forests on the lower slopes of Monte Capanne. But he had only lived there a year when he felt death approaching and instructed his religious brethren to take his body back to his diocese on the mainland for burial. When they protested that the presence there of Gummarith would make their mission certain death, he assured them of divine protection. According to the legend, the funeral boat was shrouded by a dense squall of rain which enabled the brethren to carry the body ashore and bury it under the noses of the Lombards. St Cerbone's bones were later removed to the neighbouring hillside town of Massa Marittima where they repose in a stone sarcophagus in the crypt of the church. Animated bas-reliefs, both on the coffin itself and over the west door of the church, illustrate the charming legends which are told about this saint; in Elba, the first autumn storms are called 'St Cerbone's weather'. Soon after this episode, the Lombards invaded and occupied Elba.

After barbarians by land came barbarians by sea, an even greater

threat to the islands and particularly to Elba which, with more
territory to ravage and a larger population to enslave, also offered the
sea-raiders two magnificent harbours as bases for operations against
the mainland. Pirates, mainly from North Africa, had always
flourished when there was no central power to control the sea; after
the Saracen conquests of North Africa and Spain during the seventh
and eighth centuries, Tunisian corsairs had a virtual mandate to attack
Christendom. Between A.D. 755 and A.D. 1000 the Saracens were in
occupation of Sardinia and Corsica. Their first recorded raids against
Elba came at the beginning of the ninth century and again in A.D. 849.

They might even have established themselves on the island if help
had not come from the first of the Italian city states to emerge from
the Dark Ages. The Republic of Pisa became aware of the value of the
Elban iron-mines which had lain disused for five hundred years. As
early as 874, a Pisan naval squadron intercepted a Saracen flotilla and
drove it off. Although the first official document recognizing Pisa's
sovereignty over the islands does not appear till 1138, there is
evidence of a gradual and practical extension of her control much
earlier. The little island of Palmaiola, which the ferry-boat passes in
the straits between Elba and the mainland, was fortified and
garrisoned by the Pisans in 909. Some of the Elban coastal watch-
towers may also date from this century.

By the year 1,000 the Pisans' naval strength was such that the Pope
gave them a mandate to free the Mediterranean from the dominion of
the Saracens. In the years 1004–5, they undertook operations which
dislodged the Arabs from Corsica and Sardinia. Unfortunately this
triumph seems to have gone to their heads; they then despatched their
entire navy to the Ionian Sea in response to an appeal from cities in
Calabria for help against Moorish invaders. In its absence the
Saracens, under a leader called Musetto, regained Sardinia and raided
the mouth of the River Arno, landing by night to plunder Pisa and
burn its suburbs. When their navy returned to home waters, the
Pisans made a retaliatory attack on Musetto in Sardinia, destroying his
fleet, expelling him once more from the island and forcing him to sue
for peace.

During the next ten years Musetto prepared his revenge, rebuilding
a fleet and recruiting a large expeditionary force. In 1015 he set out,
this time apparently by-passing Sardinia and making straight for the
harbour of Portoferraio in Elba. Part of his force disembarked to
occupy the island, while the main body swung north to make an

unopposed landing on the mainland near La Spezia. Here Musetto besieged and captured the ancient and formerly Etruscan city of Luni, which he used as his base while his troops ravaged the countryside right up to the closed gates of Genoa, Pisa, and other cities. However his forces were not strong enough to consolidate their gains; and eventually the Pisans, with reinforcements from Pope Benedict VII and from other neighbouring states, went over to the offensive and recaptured Luni. They then turned their attention to Elba, where the Saracen occupation force was already re-embarking on news of the defeat at Luni. They found a completely devastated island with its remaining inhabitants lurking in the woods and mountains.

It was probably after this repulse of the Saracens in 1016 that Elba was deliberately incorporated into Pisan territory and given more adequate defences. Two fortresses were built, one at Volterraio and one at Luceri, to command the bay of Portoferraio; a third was built in the western area of the island at Marciana. At Rio, Poggio, San Piero and Sant'Ilario the churches were strengthened with bastions to become fortified refuges for the local population; and it may have been at this time that Capoliveri became a walled city. For over two centuries Elba seems to have enjoyed peace under Pisan protection. The iron-mines resumed production and the granite-quarries supplied material for Pisa's churches. By the middle of the twelfth century, the finances of the Republic of Pisa were largely based on the sale of Elban iron, while the island also paid substantial tithes and an annual tribute of falcons to its archbishopric. In Elba there appeared those severely romanesque little churches whose ruins survive at S. Giovanni on the slopes of Monte Perone, S. Lorenzo below Marciana, and Santo Stefano near Magazzini. The island was divided into communes but there was also a central local administration with one, or perhaps two consuls, a 'chamberlain' (or financial secretary), councillors and syndics. A Pisan *capitano* commanded the garrison.

The Pisan regime in Elba came under attack when Genoa began to dispute the primacy of the Pisan Republic. The Elban iron-mines were one of Genoa's first objectives, and an early Genoese raid on the island took place in 1162, near Capo S. Andrea on the shore below Marciana. The real decline of Pisan power began in the thirteenth century when the naval forces of the Republic were defeated by the Genoese under Alberto Doria at the battle of Meloria in 1222. A struggle for the possession of Elba began in 1291 when a Genoese fleet of 60 galleys, under the command of Niccolò Boccanegra, landed forces in the island and conquered it in a four months' campaign. In the following year the Pisans recaptured it but were driven out again by the Genoese a few months later. In 1293 the Pisans, led by Guido da Montefeltro, once more regained possession but were under sufficient pressure to agree to pay the Genoese a ransom of 50,000 gold florins to avoid further conflict. After the defeat at Meloria, Pisa was ruled by a succession of feudal 'lords'.

FOURTEENTH AND FIFTEENTH CENTURIES

The next hundred years seem to have left Elba in peace and quiet, apart from the excitement in 1376 of offering hospitality to the reigning pope, Gregory XI, who, at the prompting of St Catherine of Siena, was transferring the papal see from Avignon back to Rome. He had made the journey by sea from Marseilles, stopping at Genoa, Pisa, and Livorno on the way before putting in to Elba where he spent a day at the island's capital, then called Feraia, which was probably a short distance inland from the modern Portoferraio. In 1387 Elba received an ominous warning of the decline of the Pisan's sea-power when some of their ships were captured by Saracen galleys raiding the Straits of Piombino, between the island and the mainland.

In 1392, the then lord of Pisa, Pietro Gambacorti, was assassinated by his secretary, Jacobo Appiano, who usurped his rule. But he died only six years later, and his son, Gherardo Appiano, sold Pisa and most of its territory to the Duke of Milan, Galeazzo Visconti, for 200,000 florins. Gherardo retained for himself the principality of Piombino, together with the islands of Elba, Pianosa, and Montecristo. This was the somewhat shabby beginning of an association between Elba and the family of the Appiani which was to last for more than two centuries. It was also the beginning of Elba's involvement in the dynastic and international in-fighting which was to govern Italian history for the next five centuries. As a foretaste of what was to come, the Genoese took advantage of Pisa's overthrow by immediately landing a force in Elba and capturing the town of Capoliveri, as a first step towards seizing control of the iron industry. Gherardo Appiano in 1402 had to invoke the aid of the lord of Lucca against the Genoese; and although, through Lucca's good offices, a peace treaty was signed in the following year, the Appiano family had to pay a ransom to obtain it and also yield to Genoa the iron-mine concession.

During its century of peace, Elba had been able to build up some military and economic strength of its own. The island was cultivated again, and its ships were engaged in commerce. But in 1442 the Tunisian corsairs began to take advantage of its lack of naval protection. Their galleys landed a large force in Portoferraio bay and began to devastate the island. The Elban defenders took refuge in the hill-fortress of Volterraio and put up a desperate resistance. They were relieved in the nick of time by a force from Piombino which landed under cover of darkness and bad weather, and the Tunisians found themselves caught between two fires. Except for those who were able to swim to their galleys, they were all slaughtered on the beaches. After this episode, the Elbans were able to beat off other Tunisian raids and even to repel a joint Neapolitan-Genoese force which attacked the island during a dynastic quarrel with the Orsini family, one of whom had married an Appiano daughter. In 1483 Elba contributed a contingent to an abortive expedition organized by the Appiani against Corsica.

As the fifteenth century ended, Piombino and its islands became briefly involved in the power structure which was being built up in Italy by the Borgia family under its head, Pope Alexander VI. The Pope's son, Cesare Borgia, Duke of Valencia, laid siege to Piombino in 1501 in the absence of the reigning Appiano, Jacobo IV, who was visiting Genoa. French intervention forced him to withdraw, but his father, the Pope, persuaded the principality to capitulate on the grounds that Jacobo IV was planning to sell it to the Genoese. In 1503, Pope Alexander died and, after a few months, the Holy See passed to one of his family's bitterest enemies, Julius II of the Farnese clan. Cesare Borgia was forced out of Italy, and Piombino and the islands were restored to the Appiani.

SIXTEENTH CENTURY

Elban history during the sixteenth century was shaped by three international developments: by Spain's successful struggle with France for control of the Italian peninsula; by the establishment of the Grand Duchy of Tuscany; and at sea by the transformation of the North African pirate squadrons into the navy of the Turkish sultanate. Beyond the island's horizons four giant figures moved the armies and the fleets about the Mediterranean board: the King of Spain, who was elected Charles V, Holy Roman Emperor, and whose imperial forces perpetrated the sack of Rome itself; Suleiman the Magnificent, Sultan of Turkey, whose armies breached the eastern defences of the Empire while his navies dominated the sea; the 'most Christian' King of France, Francis I, who allied himself with the Turkish infidel in his efforts to bring down his Spanish rival; and lastly that ruthless and able offshoot of the de' Medici family, Duke Cosimo I of Florence, who in fact came over the horizon and set his personal mark on Elba itself. But beyond these four, there was another name which has entered Elban folk-lore and survives on its map, the name of Barbarossa, or 'Red Beard', the pirate-admiral who brought fire, sword, and enslavement to the island.

There were in fact two brothers both nicknamed Barbarossa after their henna-dyed whiskers. The elder, Aroodje, sometimes described as a Maltese renegade, commanded the fleet of the emir of Tunis; he is associated with the so-called 'coup of Elba', when ships under his command in 1504 ambushed and captured off the Elban coast two papal galleys, laden with treasure for Pope Julius II, which were making their way from Genoa towards Civitavecchia. Aroodje was killed in action in 1515, but his brother, Khair-ed-Din, allied himself with Turkey, rose to be chief admiral of the Turkish naval forces, and terrorized the Mediterranean for more than a decade.

The first appearance of this second Barbarossa in Elba was in 1534 after his fleet had swept up the Italian coastline, sacking the island of Procida in the Bay of Naples, and the cities of Fondi and Terracina. He landed his men at nightfall on Elba's east coast, possibly at the beach which still bears his name and made a night attack on the ancient city of Rio. Those of its inhabitants who were not slaughtered were driven off to the ships as slaves for the galley-oar and the harem. The township of Grassera, only a short distance from Rio, heard the tumult and manned its defences, but this resistance so infuriated the raiders that they razed it to the ground. Grassera disappeared from existence during this century, though it may not have been finally abandoned until after the Turkish attack in 1553. Many of the Elban slaves were released when imperial forces stormed Tunis in the following year.

During the next decade, Barbarossa dominated the Mediterranean, inflicting three major defeats on the imperial forces and ravaging the coastlines. After the Franco-Turkish alliance of 1541 he was able to use Toulon harbour as a base. In 1543 came one of those strange moments when the story of an obscure human individual emerges from the welter of history. Barbarossa was reported to be approaching the Italian coast with the Turkish war-fleet, and in Piombino Jacobo V d'Appiano flew into a panic behind his city's earthen ramparts. He appealed for help to his nephew-by-marriage, Cosimo de' Medici, the new ruler of Florence. Cosimo who, at the age of 23, was building himself an expanded dukedom under the Emperor's patronage, was delighted to put his own garrison into Piombino. At the last minute a *libeccio,* or squall from the south-west, forced Barbarossa to take shelter with his ships in the Gulf of Feraia on the north coast of Elba.

From there he sent envoys to Jacobo d'Appiano demanding the surrender – not of Piombino but of one small boy. When he had raided Rio nine years earlier, one of his captains, known as Sinan the Jew, had carried off an Elban girl and had a child by her. The girl and her baby had been re-captured from a Tunisian galley, taken by the imperial forces in 1539, and sent to Piombino. Jacobo d'Appiano had arranged Christian baptism for the child and had retained him at his court where he became a favourite. The corsair, Sinan, had heard of this and called on his admiral to reclaim his son.

Jacobo temporized; he told Barbarossa's envoys that the child was not with him but that he would arrange for the boy to be placed in the safekeeping of a 'man of trust' with whom Sinan could negotiate. Following this reply, Barbarossa sailed away from Elba, possibly because he was satisfied, possibly because French reinforcements of his fleet had failed to make an appearance. But he was back in Elba the following year to renew his demand for the boy, and this time Jacobo said that religious scruples forbade him to surrender a baptized Christian to an infidel. Barbarossa wasted no more time. He landed his men in Elba and sacked the town of Capoliveri, hunting down its inhabitants and driving them off as prisoners to his ships. Then he turned his attention to the two forts overlooking the Gulf of Feraia; he was not able to take Volterraio but he blew up the more accessible fort of Luceri and destroyed it. At this point Jacobo agreed to surrender his boy-favourite, provided Barbarossa released his Elban prisoners. The bargain was struck and the Turkish fleet departed.

The episode gave Duke Cosimo a long-awaited opportunity. He already had his own garrison manning his uncle-in-law's city; he now persuaded the Emperor, Charles V, that it would be expedient if he were allowed to fortify Elba against further Turkish incursions. He reinforced his argument with a request for the return of 200,000 *scudi* which he had lent the Emperor out of his wife's dowry. Charles V, therefore, agreed to 'sell' to Cosimo that part of Elba which looked on to the Gulf of Feraia, and to permit him to construct a fortified city there. The transaction took place over the heads of the Appiani, who owed allegiance to the Emperor and were reluctantly forced to concur. Conveniently for Cosimo, Jacobo V had just died, and his widow was regent of Piombino during her son's minority.

In April 1548, a Florentine fleet set sail from Piombino carrying soldiers and workmen, building materials and munitions of war, and Cosimo's architect, Giovanni Battista Bellucci. The chosen site for the new *piazza forte,* or 'stronghold', was the hook-shaped promontory to the west of the entrance into the bay. It had most probably been the site of the Roman capital, Fabricia, but it was deserted hillside when Bellucci reached it, and he reports that they had to clear away the *macchia* to reach the top of the hill where the fortresses were to be established. An early map shows Feraia as a walled city on rising ground on the other side of the watercourse, now called Fosso della Madonna, and set back from the shore, no doubt as a precaution against raiders. There is no trace of it today, but it may have been in the neighbourhood of San Michele and the house called *Casa del Duca,* where Cosimo reportedly stayed when he visited Elba to see the progress of his new city. Someone – perhaps the architects – had bestowed on it the complimentary name of *Cosmopoli.* The old Feraia presumably had a waterside extension where ships put in, and this would have been called 'Porto di Feraia' or 'Portoferaio'. It may have been on the bay round which the modern part of Portoferraio is now built. Vasari, the sixteenth-century art historian, describes a fresco depicting 'smiths, architects and masons before the gate of Cosmopoli, a city built by Duke Cosimo in the isle of Elba, *with a view of Portoferaia.*' But by the end of the century, the name 'Cosmopoli' had been dropped and Portoferraio was applied to the new city.

Bellucci was transferred after four months to other projects of the Duke and in Elba he was succeeded by his uncle, Sanmarino, and by Camerino. Although the Emperor was suggesting that the Duke's footing in Elba was only provisional and was withholding any financial assistance, Cosimo pressed forward with the work as fast as possible. A German map, depicting the island in 1555, shows 'the city Cosmopoli' with a complete circuit of the walls, the two forts, *Falcon* and *Stella,* a moat protecting the fortifications on the landward side, and the harbour closed with a boom and defended by the *Torre della*

Linguella. The bronze bust of Cosimo by Benvenuto Cellini, which was installed over the entrance of the Stella fort in 1557, might indicate a date of completion nine years after the work started.

There were two reasons for haste. Henry II of France, who had succeeded Francis I in 1547, was still employing the Turkish naval forces, now commanded by another pirate-turned-admiral, Dragut, with a reputation as formidable as that of Barbarossa. And Cosimo also feared the intervention of Genoa, which was watching his Elban project with a jealous eye and might have used its friendship with the Appiani family as an excuse for interference. This second threat the Duke forestalled with a naval demonstration against the Genoese port of Livorno, and also with a neat exercise in lifemanship: he made the youthful Jacobo VI d'Appiano captain-general of his galleys, thus both subordinating him and underlining his duty of loyalty.

Dragut however was not to be deterred. In 1553, and again in 1555, he struck two hammer-blows at Elba, each time with the support of a French squadron. The 1553 attack came early in August and followed the usual pattern of Turkish terror. There were two simultaneous landings, a cattle raid in the Gulf of Feraia and a main assault in the south-east, where Capoliveri, Rio, and other towns and villages were sacked and their inhabitants enslaved. The Elbans either hid themselves in the woods and high places or took refuge in strong points like Volterraio and the Giogo fort above the iron mines, or within the new ramparts of Portoferraio. Dragut avoided any direct attack on this last, although its guns harassed his forces when they came within range and galleys, based on the new port, made a successful sortie against his smaller craft in the Gulf of Feraia. But he roamed about the island, capturing Marciana and lingering so long that the Elbans feared he might winter there. Only on August 22nd, under pressure from his French allies, did he sail away for an attack on Corsica. When he returned in 1555, he began with an unsuccessful assault on Piombino and then fell back on Elba. But the inhabitants had been warned of his coming and had already taken what refuge they could, while the island's defences had been reinforced both by Tuscan troops and Genoese galleys. This time Dragut, who was able to sail round the Elban coast with impunity, did launch an assault on Portoferraio. The Duke's general, Cuppano, enticed the attackers beneath the fort batteries and inflicted heavy casualties. Once again Dragut's French allies insisted that the real objective of the expedition was Corsica and he departed. Although

Turkish vessels were to appear again off the coast, this was their last major attack on Elba.

In 1556 the Emperor Charles V went into religious retirement, handing over the Empire to his brother Maximilian, and the throne of Spain, together with its possessions in Italy, to his son, Philip II, who had married the Queen of England, Mary Tudor. The first British intrusion into Elban affairs came with a magnificently insular missive from Queen Mary to these remote vassals of her husband's. She wrote admonishing them to live as 'faithful Catholics' and to disregard the 'devilish calumnies' of those who might call them 'Papists and heretics'. The message must have mystified a simple people who had always been Catholic and knew nothing of the Reformation that was worrying the English queen.

Philip II took immediate steps to curb the ambitions of Duke Cosimo. In 1557, by the Treaty of London, he 'restored and confirmed' Jacobo VI d'Appiano as Lord of Piombino and Elba, with full rights to the revenues thereof. Duke Cosimo was allowed to keep his new city and the land for two miles round it. In fact the Appiani were merely being transferred from his overlordship to direct Spanish control; Spanish forces were to garrison Piombino and Spain retained the right to fortify 'other Elban ports'. On the mainland, the Duke was allowed to retain Siena which he had captured, with Spanish assistance, from the French; but all former Sienese ports were controlled, like Piombino, by Spanish garrisons.

In 1561 Duke Cosimo founded a naval Order of Chivalry, the Knights of San Stefano, with the mission of keeping the seas clear of Turkish infidels. It was originally planned that they should be based on Portoferraio as the remaining principal port of Tuscany, but the noble members of the Order preferred the less provincial atmosphere of Pisa where their headquarters, the Palazzo della Carovana, survives with a statue of the Duke in front of it. In 1570, Cosimo achieved his ambition: he was crowned Grand Duke of Tuscany by Pope Pius V. When he died four years later, his second son was confirmed Grand Duke by the Emperor, now the Austrian Maximilian II.

While the Tuscan dynasty was thus established, the Appiani were gradually being ground to extinction between the millstones of Spain and the Empire. Jacobo VI d'Appiano withdrew from the Spanish-garrisoned Piombino to Marciana in Elba, where he tried to exert his authority over the island outside the Tuscan enclave. But the Spanish garrison threw a detachment into the Giogo tower which overlooked

Rio and the iron-mines, and thus excluded him from the most lucrative part of his territory. He died and three years later his successor, Alessandro d'Appiano, was assassinated during a visit to the mainland, probably on the orders of the Spanish military governor of Piombino who immediately had himself 'elected' to the lordship and took possession of the Elban mines. The people of Rio protested, and Tuscany attempted military intervention. The usurper was eventually arrested and deported by his commander-in-chief, the Spanish Viceroy of Naples, who installed Jacobo VII d'Appiano in the lordship under the regency of his mother, Isabella.

SEVENTEENTH CENTURY

An Italian historian has apostrophized Elba at this stage of its history as 'This poor island condemned to live in a permanent state of promiscuity of Powers'. Jacobo VII died aged 20 in 1603, and a new Spanish Viceroy of Naples immediately sent forces to take over Piombino and establish themselves in Elba. Under Captain Joseph de Pons, seven companies of Spanish infantry landed in the south-east harbour of Longone, pleading the excuse of bad weather, and began unloading building material and constructing a fort on the headland overlooking the harbour. Protests came in to the Spanish government from Tuscany, Genoa, France, and the Vatican; but Madrid said it was the responsibility of the Viceroy of Naples, and the Viceroy said it was necessary to protect the harbour against Turkish pirates. It seems really to have been a move to offset the Tuscan presence in Portoferraio; significantly the harbourage was henceforward named Porto Longone.

Isabella, widow of Jacobo VI d'Appiano and a more forceful character than any of her menfolk, fought hard for the reinstatement of her family, and perhaps as part of the process was re-married, at Marciana, to a member of the influential clan of the Orsini. She appealed to the Emperor and was allowed to spend all her fortune in litigation in the imperial courts. In 1626 the Emperor Ferdinand II did announce that the Appiani could be reinstated in return for a payment of 800,000 ducats. But the money was no longer available and the Viceroy of Naples forbade them to borrow it from Tuscany. Eventually the lordship passed to Niccoló Ludovisi, a member of a Roman family who had married on Appiano daughter and had paid the Viceroy handsomely for the privilege.

France still cherished an ambition to expel Spain from the Italian peninsula, and in 1646 Cardinal Mazarin took active steps to this end. After one French expedition had swept down the coast attacking Spanish garrisons in the former Sienese ports, a second and larger fleet tackled Elba and Piombino. The mainland port fell in four days but the fort at Longone held out for 37 days before its garrison surrendered and was allowed to march out with drums beating and colours flying.

Spanish retaliation was delayed for four years while the French used Porto Longone as a base for their privateers. The Viceroy of Naples was busy quelling a local uprising against the severity of Spanish taxation, and the French had to withdraw part of the 1,500 man force garrisoning the fort to deal with riots in Paris. But in 1650 a Spanish and Italian armada, commanded by Don John of Austria, was assembled at Gaeta and proceeded to Elba in May. Its forces were landed at Ortano, to the north of Porto Longone, and at the Lido beach to the south, with the intention of encircling the fort on its landward side. The French, who had strengthened the fortifications with a second wall, conducted an active defence with many aggressive sorties. The siege lasted from May 25th until August 15th when the garrison, reduced by withdrawals and casualties to 700 men, surrendered. A citizen of Portoferraio, Marcantonio Carpano, who had served with the Spanish forces, was appointed commander of the troops left to garrison Piombino and Porto Longone; he is buried under the high altar of Portoferraio cathedral.

Seven years later, a French fleet entered Portoferraio bay apparently with the intention of recapturing the island. But its commanders received news of a Spanish fleet operating off the coast of Provence and threatening their communications. They immediately withdrew, and this was the last French intervention in Elban affairs for more than a hundred years.

Towards the middle of the seventeenth century, there was a revival of corsair activity off the Tuscan coast, including an attempted raid on Elba's southern shore at Campo; but the islanders were sufficiently well armed and organized to beat the pirates off. In 1675 Cosimo III, Grand Duke of Tuscany, organized an expedition against the pirates and inflicted a decisive defeat on them in the Piombino channel, just off the little island of Palmaiola. It may have been the renewed threat of corsairs which induced the Spaniards to strengthen still further the defences of Porto Longone. They constructed a second and smaller fort on the opposite side of the entry to the harbour, at Cape Naregno. It was completed in 1678 and called after a governor with the resounding name, Don Ferdinando Gioacchino Foscardo di Roquentes e Zuniga, a name which the Elbans briskly shortened to 'Fort Focardo'.

EIGHTEENTH CENTURY

The 'promiscuity of Powers' in Elba became even more complex when the island was caught up in the machinery of the War of the Spanish Succession, the dispute between the King of France and the Austrian Emperor over which dynasty should supply an heir to the throne of Spain. Louis XIV installed his grandson as Philip V of Spain; the Emperor, whose candidate was his second son, the Archduke Charles, declared war and opened an attack on the Spanish possessions in Italy. The war reached Elba in 1708 when, following their capture of Naples in the previous year, the Austrians landed a force near Rio and proceeded to occupy as many strongpoints in the island as possible. Portoferraio was left alone out of respect for the careful neutrality of the Grand Dukes of Tuscany; Capoliveri, under the threat of the guns of Porto Longone, remained loyal to Spain; the fortress of Longone was besieged.

In the event the Austrian force, perhaps 700 men in all, was not strong enough to carry out what it had attempted. Its commander, Count Valles, gained his initial successes largely because he had procured credentials from the Prince of Piombino, a title which had drifted by inheritance from the Ludovisi to the Boncompagni family. In these he was nominated governor of the island and, as such, received the support of some Elbans, who resented Spanish rule and remained loyal to even a remote connection of the Appiani. The people of Rio accepted him, and so did places in the west of Elba such as Marciana, San Pietro, and Sant' Ilario. Capoliveri he captured in a night assault, afterwards using that walled city as his headquarters.

But the imperial forces did not have command of the sea and were forced to split up into small detachments during their military operations. The Spanish governor, General Pinel, was able to bring in Spanish and French reinforcements from the mainland, and to make numerous sorties, both to procure supplies and to punish villages supporting the Austrians. One such sortie caught a group of imperial troops among the rocks above the Sanctuary of Monserrato and routed it; the *Sassi Tedeschi,* or 'German rocks', there are named after this engagement. An Austrian assault on Fort Focardo was repulsed with heavy losses; and in May the Spaniards took the initiative with a full-scale attack on Capoliveri. After burning off the *macchia* round its walls, General Pinel led a force of five hundred men to storm it. Fifty Austrians were killed, eighty taken prisoner, and the rest fled into the countryside. On May 16th, after his last organized force had been routed in the plain of Lacona, Count Valles escaped by sea from Portoferraio. He left behind him only scattered fugitives and a garrison of forty men which surrendered the fort on Mount Giogo above Rio.

General Pinel was a choleric martinet who had been greatly enraged by the Austrians' neglect of what he called the 'courtesies of war'. Now he took his revenge on the 'disloyal' Elbans who had supported them. He pulled down the walls of Capoliveri and Rio, demolished the Monte Giogo fort, imposed heavy fines on the disloyal villages, and put many of their elders in gaol with confiscation of property. He was so severe that complaints against him reached the Spanish court and he was recalled to Madrid. But although Elba got some respite from human oppression, natural disasters were to follow. In January 1709 the island had the worst snowstorm of its history; it lasted thirteen days and caused the death of many people and even more sheep and cattle. The storm was followed by a famine and an epidemic in the same year; Elba was only saved by relief-supplies from Piombino.

During the eighteenth century the map of Europe was being continually re-drawn in a succession of international treaties, and these changing arrangements were reflected in miniature in Elba. At the end of the War of the Spanish Succession, Philip V remained on the throne of Spain, but most of his possessions in Italy and elsewhere passed to the Austrian Emperor. In 1738, however, his younger son, Don Carlos, was installed as the first Bourbon King of Naples and Sicily, with a right to maintain Spanish garrisons in Piombino and Elba. At the same time the Grand Duchy of Tuscany passed to Austria; the last de' Medici grand duke had just died, and his title and possessions were allocated to the Emperor's daughter, Maria Theresa. She married Francis of Lorraine, who was later to become Emperor himself, and Tuscany was thenceforward governed by a dynasty of Austrian grand dukes. So for the rest of the century, the Portoferraio enclave of Elba was controlled by Austrian-appointed governors, while Spanish governors, appointed from Naples, sat in Porto Longone. The interior of the island, apart from Portoferraio, was administered by the Boncompagni family in their capacity as Princes of Piombino, and as such they still enjoyed the revenues of the iron-mines.

In 1786 Britain displayed an interest in Elba. The expansion of her sea-power had underlined the advantages of Portoferraio as a Mediterranean base, and discreet advances were made to the Austrian Grand Duke of Tuscany, Leopold, concerning the possibility of a 'Portoferraio purchase'. At the same time a British naval engineer arrived in the port to take measurements and soundings and to examine the possibility of constructing a large naval dockyard in the area of the San Giovanni salt-pans. However Louis XVI of France and Charles III of Naples found out what was going on, and induced the Grand Duke to break off the transaction; but he had been reminded of Portoferraio's value, and took a renewed interest in its welfare, stimulating Elban trade by reducing the harbour dues payable by ships using this port. He also erected the lighthouse on Fort Stella, perhaps in compensation for the Cellini bust of Duke Cosimo which he had removed from the fort's gateway a few years earlier. (The bust is now in the Bargello Museum at Florence.)

The first impact of the French Revolution came for Elba on New Year's Day, 1794, when ships, commanded by the British Admiral Hotham and carrying more than 3,000 royalist refugees from Toulon, put in to Portferraio. The Austrian governor, Baron Knesevich, was reluctant to allow them ashore, perhaps because of an epidemic then raging in the town. Under pressure from Admiral Hotham he eventually did so, but most of the refugees dispersed on to the mainland during the next few months, either because of the epidemic or because they did not find the financial help they needed.

Two years later French revolutionary forces, commanded by Napoleon Bonaparte, had invaded Italy and occupied the forts at Livorno. The British, fearing they might also acquire Portoferraio as a base, demanded its surrender. Baron Knesevich after a decent show of insisting on 'guarantees', accepted a British garrison in July 1796. It was accommodated in Fort San Giovanni, an outlying sector of the city's defences between Le Padulelle and Monte Bello, which has been known as the 'English fort' ever since. According to local tradition, Lord Nelson may have used it as his headquarters. With an influx of refugees from the mainland and the arrival of the British garrison, the population of Portoferraio rose from 3,000 to 10,000; and the over-crowding gave the occupying force an excuse to spread out into Marciana, Campo and Rio. But this British occupation lasted only nine months; the Grand Duke of Tuscany complained bitterly about the double infringement on his sovereignty — by the French in Livorno and the British in Elba — and in April 1797, the two governments agreed to withdraw their men.

Two years later the French put an end to all talk of sovereignty by invading Tuscany and annexing its territory. When their troops reached Piombino a French captain was sent across to demand the surrender of Portoferraio on March 29th. A new Austrian governor consulted the leading citizens and found a majority in favour of yielding; by April 4th the city and its fortresses were occupied by French forces under the command of General Montserrat. The next day he marched some of his men towards Porto Longone, sending envoys ahead to its Bourbon governor, Brigadier Dentice. Their arrival caused a violent outburst of anti-French feeling. Dentice apparently rejected the demand for surrender but was himself forced to resign by a populace *plus royaliste que le roi,* which demanded immediate action against the invaders. The command was placed in the hands of a triumvirate; a mixed force of soldiers and armed convicts from the galleys was organized and despatched against the French. Montserrat, taken by surprise, was forced to fall back on Portoferraio while one of his detachments, which lost its way and arrived in Capoliveri, was decimated by the embattled townsfolk. This, says a local historian drily, was a mistake; a punitive French force under General Miollis arrived in Elba to 'make an example' of Capoliveri and take bloody reprisals against its citizens.

General Miollis then departed and Montserrat was left in Elba with orders to take Porto Longone by siege and to occupy the rest of the island. He constructed lines of block-houses and batteries round the fortress's landward side, with the help of impressed labour from the men of Rio. The inadequate detachment which he sent into the western and hitherto neutral sector of the island provoked an uprising which took some weeks to suppress. The siege of Longone dragged on with bombardments and counter-bombardments but the defenders showed no sign of surrender. By May they were getting supplies from British and Neapolitan ships and eventually also a new and able commander, Colonel De Gregorio, Marquis of Squillace, who succeeded in turning the tables against the French. With the help of a

Captain De Farra, who was in the service of the Grand Duke, De Gregorio succeeded in organizing a general uprising against the French. Montserrat was forced to raise the siege and defend himself in a series of engagements in the wooded hills between Procchio and the Bay of Portoferraio. His casualties were heavy, and towards the end of June he went off to Livorno to seek reinforcements. But then he was deprived of his command, and his successor in Elba could do nothing but capitulate on July 17th, and withdraw the remaining French forces from the island. After their departure the victorious Elbans turned on those who had collaborated with the enemy; many of them were massacred in Portoferraio on July 28th.

The French could not tolerate this reverse. In 1800, General Dupont, who commanded their forces in Tuscany, sent an ultimatum to Portoferraio. But the Grand Duke of Tuscany, now a refugee in Vienna, had appointed as governor an able professional soldier, Lieutenant-Colonel De Fisson, with orders not to surrender 'even when all Tuscany is in the hands of the enemy'. First the governor gained time with a long exchange of letters with the French command while he put his defences in order. In May 1801, the French landed again in Elba and laid siege to Portoferraio. It was the first time its elaborate fortifications, which had been strengthened and improved since the days of Cosimo, had been tested in organized warfare, and under De Fisson's inspired command, they withstood the test well. The siege lasted thirteen months – from May 1801 till June 1802 – the defence being assisted during its later stages by a British military force which landed on the island and harassed the French lines. But on June 4th, instructions came from the Grand Duke Ferdinand III that, under the terms of the Peace of Amiens, Portoferraio was to be handed over to the French. De Fisson pulled down his flag and left Elba with his men.

NAPOLEON AND ELBA

For the Elbans Napoleon's rule of their island began long before his presence on it. It was annexed to France in 1802 and immediately subjected to the Code Napoléon and a methodical French administration which bestowed many benefits. At last the island was united under a single rule; taxation was reformed, a road system initiated, and maritime trade improved. The ancient and increasingly tenuous connection with the Appiani had ended; the last member of the

Boncompagni family to bear the title of Prince of Piombino had died in 1801: and in 1805 Napoleon installed his sister, Elisa Baciocchi, in Piombino, and made her Corsican husband its Prince. Elba became part of the French *Département de la Mediterranée* and later a *Vice-préfetture*, dependent on Livorno. A series of French military governors controlled Portoferraio and there were no more Bourbon officers in Porto Longone. In 1813, the garrison, supported by Elban conscripts, repelled a British landing.

In 1814, on April 6th, the defeated Napoleon, with his allied enemies in control of Paris, signed the Treaty of Fontainebleau, renouncing the thrones of France and Italy for himself and his descendants. He was permitted to retain the title of '*Sa Majesté l'Empéreur*' for life; and Elba, which he was said to have 'chosen' as his future residence – no alternative was offered – was recognized as 'a separate principality for his lifetime, held by him in complete sovereignty'. The Allied Powers undertook to see that the 'Barbary States' – those old enemies of Elba – should respect his rule, and, as additional insurance, he was permitted to take with him a guard of 400 officers and men. (The number was subsequently increased to 600 because so many members of the Old Guard wanted to accompany the Emperor.)

On April 29th Napoleon embarked in the British frigate *Undaunted* and set sail for Elba. The caravan of fourteen carriages in which he and his loyal officers had crossed France had run into hostile demonstrations as it reached the south, and the Emperor had been forced to disguise himself; for the same reason he went on board at St Raphael instead of Antibes. With him was Count Bertrand, who had been Grand Marshal of the Palace, General Drouot, and Marchand, his valet. There were also three commissioners appointed by the Allies as observers. During the five-day voyage, Napoleon passed the time by designing a new flag for his kingdom. It was white with a red diagonal and, on the diagonal, three golden bees, and it was intended to recall the arms of the de' Medici, which had a red bar on a silver ground, while the bees were his own imperial emblem.

The French governor of Portoferraio, General Dalesme, had been notified by the new French government of Louis XVIII that Elba was to be the Emperor's domain, but there were conflicting reports and he was still in a state of uncertainty when the *Undaunted* cast anchor in the bay outside the harbour on May 3rd. He ordered two warning salvoes to be fired against this ship wearing British colours, and ceased fire only when it hoisted a white flag. General Drouot came ashore, accompanied by the three allied commissioners, and handed the governor a letter from the Emperor:

> General, I have sacrificed my rights in the country's interests, and have reserved the sovereignty and ownership of Elba for myself, this having been agreed by all the Powers. Kindly bring the new state of affairs to the notice of the population, and my choice of their island as my residence in view of its agreeable climate and their equally agreeable nature. Tell them I shall always have their interests at heart. (Robert Christophe: *Napoleon on Elba*)

Napoleon came ashore in the late afternoon of the next day to a hastily organized but enthusiastic welcome. General Dalesme had issued a proclamation; the municipal authorities had ordered a public holiday; devoted women had passed the night stitching together two examples of the new flag to be flown from the forts; the mayor had the keys of his wine cellar gilded to represent the keys of the city, and they were tendered on a silver tray to Napoleon as he landed on the mole outside the sea-gate. The crowd's welcome indeed became so boisterous that the official procession was obliged to take refuge at a run in the cathedral, where a service of thanksgiving was celebrated. Some of the enthusiasm may have been due to the natural Italian genius for celebrating a *festa*, but it is fair to suppose that, after so many centuries of absentee rulers, the Elbans really did welcome a monarch who was to live among them. After the service there was an official reception in the town-hall where the island's notables were presented to the Emperor, and where he afterwards retired for the night in a hurriedly furnished flat on the top floor.

The very next day Napoleon began house-hunting and was conducted by the Mayor up the 135 steps of what is now the Salita Napoleone to see a small one-storey house and garden on the ridge at the top of the town between the two forts. It was called the *Casa dei Mulini*, 'House of the Mills', because this site had originally been occupied by windmills placed there to catch the sea breezes blowing across the ridge. Napoleon liked the spot, all the more because he had been nauseated by the stench of the streets round the town-hall. Elba, like eighteenth-century Edinburgh, had no sewage system and the citizens used to throw their slops and refuse into the gutters. He immediately began planning alterations and enlargements, including a second story in which he hoped to house his wife, the Empress Marie-Louise, and their son. In fact the Austrian court was already taking steps to prevent her joining him, including the provision of an attractive officer-escort, with whom she was to have an affair.

On May 6th, Napoleon began the exploration of his principality with a visit to the iron-mines from which he was to supplement his slender revenues. (The government of Louis XVIII never paid him the annuity it had promised under the Treaty of Fontainebleau.) He met the manager of the mines, Pons de l'Herault, and was eventually to persuade him to hand over a sum of 200,000 francs, amassed for the benefit of the Legion d'Honneur, to which the mines had previously belonged. On May 21st, the Emperor took up residence in the *Casa dei Mulini*, although work on the alterations was to continue until September. It was to be furnished largely at the involuntary expense of Napoleon's brothers-in-law. He sent his quartermaster with a ship over to Piombino, then nominally occupied by the Austrians, to rifle the abandoned palace of his sister, Elisa Baciocchi, and her husband, both of whom had betrayed his cause. And from a ship which had taken refuge from a storm in Porto Longone the Emperor was able to confiscate the furniture belonging to the Prince Borghese, husband of his other sister, Paolina. The Prince had also betrayed the Emperor and was shipping his own belongings back to Rome from Turin to escape the Austrians.

Towards the end of May, the 600 men of Napoleon's Guard arrived in Elba after marching all the way across France and into Italy. They were welcomed outside the town-hall by the Emperor on horseback and were billeted in the Falcon and Star forts and in the abandoned monastery of San Francesco, halfway up the hill to the Mulini. Their commander, Marshal Cambronne, had his quarters in the Star, along with General Drouot whose windows looked down into the Mulini garden. The presence of the Guard benefited the Emperor's morale but embarrassed his purse; the men had to be paid. To some extent he offset the cost of their upkeep by employing them on public works, and especially on road-making. As a restless traveller, Napoleon was shocked by the state of Elba's communications when he arrived and gave immediate orders for their improvement.

Roads were only one aspect of 'the new era of Elba', as Pons de l'Herault was to describe it. Short though the Emperor's sojourn was, he clearly took his diminutive principality seriously at least for the first six months. He had read up all available information about it before he arrived, and gave his early attention to numerous aspects of its economy and administration — to customs and excise duties, a stamp tax, the salt-pans, the tunny fisheries, hospitals, defence works, public amusements and amenities, vineyards and *macchia* clearance, the distribution of uncultivated land, and a project for a silk-worm industry. Above all, he cleaned up Portoferraio, the city which had offended his nostrils as soon as he landed. Refuse collectors, with wicker-baskets on their backs and trumpets to announce their coming, were set to patrol the steep streets and to stop at every door; housewives who ignored them and continued to litter the roads were fined according to the size of their families. Other new regulations convey an appalling picture of the city as he found it:

> Fines will be imposed on inhabitants who ignore the latrines which the Emperor has had built, and continue emptying their chamber-pots out of the window. Fines will be imposed on prostitutes who move beyond the front of their lodgings to accost men. Fines will be imposed on persons who disobey the instructions of the medical corps and continue to sleep more than five in a bed. Fines will be imposed on individuals who wilfully or through negligence defile the drinking-water pumps installed in Portoferraio and Porto Longone by order of the Emperor. Fines will be imposed on families who do not send members suffering from a contagious disease to the hospital.
> (Robert Christophe: *Napoleon on Elba*)

The fines may have seemed vexatious, but they enabled the Emperor to present the City Council with a budget for 1814 which showed a revenue of nearly 65,000 francs and an expenditure of just over 62,000 francs, and that after having the streets paved, trees planted in the squares, street lamps erected every ten yards, grass plots placed outside the barracks, and benches along the quayside.

On June 2nd Paolina Borghese, Napoleon's favourite sister who had long been separated from her Italian husband, arrived from St Raphael on a flying visit. She stayed only 24 hours before going on to stay with the King of Naples, Joachim Murat, the former French army commander who had married Napoleon's youngest sister, Caroline, and had been rewarded by him with the Crown of the Two Sicilies. After the defeat at Leipzig, he had publicly abandoned the Emperor's cause and made overtures to the Allies, thus retaining his throne. But there is evidence of a secret understanding between him and his former master; and Paolina may, on this occasion, have been acting as a courier between them, calling at Elba just to receive a message from the Emperor. But she was there long enough to learn that Napoleon had his eyes on a summer retreat at San Martino, outside Portoferraio, and to give him some of her diamonds to help him make the purchase.

Paolina also seems to have conveyed an invitation from Napoleon to his mother, Letizia Bonaparte, pressing her to join him in Elba. She did so at the beginning of August, and was installed in a modest Portoferraio terrace-house in Via Ferrandini, just downhill from the Casa dei Mulini. She was a rich woman, and is believed to have given unobtrusive financial help to her son who often visited her to play cards. Soon after her arrival she also assisted him by her connivance in the curious episode of Marie Walewska.

This lady was a Polish countess who had become Napoleon's mistress in Warsaw in return for his promise to make Poland independent; she had borne him a son, Alexandre. During July she had written to the Emperor, explaining that she was going to Naples and suggesting a visit to him *en route*. Napoleon, who was still publicly insisting that he expected the Empress to join him and who was adopting a somewhat puritanical attitude towards the love affairs of his officers, was embarrassed. He began to look for some retired place in Elba where he could receive his mistress in secret; he thought he had found it in the mountain-hermitage of the Madonna del Monte, high up above the town of Marciana. He then wrote to the Countess, saying he would be glad to see her and her little boy on her way either to or back from Naples. On August 21st Napoleon went to stay in a house at Marciana, and was joined there on the 25th by Letizia. This public mother-and-son holiday lasted until September 1st, when the brig bringing Marie Walewska, her brother, and her son, from Naples was sighted. She came ashore after nightfall by boat at San Giovanni in the bay of Portoferraio, and was escorted by carriage to Marciana. The impatient Emperor met the party by the wayside, and they were all carried on muleback up the steep path to the hermitage. At one in the morning, they all sat down to a candle-lit meal in a marquee with Napoleon and a few of his closest associates.

The mountain idyll lasted only two days. The crew of the brig had gone ashore in Portoferraio and the news leaked out that 'a lady and her son' had come to join the Emperor. It was generally assumed that the visitors were the Empress and *her* son, the little King of Rome.

Napoleon's personal physician arrived at the hermitage to offer his services to 'Her Majesty', and the island was full of gossip and rumours. This was enough to decide Napoleon to send his mistress away immediately. On the night of September 3rd the Polish party was packed into its carriage at Marciana and sent down the hill to Marciana Marina where the brig had been anchored. Unfortunately a violent storm had arisen and the harbourmaster would not permit the party to take a boat out to the brig. A message was conveyed to its master ordering him to put to sea and sail round the island to the more sheltered waters of Porto Longone. The carriage and its escort set out on an appalling night-journey across the island, to meet it. Napoleon, who knew nothing of these happenings, became alarmed at the storm and sent messengers to recall Marie and her party.

When he heard of the planned embarkation from Porto Longone, he decided that even this was too dangerous, and set off on horseback with two aides to prevent it. But he arrived at Porto Longone too late: Marie and her party had already sailed off into the storm, and the Emperor had to wait there eight days before he had news of their safety. Perhaps wishing to stay away from the capital until the scandal had died down, Napoleon then made a five-day stay in the little island of Pianosa, lying to the south of Elba. He had visited it twice before, once during his first exploration of his principality, and once in June when he had 'annexed' it by installing a small military garrison and by planning a colony of farmers to grow wheat on its flat surface, and thus supplement Elba's inadequate grain supplies.

It was long-term planning of this kind which suggests Napoleon had begun his rule of Elba with genuine intentions of settling there. There is no firm evidence to show why or when he changed his mind. Probably several influences were at work. One was financial stringency and the failure of Louis XVIII to pay the annuity of two million francs pledged in a Declaration appended to the Fontainebleau Treaty. Sir Neil Campbell, the British Commissioner, who accompanied Napoleon to Elba as 'watchdog' for the Allies, wrote, 'If Napoleon is paid the annuity stipulated in the treaty, he will stay here quite happily.' As it was, the Emperor had to depend precariously on the money he could obtain from members of his family, and on the taxes and fines he could screw out of the Elbans. Another disturbing influence was the reports reaching him of plots to kidnap or assassinate him. At Porto Longone, after Marie Walewska's departure, he suddenly issued orders for a permanent armed escort and special guards along his routes across the island. By February an observer was writing 'Napoleon stays indoors and sees no one; this is because he fears assassins sent from France and Italy.'

He may also have been unsettled by the arrival, on November 1st, of his sister Paolina, who took up permanent residence on the upper floor of the Casa dei Mulini which had been designed for the faithless Empress. Ostensibly she was there to act as his hostess and companion, and to organize a social life of dinner-parties, dances, and amateur theatricals — a court in miniature. But privately she must have brought him news of movements and intrigues in the great world outside, and perhaps the encouragement of his dubious brother-in-law, Murat. The news from France was that the Bourbon regime of Louis XVIII was increasingly unpopular; then came disquieting rumours of another *coup d'état*.

On February 13th, 1815, one of his most loyal supporters, Fleury de Chaboulon, arrived secretly in Portoferraio with a message from the Duke of Bassano, his former Minister of the Interior. First Fleury told of a plot to bring down the Bourbons and to install the King of Rome as a puppet Napoleon II, with his mother, Marie Louise, as Regent and Joseph Fouché, that political intriguer, pulling the strings. At the word 'Regent' Napoleon exclaimed, 'Am I dead then?', and added, 'I could be in France in two days if the nation called for my return'. Then Fleury delivered his message from the Duke of Bassano: he was to tell the Emperor 'that the present Government has lost all support of the people and the army, and that discontent is rife. The hopes of the army and the nation are in the Emperor. It remains for him to decide in his wisdom what he should do.' The next day Napoleon told Fleury he was making preparations to return to France and waiting for 'the first favourable opportunity'.

Part of those preparations was an elaborate charade connected with the mid-Lent carnival then being celebrated in Portoferraio. On Ash Wednesday the traditional 'Burial of Carnival' was celebrated with a mock funeral cortège through the streets, in which all Napoleon's officers took part in elaborate fancy-dress, with the band of the Guard disguised as pierrots, and the guardsmen themselves in 'drag' as ladies of a pasha's harem. The three generals, Drouot, Bertrand and Cambronne, brought up the rear. The impression thus offered to the European governments was that of the irresponsible ruler of a musical-comedy kingdom.

The 'favourable opportunity' came the next day when Sir Neil

Campbell, by now taking his 'watchdog' duties less seriously, announced that he was leaving for Livorno and Florence where he had to confer with an Austrian diplomat. He did not mention his intention of conferring even more closely at Livorno with a certain Signora Bartoli. The Emperor urged him to be back by February 28th to attend a ball being given by Princess Paolina. Before Campbell's ship was out of sight on February 16th, the Emperor had begun to organize his own departure. His solitary brig, the *Inconstant* was brought in to be re-armed, re-fitted, and stocked for a 'three months' cruise for 120 men' – all by February 25th. Two of the largest mining industry cargo vessels were chartered from Rio; the garrison was withdrawn from Pianosa; war-chests and campaign supplies were made ready. When the generals were informed only Drouot tried to dissuade his master from 'another war'. On February 23rd, Campbell's ship, the *Partridge* hove in sight, but the Commissioner was not on board and the ship itself – the only patrol vessel on the Elba station – was bound for Naples with a party of English travellers. On that day the Emperor imposed an embargo on all ships leaving the island; no passports or health certificates were to be issued, and the guns were to open fire on any vessel putting to sea. He began to draw up the two proclamations which he proposed to issue to the people and the army of France.

On February 25th Napoleon attended Paolina's ball in the recently opened *Teatro dei Vigilanti*; it had been brought forward two days. The next day, a Sunday, he appeared at his morning levée in the green uniform of a colonel of the Guard, and formally announced his departure to the chief civil and military dignitaries. With his mother and sister he attended mass in the cathedral and afterwards handed over the island administration to the sub-prefect, the mayor, and his chamberlain. At nightfall the Emperor said farewell to his family and made his way down to the harbour. The quaysides were crowded and lanterns were lit all along the ramparts. As Napeleon was rowed across to board the *Inconstant* his troops, who were already in their transports, sang the Marseillaise. Napoleon thus left Elba on February 26th, nine months and 22 days after assuming its rule. He was about to begin the 'Hundred Days', which ended with Waterloo and his imprisonment in the much more distant island of St Helena.

Napoleon on Elba

1814

April 6th	Napoleon forced to 'choose' Elba, to be held by him in complete sovereignty under the Treaty of Fontainebleau.
29th	N. embarks in the British frigate *Undaunted* at St Raphael.
May 3rd	*Undaunted* casts anchor in bay outside Portoferraio harbour.
4th	N. lands on the mole outside the Sea Gate of Portoferraio. A thanksgiving service is followed by a reception in the Town Hall.
5th	N. starts house-hunting and finds the Casa dei Mulini.
6th	N. crosses island to visit Rio and the ironworks.
21st	N. takes up residence in the Casa dei Mulini.
26th	(Or 28th) The 600 men of The Imperial Guard arrive and are quartered in the forts and the monastery of San Francesco.
June 2nd	The Emperor's sister, Paolina Borghese, arrives from St Raphael, gives N. a jewel towards the cost of the Villa San Martino, and leaves the next day.
	During the month N. tours the island and 'annexes' the island of Pianosa.
July 16th	(About) Mme Bertrand, wife of Count Bertrand, arrives in Elba to join her husband whom she finds with N. already in residence at the Villa San Martino. She gives N. the news of the death of Josephine, his first wife, and, as a keepsake, Josephine's dress, now on view at the Palazzina dei Mulini.
August	
2nd	Letizia Bonaparte, the Emperor's mother, arrives and takes up residence in Portoferraio.
21st	N. goes to Marciana to prepare for arrival of his mistress, the Countess Marie Walewska.
25th	Letizia Bonaparte joins N. at Marciana.

Sept. 1st	Marie Walewska arrives from Naples with her brother and son and is conducted to Marciana where she is entertained by N. at the Sanctuary of the Madonna del Monte.
3rd	Marie Walewska and party are sent off to embark at Marciana Marina but are prevented by storm.
4th	Marie Walewska and party cross island to Porto Longone where they embark and leave island. N. follows them to Porto Longone and stays there awaiting news of their safety.
12th–17th	N. visits Pianosa.
Nov. 1st	Paolina Borghese arrives, to take up permanent residence on top floor of the Palazzina dei Mulini.

1815	
Jan.	Teatro dei Vigilanti opens with gala performance attended by the Emperor and costume ball.
Feb. 13th	Fleury de Chaboulon arrives secretly with news of hostility to Bourbon regime in France.
14th	N. decides to return to France 'at the first favourable opportunity'.
15th	Ash Wednesday, with parade representing 'Burial of Carnival'.
16th	The British Commissioner, Sir Neil Campbell, leaves for Livorno.
23rd	N. imposes an embargo on any ship leaving the island.
25th	N. attends ball given by Paolina Borghese at the Teatro dei Vigilanti.
26th	N. formally announces his departure to the chief civil and military dignitaries. At nightfall he says farewell to his family and in the harbour embarks in the brig *Inconstant* for his return to France.
March 1st	N. lands at Antibes.

NINETEENTH AND TWENTIETH CENTURIES

After Waterloo and the Treaty of Vienna, Elba, like the rest of Tuscany, reverted to the Austrian Grand Dukes. The islanders had not become dedicated Bonapartists – indeed the stubborn people of Capoliveri had refused to pay taxes to Napoleon until he threatened to quarter troops upon them – but they did retain a sentimental pride in the Napoleonic episode and, in 1841, a grand-duchy decree permitted Elban shipping to add the three Napoleonic bees to the Tuscan flag. But the ensuing history of the island became part of the Italian nationalist movement of the Risorgimento which was to lead, after many set-backs, to the unification of Italy under the crown of Savoy. The Star fortress became an Austrian prison for nationalist revolutionaries like Francesco Guerrazzi. who was twice confined there; but the people showed their nationalist sympathies in 1848, the year of popular but abortive risings against foreign rule. In February of that year the 'tree of liberty' was planted on a parade ground outside the old city and the communal authorities offered free hospitality to all comers, while a group of young men went off to CivitaVecchia to offer their services to Garibaldi, who was then attempting to overthrow papal rule in Central Italy. Some of them also took part in the equally unsuccessful rising against the Austrians in Lombardy, and one of them, Elbano Gasperi, won the silver medal for gallantry and became a local hero. In 1859, after the Austrians had been defeated by the Emperor Napoleon III of France, the Grand Duchy of Tuscany came to an end. In the following year Elba, like the rest of Tuscany, was incorporated into the new Kingdom of Italy.

In 1900 the character of Portoferraio was transformed when a commercial company built blast-furnaces on the high ground outside the old city and closed down the salt-pan industry along the bay of Portoferraio which had for at least three centuries provided Elba with one of its main exports. The new steel-works attracted a large working population from the mainland and with its tall chimneys disfigured the profile of the city. But although foreigners and some Elbans lamented the change, it brought prosperity and a new prestige to the island. Portoferraio, for the first time in many centuries, justified its name of 'Iron Port'.

The only episode of World War I directly to affect Elba occurred in 1916 when an Austrian submarine surfaced in the bay of Portoferraio and began a bombardment of the city and its harbour. The shells were too small to do much damage, and the main object of the operation –

to promote a mass escape of Austrian prisoners of war from the Casa dei Mulini where they were confined – was not achieved. When the guns of the Falcon fortress eventually opened fire the submarine submerged and made off; it was later able to sink a large Italian steamer in the Piombino channel.

After that war Elba shared with the rest of Italy the problem of unemployment and industrial unrest. In 1920 and 1921 the Portoferraio steelworks and the Rio iron-mines were frequently closed down by workers' demonstrations, strikes, working-to-rule, and eventually by a workers' occupation of the entire plant. The left-wing workers' movements were eventually overwhelmed in Elba, as elsewhere in Italy, by the fascist backlash which their excesses had to some extent provoked; but they survived clandestinely in the Portoferraio steel industry, and several Elban 'anarchists' were arrested and sent to confinement during the twenty years of fascist rule.

In the immediate post-war period one more landmark of the old Portoferraio disappeared: as a measure to relieve unemployment the local authorities decided to fill in the ancient moat which the architects of Cosimo de' Medici had had cut across the promontory to divide their fortified city from the rest of the island. The modern Viale Manzoni marks its course, and the drawbridge which gave sole access by land to the old city is commemorated in the Piazza del Ponticello.

Elba's tribulations in the Second World War began after the collapse of the fascist regime in 1943, following the Allied landings in Italy. In September of that year the German High Command was organizing a withdrawal of its forces from Corsica and required Elba as a base from which to support the operation. When German aircraft flew over the island demanding its surrender, a citizens' committee urged the Italian military command on the island to resist. The same committee boarded a steamer anchored in Portoferraio harbour and confiscated the cargo of provisions which it was to have carried to Corsica. On September 15th German officers arrived under a white flag to negotiate with the Italian command; they threatened bombardment from the air unless the defence yielded. No word of this ultimatum was allowed to reach the civilian population, and it was largely taken by surprise the next day when sixteen German aircraft flew over the old city and unloaded their bombs on its centre. Military casualties were heavy; 116 civilians were killed, and the streets were left in ruins. The fortress hoisted the white flag, and the next day German parachute troops began an occupation of the island.

Elba then became a target for Allied arms. On September 22nd, a passenger steamer, crowded with people who had been held up in Piombino while the Germans completed their occupation, was torpedoed by an unidentified submarine just outside Portoferraio Bay; more than 200 were drowned, including a number of demobilized Italian soldiers trying to reach their homes in Elba. Allied aircraft began bombing Portoferraio; there were more than twenty raids, the heaviest of which, on March 19th, 1944, did more damage and killed more people than the Germans had in September. The population then abandoned Portoferraio and took to the hills. The main Allied targets were the port and the steelworks, but many bombs fell outside the target area. Elbans remember with particular horror the havoc wrought in the local cemetery where so many recent casualties had been interred.

On June 17th, 1944, a French force, commanded by General De Lattre de Tassigny and composed largely of Moroccan and Senegalese troops, landed on the south coast of Elba and gained command of the island in two days of savage fighting. And for two days the African troops were permitted by their command to treat the islanders, their women, and their belongings as 'spoils of war'. Many atrocities were committed and order was only restored after some French officers had been obliged to fire on their own men.

The final disaster of the war for Elba came after the end of hostilities. The islanders, deeply shaken by a 'liberation' that might have been committed by a Barbarossa, and trying desperately to rebuild a life which had been left in ruins, were informed by the company owning the steelworks that the plant was 'uneconomic' and would be dismantled. In spite of local agitation and an attempt to restart the blast furnaces which had suffered less damage than expected under bombardment, the tall chimneys were pulled down and the jobs of 2,000 Elbans disappeared. From 1950 onwards the island's economy has been based on tourism.

ARCHAEOLOGY

During the eighteenth and nineteenth century, Elba was plundered sporadically by treasure-seekers and antiquarians who kept no proper record of their excavations, and almost invariably removed their finds. During the present century, the island has been explored more scientifically by serious archaeologists, but funds for complete investigation have been lacking and undoubtedly much remains to be discovered. In fact the only visible remains that can easily be visited are the Roman Villa at Le Grotte (p. 177), and the exhibits – labelled only in Italian – in the museum at Marciana (p. 215).

The recent development of skin-diving has revealed the existence of a number of wrecks of Roman and medieval shipping all round the Elban coast-line. But the report attributed to certain submarine explorers that a 'submerged city' exists beneath the waves, off the north coast of the island near Capo Bianco, may be discounted. Further investigation has shown that the 'walls and streets' alleged to have been discovered are nothing more than natural rock formations.

The following list of sites, both on land and in coastal waters, where finds have been made is compiled from that prepared by Dr Michelangelo Zecchini of Florence.

LAND SITES

Portoferraio Commune
Casa del Duca, at the foot of the hill of Santa Lucia, overlooking the plain of San Giovanni.

Near this house, in which the Grand Duke Cosimo is said to have stayed while Portoferraio was being built, Etruscan tombs were discovered during the last century. They contained bone fragments, a bronze mirror, pottery, and gold necklaces and ear-rings, dating from the fifth and fourth centuries B.C.

Le Grotte, on the promontory overlooking the Bay and just off the main road to Porto Azzurro.

The conspicuous but never fully excavated remains of a very large Roman villa, dating from the first century B.C., occupy the entire ridge of the promontory, which gets its name from the subterranean rooms forming part of the complex.

Hill of Santa Lucia, at its foot on the north-western side, in an area indicated by isolated clumps of umbrella pines.

The remains of what is believed to be a palaeolithic settlement have been indicated by finds of Mousterian implements – blades, arrow-heads, graving-tools, and scrapers attributed to the Gravettian and middle Aurignacian cultures.

San Martino, on a hill to the left of the road leading to the gates of the

Napoleonic villa.

On this hill, known locally as Castiglione, a drystone wall of large blocks surrounds the summit. Within the wall, which is believed to have surrounded an iron-age settlement, numerous fragments of pottery have been gathered; this site has not been excavated.

Volterraio, on the summit of a hill (1,280 feet) to the left of the road leading over the range from Portoferraio Bay to Rio nell'Elba.

This hill-fortress is the finest example of medieval fortification in Elba both for position and structure; it was constructed in 1281, underwent subsequent modifications, and is now in ruins.

Marciana Commune

Campo all'Aia, in the north-east corner of Procchio Bay.

Stone implements of the Upper Palaeolithic period have been found in the eroded areas of the lower slopes of the hill above the beach. On the beach itself, among the slag left by Roman iron-ore smelting, fragments of Roman pottery may be found.

Madonna del Monte, at a height of 2,088 feet, not far from the Sanctuary and beneath the 'Eagle' boulder.

The foundations of huts attributed to the Sub-Apennine people who inhabited Elba towards the end of the Bronze Age indicate a village constructed here about 1,000 B.C. Similar habitations have been found in a cave directly beneath the 'Eagle' boulder to the west. Both in the cave and in the hut foundations pottery vessels, loom-weights, braziers, and milk-boilers have been found. Recently, in a shelter beneath a rock close to the cave, Corinthian and Etruscan vases were discovered.

Marciana, at the top of the town.

The fine fortress is sometimes ascribed to the Pisans; the present structure was probably put up by the Appiani family in the fifteenth century.

Monte Giove, at 2,762 feet, in the saddle between the two peaks of the mountain.

Pottery vessels, loom-weights, spindles, and stone axe-heads, attributed to the Sub-Apennine Culture, have been found here and are believed to date from the eighth or seventh century B.C. when this people took refuge in the heights from Greeks or Etruscans who were beginning to exploit the Elban iron-mines.

Isola Paolina, just offshore to the west of Procchio.

Roman ruins dating from the beginning of our era have been found here and are believed to have been a trader's warehouse. On the islet itself, tiles, pottery lamps and a large urn with maker's mark have been collected.

Sant'Andrea, 9 metres from the beach and on the west side of the road.

Although now partly concealed by a deposit of building material, masses of clinkers left by Roman iron-smelting are visible. Many pottery fragments and a few intact flasks have been found among the clinkers.

San Cerbone, hermitage to be reached by a track from the cemetery at Poggio. The saint, who was bishop of Populonia on the mainland, took refuge from the invading Lombards here towards the end of his life, about A.D. 570. The present church was constructed by Jacobo II d'Appiano in 1421; the Appiano crest is partly visible today.

San Lorenzo, in a valley beneath the town of Marciana, to the west of the road connecting Marciana with Marciana Marina.

The ruins of the little romanesque church of this name go back to the Pisan period of Elban history and are ascribed to the twelfth century; walls, apse and facade survive.

Valle Gneccarina, about 1km. from the village of Chiessi up the valley leading inland.

A cache of bronze axe-heads was found here in 1930; they are technically sophisticated and are exhibited in the Antiquarium at Marciana. They were found beneath a sandstone slab and behind a boulder marked with a rough cross; they are ascribed to the eighth century B.C.

Marciana Marina Commune

Marciana Marina, at the western end of the beach.

The watch-tower, known as the *Torre Saracena* or *Torre Medicea*, is the only one in Elba with a cylindrical structure. Although sometimes attributed to the twelfth century and the Pisans, it is probably much later and may have been erected in the fifteenth century.

Rio nell'Elba Commune

Grassera, 2km. along the country road which leads out of Rio nell'Elba to the north, past the cemetery.

The site of the medieval town of Grassera, destroyed by the Turks in the sixteenth century, lies mainly to the west of the road, while the ruins of the church of San Quirico (one of the patron saints of Rio) are on the east side. Fragments of medieval pottery and a coin of the Pisan Republic have been found on the site of the town. During the last century a Roman tomb, dating from the Republican period, is reported to have been found here.

Cave of San Giuseppe, on the north side of the road between Rio nell'Elba and Rio Marina, 1km. below road junction, opposite council houses. Excavations here, begun in 1966 and continuing till 1970, brought to light a burial site of the early Bronze Age people of the Rinaldonian Culture who reached Elba in search of copper about 2,000 B.C. Human bones, copper daggers, and much pottery were found.

Rio Marina Commune

Torre Giove, on the summit of a hill (1,144 feet) to the left of the main road between Rio Marina and Cavo but more accessible from the country road between Rio nell'Elba and Cavo.

This tower, which was formerly known as *del Giogo* (i.e. Tower of the Mountain Pass), was constructed by the Appiano family in 1459 as a fortress to guard the iron-mines. It is now in ruins though both external and internal walls survive. The Appiano arms are visible carved on a stone which lies outside the walls on the east side.

Capo Castello, on private property at Cavo.

The remains of a Roman villa here, dating from the 1st century A.D., may be part of a Roman settlement called Faleria. The tank providing a water supply for the villa is to be seen on the Colle del Lentisco south-west of the site.

Capoliveri Commune

Caubbio, at the western end of Lacona beach where the watercourse, sometimes called Caubbio and sometimes Stagnolo, reaches the sea.

In 1961, a Greek tomb, dating from the fourth or third centuries B.C. was discovered here. The contents included a vase, a plate, a jug and an oil-flask. Along the Caubbio watercourse, stone implements of the middle and upper Palaeolithic period have come to the surface.

Fosse del Pino, some 270 metres north of Lacona Beach and 180 metres east of the shrine of the Madonna di Lacona, on flat ground eroded by the stream.

Numerous stone objects datable to the middle and upper Palaeolithic period have been picked up here.

Profico, some 45 metres east of the built-up area of Capoliveri, on level ground overlooking the ravine of the Profico stream.

During the last century and more recently, Roman tombs dating from the third century B.C. to the fourth century A.D. have been found in what appears to have been a large cemetery. Bronze figurines, leaden tripods, clay lamps and other pottery are among the objects that have been found.

Campo Commune

Monte Cocchero, a hill, known locally by this name (but not marked on the maps) on the ridge which divides Lacona Bay from the plain of Campo, just to the south of the main road at its highest point, opposite the 'Monument'.

A natural rocky amphitheatre on the summit (1,017 feet) has been emphasized by a group of monoliths apparently erected by human agency. Within the circle of rocks, where excavations have been hampered by the presence of unexploded Second World War missiles, a stone quern and many pottery fragments indicate a settlement of the Sub-Apennine culture dating to about 1,000 B.C.

Monte Maolo, to the south of Monte Perone, at 2,132 feet, on a level shelf below Monte Maolo.

The construction of the new road over Monte Perone revealed the site of another Sub-Apennine settlement. Finds included potsherds, loom-weights, spindles, and fragments of plaster from hut walls.

S. Giovanni in Campo, the ruined romanesque church of this name on the left of the road which climbs from San Piero to Monte Perone.

Foundations of buildings on the hillside below the church suggest this was once an inhabited area. Slightly further up the hill and to the right of the road is the *Torre di San Giovanni*, a spectacular Pisan watch-tower built on top of a granite boulder.

Seccheto, in the valley leading inland from the town.

Roman granite quarries, dating both from the Republican and Imperial period exist on the hillside. In one of them was found the granite altar, now in the courtyard of the town-hall at Portoferraio, dedicated, according to its inscription, to Hercules by the Roman Praetorian Prefect, P. Acilius Attianus. *Saint'Ilario*, along the north side of the village.

Medieval fortifications with sharply angled bastions are visible though overlaid by more modern constructions; they are believed to date from the fifteenth century.

San Piero, along the north side of the village and on the south-westward projecting spur, known as the Belvedere.

Medieval fortifications are overlaid by other more recent constructions. On the Belvedere, a twin-naved romanesque church of the twelfth century, dedicated to St Peter and St Paul, was later incorporated into the fortifications. It is believed locally to have been built on the foundations of a Roman temple to the sea god, Glaucus.

Porto Azzurro Commune

Grotta Reale, about 4km. along the main road from Porto Azzurro to Rio Marina, to the right of the road in the valley of the Reale stream.

This cave, some 22 metres deep and 2 metres wide, contains deposits from which there have been excavated the fossil remains of animals of the quaternary period, including the cave-bear, the rhinoceros, the hippopotamus, the lynx, the red deer, and roe-deer.

SUBMARINE SITES

Portoferraio Commune

Punta dell'Acquaviva, between Capo d'Enfola and Capo Bianco.

About 180 metres north of the Point, at a depth of about 100 feet, a Roman wreck is buried and scattered amphoras of the first century A.D. have been found.

Capo d'Enfola, in line with axis of Cape.

At 115 feet depth, a Roman wreck is completely buried in mud; several amphoras and two anchor stocks dating from the first century B.C. have been found.

Punta delle Grotte, in Portoferraio Bay.

At depths of between 50 and 65 feet, in the water opposite the Roman villa, amphoras and an anchor stock have been found.

Marciana Commune

Campo all'Aia, eastern cove of Procchio Bay.

In 1966, at only 6 feet depth and 27 metres from shore, a Roman wreck dating from the first or second century A.D. was found by the underwater explorer, Dr Brambilla. The wreck which was 60 feet long and 22 feet wide contained a large and varied cargo, including blocks of granite and sulphur, glass vases, perfume bottles, and a gold and ivory statuette of Bacchus and Pan.

Chiessi, some 45 metres out from the shore.

At about 160 foot depth, a large deposit of some 5,000 amphoras was discovered, together with some medieval pottery fragments. This deposit, probably left by several wrecks, has now been so thoroughly plundered that nothing remains but fragments.

Punta del Cotoncello, near Sant'Andrea.

About 90 metres north of the point, at between 50 and 60 feet depth, amphoras and potsherds are scattered on the sea-floor.

Formiche della Zanca, reef between Capo S. Andrea and Punta della Zanca.

On the north side of the rocks, at 115 foot depth, amphoras of the first century B.C. have been found. To the south of the reef other amphoras of the same period have been found at 50 feet.

Isola Paolina, 45 metres north of the islet.

Amphoras and potsherds of the first century A.D. have been brought up by fishermen from a depth of 100 feet.

Patresi, west of the lighthouse.

In 1970, at a distance of 315 metres from the lighthouse, a wreck was detected, with amphoras of varying forms and different periods scattered over a fairly wide area at a depth of 162 feet.

Pomonte, about a mile to the south-west.

In this area fishermen frequently haul up amphoras in their nets from a depth of 320 feet; sometimes ships' timbers are brought up.

Punta Polveraia, below Il Mortaio.

About 135 metres out from the Point, at a depth of 80–90 feet, ancient anchors and amphoras of the first century A.D. have been recovered.

Sant'Andrea

At a depth of 33 feet, piled up against the point potsherds may be seen which come from a Roman wreck originally containing about 150 amphoras, many of which have been recovered. A second wreck, buried in mud and containing about 1,000 amphoras, lies 135 metres away from the Point at a depth of 146 feet. Both wrecks have been dated to the first century B.C. or the first century A.D.

Porto Azzurro Commune

Barbarossa Cove

At a depth of 80–100 feet many fragments of Roman pottery and a Greco-Massiliote amphora of the sixth or fifth century B.C. have been recovered.

Mola Bay

Concealed by mud at a depth of 65 feet, there is a Roman wreck with a cargo of clay drainage pipes.

Rio Marina Commune

Capo Vite, 1·5km. north-west of the Cape.

Fragments of timber and metal cable-blocks, brought up from a muddy bottom at 234 feet, suggest the presence of a medieval wreck. Potsherds and entire vases dating from the fourteenth and fifteenth century have been brought up from the same area.

Capo Pero, near Cavo.

Roman amphoras of the first century B.C. have been found here.
Capo d'Arco, otherwise known as Punta delle Cannelle.
Amphoras of various shapes, dating from the first and second centuries A.D. have been found just offshore.
Ripabianca, between Rio Marina and Cavo.
Small Roman amphoras of the Imperial period and medieval vessels of the fourteenth and fifteenth centuries have been found just offshore.

Rio nell'Elba Commune

Punta dei Mangani, on the north-west coast just south of Monte Grosso.
A few metres offshore, at a depth of about 180 feet, lies a still unexplored Roman wreck. In the area amphoras of the first century B.C. and the second century A.D. have been found.

Capoliveri Commune

Isola Corbella, just south of the tip of Capo Stella.
A virtually unexplored Roman wreck lies here at a depth of 146 feet. It is buried in mud and so far only an anchor stock and a lead weight have been recovered.
Isole Gemini, south of Pareti.
Roman amphoras of the second century A.D. have been found in this general area at depths varying from 65 to 130 feet.
Punta Perla, just south of Porto Azzurro Bay.
Roman amphoras are scattered on the sea-floor at a depth of approximately 100 feet.
Punta Ripalti, southernmost tip of Calamita peninsula.
Amphoras of the sixth and fifth centuries B.C. can be found scattered at a depth of 115 to 140 feet.
Spiaggia degli Stecchi
One Roman amphora has been found here at a depth of 65 feet.

Campo Commune

Galenzana, in the vicinity of Capo Poro.
Only a few metres from the shore amphoras of the first century B.C. have been recovered from a depth of 80 feet, together with a leaden anchor stock.
Punta Le Tombe, west of Fetovaia.
About 270 metres offshore, at a depth of about 160 feet, a Roman wreck, still unexplored, lies among amphoras of the first century B.C.
Scoglio della Triglia
A Roman anchor stock was found here.

POPULATION

The population of Elba is approximately 28,000, out of which one-fifth lives in the towns while the other four-fifths are dispersed through the countryside. The history of Elba has resulted in the existence within this population of several differing strains, although the distinction between them is now being broken down by an improved network of communications and increased interchange with the mainland. Portoferraio and its neighbourhood have a predominantly Tuscan atmosphere ever since the walled city was founded by Grand Duke Cosimo in the sixteenth century; indeed its original inhabitants migrated there from the Tuscan mainland, and their descendants today still use an exaggerated version of the aspirated Tuscan 'hard C' at the beginning of such words as *casa* or *commune*.

In eastern Elba the people of the mining area round Rio nell'Elba still enjoy the reputation for rugged independence that they have had throughout the long history of the mines. In Porto Azzurro and Capoliveri, which were so long governed and garrisoned by Spaniards, there is a dignified and leisurely approach to life which seems to recall Iberian traditions. Along the south coast many fishing families hailed originally from Naples. In Marciana and the villages of Western Elba, local experts claim to detect a more ancient Elban population: certainly the people seem more reserved and less interested in the visiting tourist, although they show the dignified courtesy which is characteristic of all Elbans towards the foreigner. Finally, in some of the more remote coastal districts, it is occasionally possible to see a physical type which reminds one of the many raids on Elba by pirates from the North African coast: it is related that when the African forces of the Free French 'liberators' of Elba were running riot in the island, some Elbans went along the cliffs to shout down to one such community, 'Your cousins have arrived.'

ECONOMY

Elba's economy was transformed by the Second World War. Before the war, and indeed up to 1944, it had been primarily an industrial economy: about 1,000 men were employed in the iron-mines in the eastern part of the island, and some 2,000 more in blast-furnaces and workshops at Portoferraio where the iron-ore was smelted and processed. There was also a cement works at Portoferraio employing several hundred people. After the German occupation of the island in 1944, the ironworks and other industrial plants became a target for Allied bombers and were eventually abandoned. And after the war was over, the Italian authorities decided to dismantle the Portoferraio ironworks on the grounds that they were 'uneconomic', regardless of the fact that they had, directly or indirectly, provided a livelihood for a large proportion of the Elban population. Since then, Italsider, the state concern which leases the iron-mines, has shipped their entire output to the mainland. Today the mines employ less than 500 men, and their output is restricted, under the present production plan, to approximately 400,000 tons of ore a year. The cement works were also closed down as uneconomic, although they are to be replaced by a factory under the joint sponsorship of Italsider and Fiat.

After a few difficult years, in which the island population decreased as the younger generation either migrated abroad or went off to seek employment on the mainland, the provincial authorities decided to convert Elba into a tourist resort. The Ente Valorizzazione Elba was founded in 1952 to develop tourist facilities; and plans were drawn up for a progressive expansion of accommodation, motor-roads, and ferry communications with the mainland. The result has been that an island which, in 1950, was completely off the beaten track for Italian tourism, had become, by 1970, a major holiday centre attracting over a million visitors during its annual six-month season. Some 50 per cent of these visitors are Italians; of the rest, 20 per cent are German, 10 per cent British, and 5 per cent French. Today there are nearly 100 hotels in Elba, ranging from the fourth to the first categories, some eighty-five pensions and lodging-houses, as well as motels, camping-sites, villas and blocks of furnished apartments, usually known as 'residences'. This tourist industry has become the basis of Elba's economy, although it is still mainly confined to the island's seaboard; it has also given an important stimulus to a number of subsidiary trades such as quarrying and building, carpentry and plumbing, the restaurant and amusement businesses, boat building and road construction.

However an ancient and unbroken tradition of agriculture underlies the tourist industry, as it underlay the iron industry before it. It has already been noted that four-fifths of the island's population lives outside the main centres, and they are largely concerned with country pursuits, above all with vine growing and wine production. Although some of the highest and most remote hillside vine terraces have been abandoned, owing to a shortage of people willing to work them, Elban wine production is still important and provides the only island export, apart from iron-ore. However, in spite of a wine growers' consortium which prepares high quality wine from the grapes supplied by individual farmers, the Elba wine industry is still run mainly on a family basis; lack of proper equipment and financing means that it has only developed about one fifth of its estimated potential. There are also a few low-lying areas of the island – the plains between Marina di Campo and La Pila, and the valleys between Portoferraio and Porto Azzurro – where grain crops are cultivated, though not in sufficient quantity to meet the island's needs. The forests of sweet chestnut trees on the northern slopes of Monte Capanne, which used to provide an important subsistence food, are now neglected; small family parties will go chestnut-gathering during the season but there is no attempt at serious harvesting.

Although sea-food is a prominent feature of the Elban cuisine, and although there is an abundance of fish in the local waters, the number of local fishermen is very small. Sea-faring Elbans prefer to work in maritime transport. At one time tunny fishing was an Elban industry, and the last of the island's tunny-fishing grounds survived until quite recently off Capo d'Enfola. It was closed down by order of higher authority on the mainland, the official reason being that the tunny were no longer frequenting these waters. Local Elbans will tell you that the real reason was the jealousy of other Italian tunny-fishing centres.

GOVERNMENT AND ADMINISTRATION

Elba now forms part of the territory of the administrative province of Livorno, and the Prefect of that province has an office in Portoferraio. All the separate police forces with which Italy abounds are represented on the island: the *Carabinieri*, a semi-militarized national force, the *Pubblica Sicurezza*, another national force roughly equivalent to the C.I.D., the *Guardia di Finanza*, or customs and excise police, and the two local forces, the *Polizia Municipale* and the *Polizia Stradale*, which are concerned with the enforcement of local regulations and with traffic control and road incidents respectively.

Local administration is based on the territorial unit known as the *Commune*, with an elected mayor and council operating from its chief town (*capoluogo*). Other towns or villages within the same commune are known as *frazioni* (sections). There are altogether eight communes in Elba: Portoferraio, Campo nell'Elba (with Marina di Campo as its *capoluogo*), Capoliveri, Marciana, Marciana Marina, Porto Azzurro, Rio nell'Elba, and Rio Marina. The headquarters of each commune is known as the *Palazzo Municipale* (Town-Hall), or more colloquially as the *municipio*.

RELIGION

With one exception, all Elba's churches are Roman Catholic, the religion of the State, established by Concordat with the Vatican. The exception is a church in Portoferraio belonging to the Waldensians, that most ancient of all Protestant communities which rejected the authority of the Pope in 1170 and survived centuries of persecution to join in the Reformation.

The so-called *Duomo* (cathedral) in the old city of Portoferraio is not technically entitled to the name; it is a parish church, and the senior ecclesiastic of the island is a Vicar-General, usually of monsignorial rank. In addition to the other parish churches of the Elban towns and villages, there are a number of isolated shrines and sanctuaries, many of them dedicated to the Virgin Mary. The most renowned is that of the Madonna del Monte, above Marciana; there are also the shrines of the Madonna del Buon Consiglio and the Madonna Serrapinella on the mountain slopes below Poggio; of the Madonna delle Neve above the plain of Lacona; of the Madonna delle Grazie on the shore below Capoliveri; and of the Madonna di Monserrato in a mountain gorge north of Porto Azzurro. Each of these shrines is the goal of local pilgrimages on church festivals connected with the Virgin Mary. There are also other isolated shrines dedicated to saints, notably that of Santa Lucia on a hill overlooking the plain of San Giovanni outside Portoferraio, to which a traditional pilgrimage is made on Ascension Day.

LANGUAGE

Elbans speak Italian, usually with a Tuscan accent and with certain specialized local and dialect words incorporated into the vocabulary. For example, the word *fosso*, which normally means 'ditch' or 'entrenchment', is applied by the Elbans to the mountain torrents which run down their hillsides in the winter months but are apt to dry up in summer; another specialized local word for 'watercourse' is *uviale*.

Like most Italians, the Elbans respond enthusiastically to the foreigner who has even a smattering of their language. They are not outraged or affronted by errors of grammar and pronunciation. Since the development of the Elban tourist industry, most hotels have an English-speaking member of the staff, but an English-Italian phrase-book (e.g. *Travellers' Italian*, Cape) will be a great help in shopping, ordering meals, etc.

CUSTOMS AND FOLKLORE

As in many other formerly out-of-the-way parts of Italy, the spread of popular education in Elba and the pseudo-sophistication induced by television have tended to eradicate old customs and beliefs which flourished within living memory. So far as they survive it is in an embarrassed, subterranean way which is not easy for the visiting foreigner to detect. For example, 'until a few years ago' the young men of the Campo commune would celebrate the month of May by planting a branch of peach or almond blossom in the ground outside their sweethearts' houses, singing a special song as they did so; this custom was called *piantare il Maggio* (planting the May). No one will now admit to knowing the words of the song; and if the custom persists as it is said to do, in the villages of San Piero and Sant'Ilario, it is on the quiet. Similarly, in Rio nell'Elba, the boys and girls would salute the spring by exchanging gifts of specially baked breads. The boy's gift-bread was called *il cerinito*, the 'little taper', and the girl's was called *la sportella*, the 'little doorway', and each had an explicit sexual symbolism. In Capoliveri during Holy Week, until the beginning of this century, the young men indulged, after suitable festivities, in a 'bloody race' through the town, slashing at each other's naked shoulders with whips. This was almost certainly a degenerate survival of some form of flagellant procession introduced by the Spaniards during their period of occupation of that area.

The more innocuous custom of singing serenades, to the accompaniment of mandolins and guitars, under girls' windows during summer evenings, was widely practised in Elban villages as in other parts of Tuscany. And it is pleasant to record that it has not entirely died out; there is still a small group with mandolins and guitars which keeps up the custom in Rio Marina.

Nineteenth century Elban historians record a number of local beliefs and superstitions. Newly-born babies must not be left alone or unwatched until they have been christened, for fear that they will be frightened or harmed by a bearded female ghost wearing a pointed hat and known by the significant name of *La Pagana* (The Heathen Woman). The Elbans also seem to have cherished a number of peculiar beliefs about Ascension Day, the festival on which the people of Portoferraio still like to make a pilgrimage to the shrine of Santa Lucia outside their city. At midnight before the festival, it was said, the sea stands still and the waves stop moving towards the beach. A hen's egg laid during the festival will keep uncorrupted for many years, and is of great value to fishermen because, if thrown into a stormy sea, it will reduce the force of the waves. An egg laid during Ascension Day High Mass, at the moment of the Elevation of the Host, will be found to have the emblems of the Passion imprinted on its shell.

FOOD AND DRINK

Elba is too near the mainland to have developed a separate or insular cuisine. It offers its visitors the typical Italian menu, enlivened with Tuscan specialities and with a special emphasis on sea-food, freshly caught in the offshore waters. One of the Tuscan sea-food dishes in which the Elbans specialize is *cacciucco*, a form of fish soup or stew, resembling bouillabaisse. Another is *seppie* (cuttle-fish) cooked in their own ink – a dish which tastes better than its alarming appearance might suggest. *Gamberi* (prawns) and *polpi* (octopus) are the subject of various recipes; they are often served together, dipped in batter and fried, and very good they are too. Other fish you are likely to be offered include *dentice* (sea bream), *nasello* (whiting) and *triglia* (red mullet).

Elba does have a speciality, however, and that is wine, which has always been produced in abundance on its mountain slopes. At the beginning of the nineteenth century, the English traveller, Richard Colt Hoare, visiting Elba before Napoleon was sent there, noted that 'the produce of corn does not amount to more than three months consumption of the inhabitants, but the wine is more than sufficient'. Until fairly recently the wine was produced by such 'hit or miss' methods that it did not travel or even keep well, and could not be considered as more than a local curiosity. Now, however, special efforts are being made to modernize production and marketing, and Elban wine has become one of the island's main exports with *denominazione di origine controllata* on its label, although little of it gets beyond the Italian frontiers.

Elba produces all varieties of table wine – red, white, rosé and sparkling – and two desert wines, *Aleatico* and *Moscato*. Of the table wines, only the red and the white deserve serious consideration. The rosé is undistinguished, and the sparkling variety is only one more version of the Italian wines left to complete their fermentation in bottle, and thus acquire the *frizzante* characteristic so popular with Italians.

The red and white table wines are more interesting. In the authors' view the two best are *Alicante* and *Chabry*, both comparatively recent additions to Elban production. Alicante is an excellent full-bodied dry red wine with a fairly high alcoholic content made from the Grenache grape and obviously modelled on similar wines made in the South of France. Chabry is a white wine of great elegance and delicacy, produced from grape juice separated at an early stage from the grape skins. The most familiar Elban table wines, Elba Rosso and Elba Bianco, are made to standards which require 75 per cent of the San Gioveto grape in the red and 75 per cent of the Procanico grape in the white. On the whole the red seems slightly superior as the Biancone grapes, blended with the Procanico, in Elba Bianco give it a faintly resiny flavour. *San Gioveto*, generally called *San Giovese* on the mainland, is an excellent red-wine grape which is one of the main constituents of Chianti; the Elbans also make an unblended San Gioveto which is both agreeable and robust. *Procanico*, otherwise known as *Trebbiano*, is a good but undistinguished white-wine grape, widely used in all parts of Italy, which produces sound, well-balanced wines without much bouquet; the unblended Procanico made in Elba has a slight acidity which makes it go well with sea-food.

Elba's two dessert wines, the red *Aleatico* and the white, or more properly golden, *Moscato*, are well known in Italy. Both are made from grapes of the Muscat family and each has the unmistakable Muscat flavour. When properly produced, neither of them is fortified by the introduction of spirit but each has been allowed to reach an alcoholic strength of at least 16 degrees by the fermentation of 'enriched' must. They are undeniably sweet but they have plenty of character, and either of them will make a pleasant accompaniment to fruit or after-dinner coffee. They are often sold to tourists in fanciful souvenir bottles which may add something to their price but nothing to their quality.

ELBA
Diagram of Routes, Excursions and Walks

▬▬▬	Routes
──	Excursions
----	Walks

Vitic

Marciana Marina

3C

Sant'Andrea
Zanca
3

Il Mortaio
MADONNA
DEL MONTE
3A

Colle d'Orano
Marciana Alta
S. CERBONE
3B
Poggio

3

MADONNA
BUONCONSIGLIO
4

Biodo

Procchio

Monte Perone
E
3B

Monte Capanne
2A
S. Ilario

Monume

Chiessi
2A
2

Pomonte
Monte Cenno
S. Piero
Monte Tar

3
Seccheto
2A
3
Marina di Campo

2B
2B

Fetovaia

2 km

Cavo

1C

1C

Nisportino

D

Nisporto

PORTOFERRAIO

D

Rio nell'Elba

Rio Marina

B

Bagnaia

1C

vio Boni

Magazzini

D

Volterraio

D

Cima del Monte

1

D

Ortano

A

E

S. STEFANO

lla San Martino

Monte Castello

1E

MADONNA DI MONSERRATO

Monte Orello

1A

1C

2

1

PORTO AZZURRO

1

nte Fonza

1D

1B

Naregno

Capoliveri

1B

Monte Calamita

1D

1D

INTRODUCTION TO ROUTES

In an island as small as Elba and as well provided with a circuit of motor-roads, any description of 'routes' through its territory must seem slightly artificial; all parts of the island are accessible by car in a single day. But since this Guide is primarily for the traveller who is making more than a brief visit and wants to get to know Elba in some detail, this section of the book is divided into five parts, each dealing with a separate area.

The first part, Portoferraio and Environs, deals with the island's capital, Portoferraio – a historic city notable especially for its Napoleonic associations – together with excursions to places of interest in its immediate neighbourhood. Next, Route 1 deals with the main road from Portoferraio to Porto Azzurro and the excursions that can be made using Porto Azzurro as a base. Route 2 describes the road from Porto Azzurro to Marina di Campo on the south coast and possible excursions to be made in that area. Route 3 takes the traveller round the western end of Elba from Marina di Campo to Marciana and Marciana Marina, and lists excursions in and round the massif of Monte Capanne. Route 4 completes the circuit of the island, with a brief description of the road linking Marciana Marina with Portoferraio (see Diagram of Routes, p. 146).

Three other motor-roads which do not form an essential part of that circuit but are nonetheless important are mentioned in the appropriate context. One is the road along the east coast from Porto Azzurro to Cavo; the second is the link between Procchio and Marino di Campo across the centre of the island; the third is the scenic mountain road over Monte Perone which links Marina di Campo with Poggio and Marciana.

Provided you have transport – car, motor-scooter, or the local bus system – there is nothing to prevent you from going directly to the 'base' of any of the five sections and then making one of the excursions listed in that section. Most of them take from half to a full day.

WALKING
Since the authors are convinced that one of the least known and most rewarding aspects of a stay in Elba is the opportunity it offers for exploratory walks, or drives combined with walks, into the relatively

unexploited interior, each route-section also describes a number of optional walks as subsidiary excursions. Many of them have been personally explored but the list is not intended to be exhaustive; the keen path-finder will certainly be able to discover more, especially in the mountains. The serious walker may be surprised, and perhaps a little amused, by the shortness of the distances involved. He should however reckon on three other factors as well as the map distance: the steepness of many hills, the roughness of the going, and the heat of the Mediterranean sun, especially after a picnic lunch which has included a bottle of wine. A five mile walk in Elba may seem in retrospect the equivalent of ten miles in a cooler climate and over an easier terrain. The diagram of Routes, Excursions and Walks (p. 146) is only a rough indication of their whereabouts; serious walkers will require a larger scale and should consult the following section on Maps.

MAPS

Tourist pocket-maps of Elba abound in the local shops. They are generally reliable about the main motor-roads (though some of them were published before the system was completed) and reasonably accurate about the secondary system of what are called in this Guide the 'country roads' with only roughly metalled surfaces. But although most of them indicate the existence of footpaths (*sentieri*) and bridle-tracks (*mulattieri*), they tend to be wildly inaccurate or vague about their location. The authors found the best available map for the serious exploration of Elba is that published by the Military-Geographic Institute in Florence on a scale of 1:25,000 (roughly 700 yards to one inch). The Institute has published a complete survey of Italy on this scale. It is very detailed and for most areas, including Elba, is printed in three colours – blue for water, pink for contours, and black for all other features. It is not very easy to read without a magnifying-glass and, as far as Elba is concerned, not very up-to-date, being based on an aerial survey carried out in 1954. But, granted these shortcomings, it remains the most accurate and informative map available. A new edition, printed in five colours and based on more recent surveys, is now in process of being published and will be a great improvement, but at the time of writing it had not yet covered Elba. The current three-colour map for the island comes in seven sheets (*tavolette*), and should be quoted when ordering as 'Folio 126, Tavolette I, II, and III, SE Cavo, NE Porto Azzurro, SE Capoliveri,

NO Portoferraio, SO Marina di Campo, NE Marciana, SE Pomonte'. It may be purchased from Istituto Geografico Militare, 50100 Firenze, Viale Filippo Strozzi 14; the price at time of writing was 700 lire per sheet or 4,900 lire for the set.

EQUIPMENT

As already indicated (p. 60) visitors to Elba intending to do much walking should equip themselves with stout shoes with non-slip rubber soles. Both sexes should preferably wear trousers of some tough fabric which will withstand the thorny vegetation of the *macchia*, especially the prickly broom. Incidentally walkers should be wary of patches of burnt-off *macchia*. Although these are easier to cross, the charred stalks leave persistent dirty marks on clothing. A light ruck-sack for picnic lunches is useful and its pockets should contain insect repellent and some remedy for wasp stings; these insects can be a nuisance especially in late summer. Sunglasses or shady headwear are also advisable.

PORTOFERRAIO

Population	10,800
Air and sea connections	See p. 34
Buses	The bus station is at Calata Matteotti (*Map* **16**); see p. 37 for information about bus timetables and routes.
Taxis	The main rank is at the landward end of the Molo Massimo (*Map* **19**); see p. 38
Hotels and pensions	See p. 44
Restaurants	See p. 58
Information	The Ente Valorizzazzione Elba (E.V.E.) is at Calata Italia 26 (*Map* **18**)
General post office	Piazza della Repubblica (*Map* **8**)
Central telephone exchange	Viale Manzoni (*Map* **9**); for making international calls.
Markets	The covered market (*Map* **15**) is open every week-day; see p. 66. There is also an open-air market in Piazza della Repubblica on Friday mornings.
Civil Hospital	(*Map* **5**); see p. 64

Protestant church	Waldensian sect only; services in Italian.
Entertainment	See p. 69
Festivals	April 29 San Cristino (patron saint).
	May 5 Commemoration of Napoleon at Church of Misericordia.
	August 29 Misericordia procession to Church of San Rocco.
Beaches	The nearest beaches are Le Ghiaie (p. 154), Le Viste (p. 167), and Grigolo (p. 169).

Portoferraio, the capital of Elba, lies on the island's north coast; it occupies the promontory to the west of the entrance to Portoferraio Bay (Golfo di Portoferraio) and owes much of its historic importance to its command of this large and almost land-locked anchorage. Its name means literally 'Iron Port' and associates it with the age-old mining industry in the eastern part of the island. But, although there were blast-furnaces in Portoferraio during the first part of this century, they have now gone and Elban shipments of iron ore go directly to the mainland from Rio Marina on the east coast. There is evidence to suggest that the 'Iron *Port*' was originally subordinate to a medieval town called simply Feraia (see History, p. 108). No known trace of this medieval town exists today.

The visitor arriving from the mainland by ferry is able to see that Portoferraio is built round two separate harbours. On his right, as the ferry enters the bay, he sees the old fortified city, constructed on the tip of the promontory by Duke Cosimo de' Medici in the sixteenth century round a deep horse-shoe-shaped basin, originally designed to be closed by a boom. The ferry by-passes this and ties up at a broad pier (the Pontile G. Massimo) in a second and more open harbour round which the more modern section of Portoferraio is built. Here is the quay-terminus (*Map* **21**) for the various ferry services connecting Elba with Piombino and Livorno. There is a taxi-rank and a parking area for motor vehicles entering or leaving the ferries. A broad and busy esplanade, the Calata Italia, runs along the sea front; on its landward side are two conspicuous multi-storeyed office blocks with shops, banks, cafés, and tourist agencies at ground level. The block seen to the right as visitors land, and familiarly known as 'Il Grattacielo' (The Skyscraper) (*Map* **19**), contains the offices of the port authority and the official tourist organization, the *Ente per la Valorizzazzione dell'Isola d'Elba*, or E.V.E., which can provide general information about accommodation and tourist facilities.

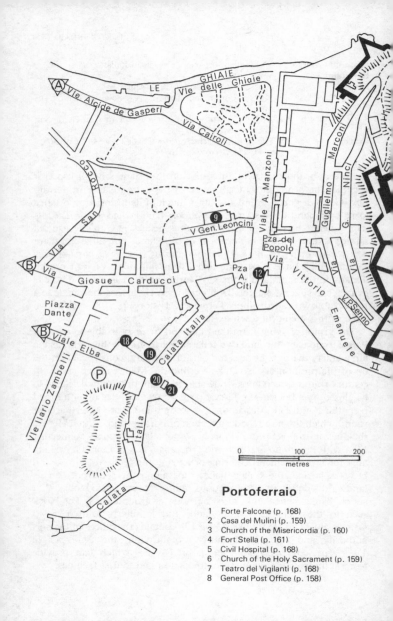

Portoferraio

1 Forte Falcone (p. 168)
2 Casa del Mulini (p. 159)
3 Church of the Misericordia (p. 160)
4 Fort Stella (p. 161)
5 Civil Hospital (p. 168)
6 Church of the Holy Sacrament (p. 159)
7 Teatro del Vigilanti (p. 168)
8 General Post Office (p. 158)

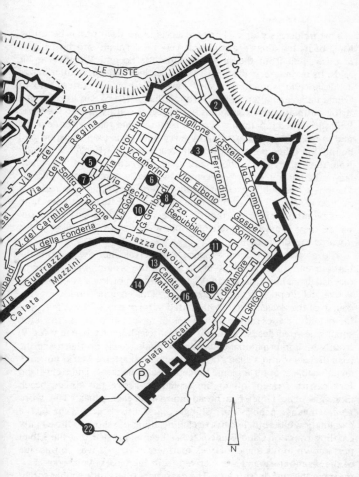

9   Telephone Exchange
10   Town Hall (p.158)
11   Cathedral (p.158)
12   Public Mail Box
13   Porta a Mare (p.156)
14   Molo Mediceo (p.156)
15   Covered market (Galeazze) (p.169)
16   Bus Station (p.150)
17   Porta a Terra (p.156)

18   Bus Office
19   E.V.E. Information Office
20   Taxi Rank
21   Ferry Terminus (p. 151)
22   Torre del Martello (p. 156)
P   Parking areas
A   Exit to Viticcio & Capo d'Enfola
B   Exit to Bivio Boni & rest of island

This modern sector of Portoferraio is more useful than beautiful. Most of its buildings are comparatively modern and much of it was reconstructed from the ruins left after the Second World War air raids. Its main artery, the Via G. Carducci, leaves the triangular Piazza del Ponticello (sometimes called Piazza Citi) at the eastern end of Calata Italia, and after passing through the district of San Rocco and a string of unattractive roadside suburbs, turns southwards to the Bivio Boni (Boni road junction) where the island's main road system may be said to begin. Visitors arriving by ferry with their own transport and bound for other parts of Elba can reach the Via Carducci directly from the pier by taking the broad, divided avenue, Viale Elba, which leaves the harbour-front between the two multi-storeyed office blocks. There is a free public parking lot on the left side of this avenue, but if no stop is planned cars should take the first main turning to the right, Via Colombo. This brings them into the Via Carducci at a T-junction, where they should turn left and follow the main stream of traffic towards the Bivio Boni.

The pleasantest part of modern Portoferraio lies away from the harbour and the bay, on the north side of the promontory. It may be reached by taking the broad Viale Manzoni northwards out of the Piazza del Ponticello (or Piazza Citi). This avenue, following the course of the ancient moat which used to form part of the defences of the old city, passes on the right a line of naval barracks; on the left a small side-street leads up to the central telephone exchange (*Map* **9**) from which international calls may be made. At its northern end the road divides round a shady little public park (Parterre Mario Foresi) – an agreeable spot for a picnic lunch beneath the trees. The right-hand fork carries straight on to the esplanade above the Ghiaie beach (Spiaggia delle Ghiaie), a broad northward-facing bay. The word *ghiaie* means 'pebbles' or 'shingle', and this beach is in fact a dazzlingly white shingle bank stretching along the shore to the equally dazzling rocks of Capo Bianco. It has been suggested that the Elban port known to the ancient Greek mariners as *Argoos* was on this side of the promontory and was derived from the Greek word-root *arg-*, meaning 'bright' or 'shining'. The coast here offers little shelter for an anchorage but the shingle would have been convenient for beaching small ships.

The road forking left from the northern end of Viale Manzoni, Via Cairoli, leads uphill to Capo Bianco past hotels and pensions and then along the north coastline to Capo d'Enfola (see p. 173).

The main attraction of Portoferraio for visitors is the old, walled city with its Medicean and Napoleonic associations. It was constructed in the middle of the sixteenth century on what seems to have been then a deserted site by Cosimo I de' Medici, later to become the first Grand Duke of Tuscany, and in his honour it was known at first as 'Cosmopoli', though it reverted to the local name of Portoferraio in the next generation. Cosimo had been authorized by the Emperor Charles V to build a *piazza forte* or 'stronghold' in the territory of Feraia, as a defence against the North African corsairs who served as the fleet of the Sultan of Turkey and used Portoferraio Bay as an anchorage and base of operations (see History, p. 108). The duke's architects, first Belluzzi and later Camerini, designed a fortress-city as a single unit to fit the contours of the hill at the end of the promontory. The work began in 1548 and was completed within ten years. The elaborate fortifications were constructed to meet the new siege tactics of the age of fire arms; extended and improved during the seventeenth and eighteenth centuries, they were regarded as a model of their kind.,In fact the city successfully withstood a thirteen-months' siege by French forces in 1801–2.

Inside its solid defences-in-depth, the city has the appearance of a steeply raked theatre auditorium, focussing on the harbour-basin which it encloses on three sides. The street plan climbs up from sea-level towards the natural ridge along the north side of the promontory with flights of steps where the slope gets too steep for streets. Along the northern side the ground drops again as cliffs or precipitous slopes into the sea; it was made even more difficult of access by outworks and the two bastioned forts which crown the two highest points of the ridge. At its eastern end, overlooking both the harbour entrance and the sea outside, is *Forte Stella* (Star Fort), so named after its spiked ground plan. At the western end of the high ridge is *Forte Falcone* (Falcon Fort), overlooking the landward defences. From Forte Falcone the natural ridge swings southwards to form the headland dividing the two harbours of present-day Portoferraio, and the fortifications follow it.

TOUR OF OLD PORTOFERRAIO

(All map references are to the map of the city, p. 152–3.) A tour of the walled city should be made preferably on foot, and begins most logically and conveniently at the *Porta a Mare* or 'Sea Gate', giving on to the harbour. To get there, either by car or on foot, from the modern ferry landing-stage (distance about 1km.), turn right along the Calata Italia to the Piazza del Ponticello (or Piazza Citi), and from there follow the Via Vittorio Emmanuele along the seafront and round the headland dividing the two harbours. As you enter the old harbour-basin, the name of the esplanade changes to Calata Mazzini and you see the fortifications of the Medicean city looming on your left; to the right is a comparatively modern jetty, the *Molo del Gallo* (Weathercock Pier). Along this stretch houses, shops, cafés and even a modern hotel have been incorporated into the massive curtain-wall which screens the town from the harbour: the Café Roma here has long been a centre for Elban society and gossip.

As you reach the centre of the horseshoe-shaped curve of the harbour, you come to the broad jetty constructed by Duke Cosimo's architects and called the Molo Mediceo (Medici Pier). Opposite it, across the road, is the Porta a Mare (*Map* 13) designed as the main entrance to the town. Two further passages have recently been cut through the rampart for motor traffic to enter and leave the city, but parking space within the walls is very limited, and if you have arrived at this point by car and intend to continue the tour on foot, it is advisable either to find a parking space along the harbour-front, or to follow the esplanade right round the harbour to its termination at a gateway leading into the square of a naval barracks. The local bus services turn round in this square, and part of it has been marked out as a parking-grid.

Standing on the *Molo Mediceo* (*Map* 14) and looking down the harbour, you see to your left front the octagonal tower (*Map* 22) designed by Camerini as part of the original defences and the terminus of the chain boom which could close the basin in time of emergency. The tower has been given several names during its existence, *Torre della Linguella* because it stands on a 'little tongue' of land; *Torre del Martello* because it resembles the head of a hammer; *Torre di Passanante* because it served as the prison for a notorious character of that name who attempted to assassinate King Umberto I.

Turning round to face the town, you find it screened by the tall wall of buildings which was once the harbour rampart; a series of loggias at second-floor level indicate the original sentries' walk. Immediately in front of you is the Porta a Mare, an imposingly simple gateway which is one of the two original entries to the city. (The *Porta a Terra* (*Map* 17), or Land-gate, is an unobtrusive tunnel under the fortifications.) Prominent above the gateway is the Latin boast of the city's founder; translated it reads, 'Churches, walls, houses, fortresses, harbour, Cosimo, Duke of the Florentines, erected them all from their foundations upwards, A.D. 1548.' This is perhaps the most emphatic evidence that no trace of an earlier city survived on this spot in the sixteenth century, although Roman remains found during recent building excavations suggest it may have been the site of the Roman capital of the island, Fabricia. A second Latin inscription records that the gateway was given its present form by one of Cosimo's Medici successors: 'Ferdinando II, Grand Duke of Tuscany, completed it in A.D. 1637, the year in which he took Victoria, Princess of Urbino, as wife, by happy omen.'

These inscriptions met the eye of Napoleon Bonaparte when he landed on the jetty in the afternoon of May 4th, 1814, to take possession of the tiny principality granted to him by the Treaty of Fontainebleau after his abdication from the thrones of France and Italy (see History, pp. 117–127). They were translated for him as he stood there by the deputy mayor of the town, Joseph Hutré, who formed one of the welcoming group of local dignitaries. Napoleon had arrived a day earlier but had waited on board the British frigate *Undaunted* to allow time for a suitable reception to be organized. The Elbans, encouraged by the French military governor and the local authorities, had done their best: the harbour front was crowded, and a flock of small boats, one carrying a girls' choir and another a guitar band, had escorted the Emperor into the harbour while Napoleon's newly designed flag was hoisted on the battlements and the fortress artillery replied to the 21 gun salute of the *Undaunted*. After a formal welcome from the local authorities and the Vicar-General of the island, Monsignor Arrighi, Napoleon went forward under a gilt canopy through the Sea Gate.

The modern visitor who follows his footsteps finds himself in an open space called the *Piazza Cavour* (formerly the *Piazza Granguardia*), which is more like a wide curving street than a conventional square. It is now the main commercial centre of the old city, and many of the shops and cafés which are built into the harbour rampart have second frontages on the piazza. Just inside the gateway are two useful kiosks which sell English-language newspapers, usually 24 to 48 hours old, paperbacks, maps and local guides.

Still following Napoleon's processional entry, the visitor should then take the narrow street opposite the Sea Gate across the piazza into the *Piazza della Repubblica*, an oblong tree-lined square which in the Emperor's day was called the Piazza d'Armi or Place d'Armes. It was here that, during his nine months' rule of the island, Napoleon was wont to review his miniature army with a total strength of some 1,000 men. But on the day of his arrival, he passed through the square with undignified haste: the over-excited crowd threw fireworks at his procession which, led by the two generals, Drouot and Marshal Bertrand, took refuge at the run in the cathedral church. This is at the right-hand end of the square as you enter it from the direction of the Piazza Cavour; and it was here that Monsignor Arrighi, who was a Corsican like Napoleon, conducted a service of thanksgiving with the Emperor kneeling at a purple-draped prie-Dieu in the central aisle while the *Te Deum* was sung.

The Cathedral (*Map* 11), so-called only by courtesy, is in fact an unpretentious eighteenth-century church in the Florentine style which contains no significant art treasures but offers a peaceful refuge from the summer sun. Its monuments include a moving epitaph composed by a bereaved husband for his young wife, to be found in the north aisle.

At this end of the Piazza della Repubblica, just above the cathedral, is the oldest hotel in Elba, the *Albergo Ape Elbana* (Elban Bee Hotel). In Napoleon's day, it was called the Auberge Bonroux and was enlarged to accommodate the many nobilities who made the pilgrimage to Elba either to pay their respects to the Emperor or merely to gratify their curiosity.

At the other end of the Piazza is the general post office (*Map* 8) with its main entrance round the corner at the left-hand end of the building looking on to the adjacent *Piazza Joseph Hutré.* (The post office handles telegrams and has *poste restante* facilities but does *not* provide telephones, which are controlled by a separate administration.) On the building's façade is a modern bas-relief by the sculptor Arturo Dazzi, commemorating Pietro Gori, poet and Risorgimento figure, who died in Portoferraio in 1911.

Also facing on to the Piazza Hutré, on the side at right-angles to the post office, is the *Palazzo Municipale* (Town Hall) (*Map* 10), and it was here that Napoleon came after the thanksgiving service. The Elban authorities, suddenly faced with the problem of housing their new ruler, had cleared out its top floor and equipped it with borrowed furniture to provide an apartment for the Emperor. Ten years earlier the same rooms had accommodated a Major Hugo, sent as governor to the island after its annexation by France. One of his three children who used to play in the courtyard of the building was Victor Hugo, the French novelist and poet. Today the same top floor houses the *Foresian Library*, a collection of books and manuscripts, largely dealing with the history and topography of Elba, donated to the municipality by Mario Foresi, historian and member of a well-known Elban family. The library may be consulted by special arrangement through the Ente per la Valorizzazzione dell'Isola d'Elba, (p 59).

In the courtyard stands a Roman sacrificial altar, carved in granite and bearing the symbols of Hercules; it was found at Seccheto on the south coast of Elba. On the outer facade of the building is a stone tablet commemorating the air-raid by means of which the Germans enforced the surrender of Elba in the Second World War after the collapse of the fascist regime in 1943. It offers a fine example of monumental rhetoric:

> The desperate screech of the sirens was drowned in the terrifying roar of the insolent invader who, with bestial fury, rained down fire and sword from the heavens above our peaceful rooftops, strewing the streets with ruins and the dead. The people of Portoferraio, under the auspices of their civic administration, placed this marble stone as a perpetual memorial of so barbarous an attack ten years afterwards, to honour the fallen and to pray for peace and concord among nations.

Napoleon did not appreciate the town hall as a residence. There were no toilet facilities and the streets outside were overflowing with the filth of a town without sewers or refuse collection. On the morning following his landing he immediately began a search for a more desirable dwelling. He was eventually conducted up to the highest level of the town to see a building on the ridge between the two fortresses, the *Casa dei Mulini* (House of the Windmills) (*Map* 22), which, after enlargement and alterations, became his principal residence. Today it is officially known as the Palazzina Napoleonica dei Mulini, and to reach it, the visitor should climb the steep street leading out of the Piazza Hutré which is now called Via Garibaldi; when Napoleon climbed it, it was Via del Buon Gusto (Good Taste Street). It continues to the point where the slope is so steep that the road becomes a flight of 135 broad stone steps, with the name *Salita Napoleone*.

On the left, just before the steps begin, is the *Church of the Holy Sacrament* (*Map* 6), known locally as the 'Chapel of the Whites'.

The inhabitants of Portoferraio all belong to one or the other of two religious confraternities, the 'Whites' and the 'Blacks', which do charitable work among their members and above all escort their funerals to the cemetery. The church is undistinguished architecturally but contains a number of minor works of art, a marble high altar by an unknown sculptor, a painted ceiling depicting the Assumption of the Virgin Mary by the seventeenth-century painter, Sagrestani, a sixteenth-century embroidered vestment, and a bronze copy of Napoleon's death mask.

The church of the other confraternity, the 'Blacks', officially known as the *Church of the Misericordia* (*Map* 3), is on the right, half-way up the Salita Napoleone. When the main door is not open, it can usually be entered from the Via Ferrandini, which runs off at an angle to the Salita. It contains one exquisite work of art, a miniature sculpture of the Virgin and Child, attributed to the renaissance artist, Tino di Camaino. It stands on a pedestal attached to a pillar on the left of the main door. But this church has also become Elba's shrine to the memory of Napoleon – a sort of local *Les Invalides* – thanks to the bequests of Prince Anatole Demidoff who married the Emperor's niece, Mathilde Bonaparte, daughter of his youngest brother Jerome. He left a fund which provides an annual payment of 500 francs to the local clergy, 400 francs for the poor of the parish and 100 for a mass to be celebrated on the anniversary of Napoleon's death, May 5th. He also gave the church a replica of the Emperor's coffin at Les Invalides, inside which are kept bronze casts of Napoleon's death-mask and hand. These are normally kept in an alcove draped with one of the Elban flags designed by the Emperor, to be exhibited by the sacristan at visitors' request. But once a year, at the memorial mass on May 5th, the replica-coffin is taken from the alcove and exhibited to a congregation which traditionally includes the Mayor of Portoferraio and the civil and military authorities of the island: to preserve the correct martial atmosphere, at the Elevation of the Host, a detachment of troops presents arms and a bugle is blown.

At the top of the Salita Napoleone, you reach the Via della Stella which leads to the right across the top of the town and up a ramp to the fort of the same name. But opening off this street to the left is the entrance to the outer courtyard (and parking lot) of the Palazzina dei Mulini. Motorists can reach this point from Piazza Cavour at the bottom of the hill by ascending Via Garibaldi as far as the foot of the Salita Napoleone and then turning sharp right along Via Elbano

Gasperi. The first (and even sharper) turning to the left leads diagonally uphill to Via Stella and the entrance to the Palazzina.

Forte Stella (*Map* 4)

Before entering the Napoleonic residence, the visitor may care to admire the view over the town rooftops from Via Stella and look round the fort. Its buildings are now private homes but it is possible to stroll through its courtyards up to the covered wall which supplied the defenders in time of siege. Within its ramparts and looking out over the harbour entrance is the elegant small lighthouse which was erected by the Austrian Grand Duke of Tuscany, Leopold of Lorraine, and first lit on November 15th, 1789, the year of the French Revolution which was to bring such changes to Elba. It was this Grand Duke who had earlier removed from the niche over the main gate of the fort a bust, made by Benvenuto Cellini, of the Grand Duke Cosimo, now to be found in the National Museum at Florence. During the Napoleonic rule, Fort Stella housed the Grenadiers of the Imperial Guard and also provided appartments for the Guard's commander, Marshal Cambronne, and for Marshal Bertrand, Grand Marshal of the Emperor's household. But for Italians the fort is perhaps more noteworthy as the prison in which several nationalist revolutionaries of the Risorgimento were detained by the Austrian rulers of Tuscany. It was their movement which was eventually to unite Italy under the House of Savoy and put an end to all the foreign dynasties in the land, including the Austrians in Tuscany.

Palazzina dei Mulini (*Map* 22)

Open 9.00–13.30
15.00–18.00 } April 30th–October 1st: 9.00–14.00 Winter months.

Closed Tuesdays

Entrance 100 lire (this also gives same day admission to the Villa San Martino (p 170))

Outside the Palazzina dei Mulini is an inscription which, with considerable aplomb, links the Risorgimento with Napoleon Bonaparte.

This august and sovereign house, where an empire collapsed and was revived, was occupied for nearly a year, during his first exile, by Napoleon the Great. The divided Island of Elba having found unity through him, he solemnly pointed the way to the unity of Italy. Nostalgic for the epic of his glory, he here conceived the bold undertaking which took him away from these heights to land him on distant shores.

Before exploring the interior of the Palazzina, it is worth looking at the exterior from the little garden on the cliff top. When Napoleon was first brought here, there was only a one-storey building formed by linking two small houses together. They stood on the site where two windmills had formerly ground the garrison's corn, catching the sea breezes blowing across the ridge in their sails. The Emperor was delighted by the fresh air after the stench in the lower part of the town, and also by the view across the open sea to the north. He immediately envisaged the possibility of adding the second storey which exists today. The building to the right of the Emperor's residence, as seen from the garden, was originally the barn in which the corn and flour of the windmills were kept. In Napoleon's day it was enlarged and decorated to become a ballroom with a stage for amateur theatricals. Traces of the decorations survive but the interior is in a state of decay and is not shown to visitors.

The Palazzina itself, even after Napoleon's additions and improvements, was clearly little more than a comfortable middle-class residence of its time. It suited Napoleon not only because of its airy and commanding position above the town, but also because, as a military commander, it gave him easy communications with the two fortresses. He moved into it on May 21st, 1814, less than three weeks after his arrival in Elba. Its interior today is a somewhat melancholy compromise between a Napoleonic memorial museum and a reconstruction of its appearance during the Emperor's tenure. After Napoleon had reached Paris during the Hundred Days following his escape from Elba, he gave the Palazzina to the town of Portoferraio to be made into a museum, and gave his books to the town hall to become the nucleus of a library. But when the Austrian Grand Dukes regained Tuscany after Waterloo, they seized the building and its contents, sold the furniture to dealers in Florence, and even obtained part of the library. In the middle of the nineteenth century, Napoleon's devout nephew-in-law, Prince Anatole Demidoff, collected some of the dispersed furniture and sent it back to Elba together with other pieces from his own collection. But, on his death, the furniture was again auctioned off to pay his debts. Some of it was recovered before the First World War, and put on exhibition at the town hall, but it was badly damaged when that building was bombed in 1944. Finally, in 1952, when the tourist industry had become important to the Elban authorities, a determined effort was made to restore the furniture which was available and to procure other pieces from Florence. After all these vicissitudes, it is not surprising that only eight of the twenty rooms in the house have been partially or completely furnished, and that their contents are somewhat heterogeneous. They are worth viewing for the sake of what does survive and also for the interesting collection of historic documents, prints and portraits hanging on the walls.

The ordinary visitor is permitted to go round the house without a guide and to linger where he pleases provided that he stays within the ropes which cordon off the main apartments. It is suggested that he completes the tour of the ground floor first, the part occupied by Napoleon himself, and then the upper floor originally intended by Napoleon for his wife, the Empress Marie Louise, and his little son, the King of Rome, who in fact never joined him (see History, p. 120).

GROUND FLOOR

The first ground floor room to be entered after the little waiting-room is Napoleon's *grand salon*, which stretches right across the house from front to back. It contains a large settee, a set of white and gold armchairs, and a small mahogany table. The equestrian statuette of Napoleon on the table was made during the reign of Napoleon III, under the Second Empire, and the Sevres porcelain also dates from that period. The four chests of drawers, inlaid with brass and ivory, are also post-Napoleonic, and date from about 1840. On the wall hangs a reproduction of David's popular painting, 'Napoleon crossing the Alps'. The ceiling used to be painted in the *trompe-l'œil* style as a military marquee, adorned with trophies of arms, but this has been overpainted, presumably to conceal the damage of time and damp.

The next room, Napoleon's *study*, contains a writing-table, cupboard, and armchair, which could conceivably be part of the original furnishings; they date from the Directoire period, the first post-Revolutionary government of France, preceding Napoleon's rise to power. On the table is a frame holding a proof of the two proclamations, addressed by Napoleon to the people and the army of France after he had escaped from Elba; they were printed in Portoferraio. On the wall is a town plan of the city as it was in 1814, showing the salt pans which were then one of the main local industries.

The room beyond now contains a set of showy gilt armchairs and settee in Italianate style; it was Napoleon's *Petit Salon*, or small drawing-room, and a doorway in its rear wall leads into Napoleon's bedroom on the other side of the house.

The next room, *Camera dei Valetti*, or Servants' Room, has no furniture apart from a glass-fronted cupboard containing a service in English pottery, bearing the Imperial crest. On the walls hangs a set of contemporary caricatures, and an interesting print of Portoferraio dated 1796, showing the two windmills which formerly occupied the site of the Palazzina. It dates from the brief British occupation of the island in 1796–7. There are also some autograph letters of Napoleon III and the Empress Eugenie. One of them, from Napoleon III, was written in 1870 after his defeat in the Franco-Prussian war during his temporary imprisonment in Germany: it thanks the Mayor of Portoferraio for his offer of the Palazzina as a refuge.

A small passage under the staircase leads into a lobby opening into the garden. The visitor's route takes him past Napoleon's bathroom, now not shown because completely empty, into the *Guardaroba*, or Wardrobe Room, where Napoleon's robes and uniforms were kept under the supervision of a Signora Squarci, wife of an Elban doctor. One wall of the room is now covered by the Elban flag designed by the Emperor and hoisted over Fort Falcone on May 4th, 1814, at the moment when Napoleon landed. It has the red diagonal stripe on a white background which was intended to recall the arms of the De' Medici family, and superimposed on it the three golden bees which were the symbol of the Napoleonic empire. On a corner table is a sword worn by Napoleon and in a glass case the keys presented to him on landing by Mayor Traditi; they had been gilded and were supposed to be those of the Sea Gate, although they actually belonged to the Mayor's cellar. There are portraits of Marshal Bertrand, General Cambronne, and also of a Polish officer, Colonel Germanowski, who was one of the three Allied Commissioners who accompanied Napoleon to Elba. (Only one of them, Sir Neil Campbell, the British Commissioner, actually remained on the island with him.) There is also a portrait of M. Pons de l'Herault, the manager of the iron-mines whom Napoleon visited soon after his arrival in search of funds to finance his administration. Other pictures include another view of Portoferraio, showing the salt pans, the scene of Napoleon's departure from the island on February 26th, 1815, and a photograph of the Emperor's dog, stuffed and preserved in Paris.

The door out of the Guardaroba leads to a small *ante-room* now containing only two round heating-stoves and, on the wall, an interesting group of orders issued by General Drouot, who was Napoleon's governor of the island, and counter-signed with comments by the Emperor himself. It was here that Napoleon's personal bodyguard, St Denis, used to sleep on a mat on the floor outside the door of the Emperor's bedroom which lies beyond. St Denis had taken the name of 'Mameluke Ali', to recall Napoleon's victories in Egypt and perhaps also because he had taken the place of a genuine Egyptian bodyguard, Roustan, who deserted his master after the Treaty of Fontainebleau.

Napoleon's *bedroom* retains virtually all its original furniture, the magnificent suite which formerly belonged to his sister, Elisa Baciocchi, whom he had installed with her husband in the principality of Piombino. Although the Baciocchi couple had abandoned the Emperor's cause at the time of Fountainbleau, they had been turned out of Piombino by the Austrians who occupied the city. Their palace there was standing empty when Napoleon reached Elba, and he despatched his quartermaster and a party of his men to raid it and remove the furniture under the nose of the Austrian general, Starhemberg. The cargo they brought back included this suite as well as much else which has since disappeared; the Emperor is reported to have remarked: 'I've punished my sister and robbed Austria at one stroke.' The Princess Elisa had not enjoyed a high reputation with her subjects in Piombino, and when the Emperor asked one of them what his sister had done during her reign, the reply was, *'Faceva l'amore'* (She made love). The suite includes a marble-topped console-table, an Empire writing desk, a white and gold armchair, two stools, a clock, two bedside tables disguised as classic columns, and the vast, flamboyant bed. Napoleon used to lie in the evenings holding long conversations with an old Corsican friend, Poggi, whom he had appointed chief of the Elban police. On the bed today lies a green velvet dress, embroidered with tiny golden flowers, which belonged to Napoleon's first wife, Josephine, the beautiful Creole whom he divorced in order to marry the daughter of the Emperor of Austria. When Marshal Bertrand's wife joined her husband in Elba, she brought this garment with her to give to Napoleon as a memento of Josephine who had just died.

Beyond the bedroom is Napoleon's *library* which still contains all of its original collection of books, except for those taken by the Grand

Duke Leopold III after Waterloo. The four glass-fronted bookcases contain an extraordinary variety of reading-matter although the visitor is not permitted to take them from the shelves. There is a complete set of the *Moniteur Universel* from the outbreak of the French Revolution to 1813, the works of Cervantes, Fénélon, La Fontaine, Voltaire, Rousseau, and Plutarch. But, in addition to these classics, there are technical works on cattle diseases, on botany, distilling, and the 'dying of red cotton'. The large collection of fairy tales, called *Le Cabinet des Fées*, moral tales for young females, the stories of Boccaccio, Young's *Night Thoughts*, translated into French, and a book with French on one page and English on the other, entitled *The Hundred Thoughts of a Young Lady* are also there.

From the library the visitor enters the other side of the Grand Salon. and the tour of the ground floor then ends with the so-called *Officers' Room* which has, framed on its walls, newspapers and broadsheets issued during the 'Hundred Days' and the two proclamations, addressed to the People and the Army of France, which Napoleon drew up during his last days on the island and had printed by a local firm. Beyond the Officers' Room a corridor used to lead to the kitchens which do not survive today. There is, incidentally, no dining-room because it was customary in Napoleon's day to set up tables and serve a meal in whatever room was found to be convenient.

UPPER FLOOR

Retracing his steps through the library, bedroom and wardrobe, the visitor can return to the narrow staircase of twenty pink marble steps which leads up to the upper floor, constructed under Napoleon's orders while he was already living on the ground floor. When the Empress Marie Louise failed to join her husband, it remained empty until November 1814, when it was taken over by Napoleon's favourite sister, the Princess Paolina Borghese, who came to join her brother and to act as his hostess and companion. There is first a suite of four small rooms, originally planned for the Emperor's son, and now quite empty except for a few pictures.

Then, over the central portion of the ground floor, there is a large and lofty *salon*, stretching across the entire width of the house, which became Paolina's state drawing-room where many of her entertainments were held. The massive Empire chandelier hanging from the ceiling is part of the original decor, as well as the enormous mirror on one of the walls. The ceiling, like that of the Grand Salon downstairs, was originally painted in a Florentine style, with spears and pikes supporting an awning and brightly clad Victories holding laurel wreaths. But this too has been painted over to conceal the damage and stains resulting from a leaky roof. During the air-raids of 1943–4, the Palazzina escaped a direct hit, but the windows were blown out and the roof badly damaged. The smaller rooms on the far side of this drawing-room were Paolina's private suite; they are unfurnished and not shown to visitors. A private staircase from them leads down into the garden.

GARDEN

Perhaps the chief attraction of the Palazzina is the garden which is still in much the same state as it was in the Emperor's time. Now, as then, its lawns are bordered with geraniums in ornamental pots while a statuette of Minerva stands in the centre. On the seaward side a low wall runs along the top of the cliffs; the two marble seats set in it opposite the house are reputed to have been where Napoleon sat gazing nostalgically northwards towards France beyond the horizon. But the garden also saw him in his lighter moments, playing blind-man's-bluff with his sister's ladies-in-waiting and insisting on a kiss as forfeit, even dressed as a clown in a paper costume designed by Paolina.

The walk along the façade of the house leads to the wrought-iron gates of an upper garden immediately below the walls of Fort Stella. In Napoleon's day this was the kitchen garden; now it is a lawn surrounded by flower beds and has, as its centre-piece, a replica of the nude statue of Paolina, posing as the nymph Galatea, by the Italian sculptor, Canova. (The original is in the museum attached to the Villa San Martino, see p. 171.)

The garden also extends in the other direction, beyond the building which used to be theatre and ballroom, and at its western end looks down on a small pebble beach at the foot of the cliff, called *Le Viste* (The Prospects). This was one of the first attractions of the site for Napoleon who used to go down there to bathe when he first took over the house. Later, however, after the soldiers of his Guard had arrived and begun to use the same beach, he gave it up, perhaps ashamed of his increasing corpulence. Instead, he began bathing in the privacy of a cave in the cliffside; a flight of steps still exists leading down from tnis part of the garden to a door in the cliff-face, and probably indicates his route to the cave.

Forte Falcone (*Map 1*)

After leaving the Palazzina dei Mulini, there is a pleasant walk along the cliff-top towards the Falcon Fort. The fort itself is controlled by the Italian naval authorities and is not open to the public, but it is possible to scramble a short distance along a rough path between its outer and inner ring of fortifications.

The tour round the town may be resumed by taking the Via della Regina which forks left away from the road leading up to the fort and swings across the western slopes above the old city. It should be followed as far as the top of a long flight of steps leading downhill on the left and known as the Salita del Falcone. Make the descent as far as the little piazza which makes a 'landing' level with the next transverse streets. This is Piazza V. Hugo, named after the writer who spent some of his early years in Elba and offers an admirable look-out over the city. It also lies in front of a now nondescript building closely associated with the Napoleonic story. This is the *Teatro dei Vigilanti* (Theatre of the Watchmen) (*Map 7*) which was opened by the Emperor in January 1815 just a month before he escaped from the island. The site had been occupied by a deconsecrated church of San Francesco, used since 1801 as a military storehouse. The cost of adapting the building was met by selling the ownership of boxes and seats outright in advance. The demand for them was so great that the successful purchasers formed themselves into the *Accademia dei Fortunati* (Academy of the Fortunate), with their motto '*A noi la Sorte*' (We are the lucky ones) inscribed on the building's façade. A theatre company was imported from Livorno and Napoleon was present on the opening night, accompanied by Letizia Bonaparte (Madame Mère) and his sister, Paolina Borghese, dressed for the occasion in Italian peasant costume. The evening ended with a fancy-dress ball and seems to have been part of Napoleon's tactics to conceal his plans for an early escape. Today the theatre is disused and not open to visitors, although enough of the interior is said to survive to make restoration possible. Next door to the theatre, at the beginning of Via V. Hugo, is Elba's ancient *general hospital* (*Map 5*), some parts of which go back to the foundation of the city by Duke Cosimo.

From this point there is a choice of two routes. If the visitor is on foot and prepared to walk back to the modern sector of Portoferraio, he can turn right out of the piazza and follow the Via del Carmine and the Via Lambardi downhill to the old *Porta a Terra* (Land Gate) (*Map 17*) which takes him through a tunnel under the fortifications back to the Via Vittorio Emmanuele on the sea-front.

If, however, he wants to stay in the old city, he should go down the rest of the flight of steps below the little piazza back to the Piazza Cavour. From here he can visit another of the ancient buildings of the Tuscan Grand Dukes which has successfully been adapted to a modern function. This is the *Galeazze* (Great Galleys) (*Map 15*), a huge naval arsenal built as a storehouse for the oared galleys of the Tuscan fleet based on Portoferraio, which has now been converted into a covered market. To reach it, walk the length of the Piazza Cavour and follow the narrow street (Via G. Colombo) leading out of it at the far end behind the harbour curtain-wall. The entrance to the market is on the left just before this lane enters the Via dell'Amore, which runs uphill along the eastern flank of the town. At the foot of Via dell'Amore a tunnel leads through the harbour curtain-wall back to the quayside. At the upper end of Via dell'Amore a flight of steps gives access to a little maze of picturesque streets and alleys on the slope below Fort Stella; almost any horizontal street to the left will bring the explorer back to the neighbourhood of the cathedral and the Ape Elbana hotel. It is also possible to find your way down alleys and flights of steps to the right to one of Portoferraio's less frequented and less attractive beaches, the *Grigolo*.

From Piazza Cavour, the Porta a Terra (Land Gate) (*Map 17*), can be reached by following the Via Guerazzi which leads out of the western end of the piazza. It follows the inner side of the harbour curtain-wall past the modern Albergo Darsena (Harbour Hotel), which has been built into the wall, to the corner with Via Lambardi where the entrance to the tunnel will be found.

EXCURSIONS FROM PORTOFERRAIO

EXCURSION A: VILLA SAN MARTINO

Route	Follow main road (Route Exit A) to Bivio Boni (Boni road-junction) (3km.) and continue straight ahead as if for Procchio. After another 2km. take a sign-posted left-hand fork to the gates of the Villa (5km.). Although the distance is not great this route is not recommended as a walk since it follows the busy main road which goes through Portoferraio's unattractive suburbs.

| **Open** | 9.00–13.00 | April 30th–October 1st: | 9.00– | Winter |
| | 15.00–18.00 | | 14.00 | months. |

Closed	Mondays
Entrance fee	Lire 100 (for a ticket which is also valid for admission on the same day to the Palazzina dei Mulini; since that is closed on Tuesdays the double visit cannot be made on Mondays or Tuesdays.)
Restaurants	Open-air café at Villa gates; farmhouse restaurant a little way up the hill on right of road, open only from May to September.

Napoleon had scarcely installed himself in the Palazzina dei Mulini when he began hankering for somewhere else to reside, away from the heat and noise of the city. He thought he had found what he wanted in the Forest of San Martino, just outside the city, where an Italian officer was ready to sell him an old barn 'ripe for conversion'. But the costs of purchase and conversion were estimated at 180,000 francs – more than the Emperor could afford. His sister, Paolina Borghese, paying a flying visit to Elba on June 1st, 1814, heard of his predicament and contributed a cluster of diamonds from her jewel-case as a gift towards the cost. Napoleon immediately sent an architect, twenty masons, and twenty men from his newly arrived grenadier guards to the site, and the barn was rapidly transformed into a small country-house, looking down the long, straight San Martino valley to the Bay of Portoferraio. Since it was on a steep slope, the house was constructed to be entered on two levels; on the upper floor a 'front door' giving access to the main living quarters from behind the house; on the lower floor, the kitchens, storerooms, and bathroom.

The nineteenth century did not do well by Napoleon's country villa. Prince Anatole Demidoff, who married the Emperor's niece, Mathilde, took the villa over and built in front of it a pompous museum, constructed of the stone known in Elba as 'yellow granite' and adorned with pillars and pilasters, together with a bronze frieze of emblematic eagles, bees, and the letter N. It was constructed in 1852 to house the Prince's collection of Napoleonic relics, the collection which was sold by auction on the owner's death. Today the museum does nothing but hide the Villa's front from the visitor toiling up the steep drive between rows of cypresses. It houses nothing but a mediocre municipal collection of pictures, mostly of the nineteenth century, and the original of Canova's nude statue of Princess Paolina Borghese. The landscape is further disfigured by a monstrous gingerbread-coloured pension at the foot of the drive, now serving as a Catholic hostel. The museum spoils the approach to the Villa, the pension the view from it.

In spite of these drawbacks, the Villa is worth a visit. It is reached by a path and flights of steps which lead round the left-hand end of the museum to the higher plateau giving access to the upper floor of the house. It is set at the head of the valley in a wooded bowl of acacia trees and evergreen oaks. On entering the visitor finds the house much better furnished than the Palazzina. Much of the furniture was taken by Napoleon from his brother-in-law, Paolina's husband, Prince Borghese. The Prince, who was separated from his wife, had removed his belongings from his house in Turin, to save them from capture by the Austrians after The Treaty of Fontainebleau, and despatched them by sea to Rome. The vessel carrying them put in to Porto Azzurro in bad weather, and its cargo was commandeered by the Emperor. The result is a mixture of styles with French Empire and Italian eighteenth century predominating. The Emperor had walls and ceilings decorated by an Italian artist, Ravelli, and these decorations have also suffered much less than those of the Palazzina.

After an *ante-room*, with a small bust of Napoleon in the corner, the visitor enters what is called *Marshal Bertrand's bedroom*. Appropriately, since the Marshal's wife joined him in Elba, it contains a large double bed. Next comes a small *drawing-room*, and then what is now called 'the dining-room', though in Napoleon's day it was the *Council Chamber* in which Napoleon occupied a gilt chair while his ministers sat on others of different colours. Ravelli painted the ceiling, according to the Emperor's directions, with a design of two doves flying in opposite directions with ribbons in their beaks thus tightening the love-knot that is between them. The emblem was supposed to represent the Emperor and his wife Marie Louise whose love was increased by the distance between them. In fact the Empress, while still writing tearful letters to her husband, was in Vienna where her affections were transferred to her chamberlain, General Neipperg.

From the Council Chamber the visitor passes directly into Napoleon's *bedroom* where a single bed contrasts with the elaborate 'temple of love' in the Palazzina. The walls are painted with simulated hangings. Next to the bedroom is the Emperor's *study* but the passage to it also gives access to the *bathroom*, which is not normally shown to visitors. The floor hinges up to reveal a short flight of stairs down to the lower floor of the house. The bathroom there has, directly above the tub, a fresco of a nude woman and the enigmatic motto, 'Qui odit veritatem odit lucem' (He who hates the truth hates the light).

After passing through the study and another ante-room the visitor finally reaches the large, cool *reception room*, decorated with elaborate frescoes by Ravelli of Napoleon's triumphant Egyptian campaign and originally further refreshed by an octagonal pool in the centre of the floor. To the right of the exit, a piece of plate-glass, fixed to the wall, protects Ravelli's signature – 'Ravelli fecit 1814' – and also the autograph words said to have been added by Napoleon with the painter's brush, 'Ubicumque Felix Napoleo' (Wherever he may be, Napoleon is fortunate).

From the interior the visitor may go out on to the flat roof of the Demidoff museum and see both the façade of the upper floor and also the view that the Emperor enjoyed from his windows. A narrow flight of covered steps leads down from this terrace to the interior of the *museum*, a large cool space empty, apart from the Canova statue, a few items of furniture, and the mainly mediocre paintings. Only three of them are worth noting, a Tiepolo, a Canaletto, and a Horace Vernet. In the garden outside there appears to be no trace of the elm which Napoleon ostentatiously planted in front of the British Commissioner, Sir Neil Campbell, saying, 'When my elm is tall enough, I shall use its trunk for the mast of a ship in which I shall set off again to conquer the world.'

Returning along the road from the Villa gates, you may see to your right, across the stream in the bottom of the valley, the small hill, known locally as *Castiglione*, where drystone walls surrounding the summit indicate the possible site of an Iron Age settlement (see p. 132).

EXCURSION B: VITICCIO AND CAPO D'ENFOLA

Route Leave Portoferraio by Route Exit B and continue to Viticcio (7km.) and/or Capo d'Enfola (7·5km.).

Restaurants There are two pensions and a café-bar at Viticcio which are open during the season but closed from October to early May.

This is a pleasant short outing along the north coast of Elba's central section, offering fine scenery and the possibility of bathing and rough walking or picnicking.

From the Piazza del Ponticello (Piazza Citi) take the Viale Manzoni which runs north towards Le Ghiaie beach, and where the avenue divides, follow the left fork, Viale De Gasperi, uphill to the district called Le Padulelle. Just before the top of the hill is reached, a mule-track on the left side of the road leads back and up the side of the hill to the remains of the *Forte Inglese* (English Fort), so called because when British forces occupied Elba in 1796–7 this outlying sector of the Portoferraio defences was their first billet. The remains of the fort, damaged by the Second World War air-raids, stand on the hillside above the western end of the Le Ghiaie beach; they are of no particular interest apart from their associations.

Passing Le Padulelle Pensione and the Adriana Hotel, the road crosses the base of Capo Bianco (White Cape) and follows the coastline above the rocky shore beyond it. It then swings left round Monte Bello, a symmetrical mini-mountain on the sea's edge. Its height is only 155 feet but it seems to offer opportunities for rock-climbers.

Beyond Monte Bello, the road twists along the hillside above the sea; to the left is the wooded massif of Monte Poppe (806 feet), a rather inaccessible area of Elba traversed only by mule-tracks. A longer curve inland takes it across the valley of the Fosso Acquaviva, and just after it has crossed the watercourse, a track, negotiable by cars, leads off to the right, following the stream, down to the Acquaviva camping site on the shore, just above a shingle beach.

The main road continues along the hillside, passing a second track down to the shore, until it reaches a fork. Here the left-hand turning takes you to Viticcio, while the right-hand turning runs twisting downhill past a caravan campsite to the narrow neck of land at the foot of Capo d'Enfola.

Viticcio

Viticcio is a tiny fishing village in the centre of the bay of the same name, looking due west along the north coast of the island. It is consequently famous for its sunsets in which the group of peaks round Monte Capanne are silhouetted against the sky. The road ends at the village in a spacious parking lot behind the houses. Narrow winding alleys lead down to a small public beach of sandy gravel. There are two pensions and a lodging-house (see Hotels, p. 44).

From the left-hand, or south-western end of the beach, a mule-track for walkers only leads across the Punto Penisola into the next bay, Golfo della Biodola, terminating in the village of Forno (about 1km.). **Forno**, which means 'furnace', is so called because of the remains of primitive iron-ore kilns found in the locality (see p. 175).

Capo d'Enfola

Capo d'Enfola is a spectacular wooded hill, connected with the rest of the island by a narrow isthmus of rock and coarse sand; it has even been suggested that the word 'Enfola' is a corruption of the Latin word '*insula*', meaning 'island'. The ruined buildings (unsafe to enter) and balks of timber to be seen at the foot of Capo d'Enfola are remains of what was until recently Elba's thriving tunny-fishery. 'Economic reasons', which are not understood or appreciated by the Elbans themselves, led to its being closed down. The wooded slopes of the cape are now being developed for villa sites, but a track, open to the public, twists uphill to a point just below the top of the promontory (439 feet). The track is narrow and steep and although cars can get up it, it is more suitable for walkers. It passes several concrete block-houses, half-hidden among the trees. These were constructed by the Germans during their occupation of Elba in 1943–4, and when the island was liberated by Free French forces in June 1944, two German soldiers heroically defended the hill against all-comers for two days, until their ammunition ran out.

On returning to Portoferraio, an alternative route can be followed by taking a road going off to the right, opposite Monte Bello. This joins the main road leading out of Portoferraio at a point about halfway between the city centre and Bivio Boni (Boni road-junction).

EXCURSION C: BIODOLA BAY

Route   Take the road (Route Exit A) for 3km. to Bivio Boni
                      (Boni road-junction), and here continue straight on, as
                      for Procchio. After 6·5km. take a signposted turning to
                      the right downhill to Biodola Bay.

Restaurants   There is a modest but cheerful open-air snack-bar at
                      Scaglieri, as well as the restaurant of the Pensione
                      Danila.

Biodola Bay (Golfo della Biodola) is one of the most secluded and
scenically attractive bays on Elba's north coast. Like the Bay of
Viticcio, from which it is divided by the Punta Penisola, it has a
western outlook; unlike Viticcio, it has a broad sandy beach. This
asset, together with the fact that it is off the main road, has made it the
site of one of Elba's few first-class hotels, the Hermitage, which has
appropriated a substantial section of the beach for its guests.
However, part of the beach remains public, and the bay also includes
the more popular resort of **Scaglieri,** with its own beach, and above
the rocks at the north-eastern end of the bay, the hamlet of Forno.

Near the foot of the steep descent down to Biodola Bay, the road
divides, the left-hand fork going to the La Biodola beach with a
conveniently large parking-lot, and to the Hermitage Hotel. The right-
hand fork goes on to the little family resort of Scaglieri where there
are also parking facilities and an inexpensive restaurant. From
Scaglieri, a country road leads on along the coastline to Forno and
from here those who enjoy rough walking can find a path which leads
up over the headland and down into the next bay at Viticcio.

Above Forno signs point towards 'Quagliadromo' (apparently
indicating a quail-shooting range). Where the track ends in a rough
scoop towards the end of the promontory, a narrow, single-file
footpath leads upwards through the *macchia* to the right. The path
climbs steeply to the ridge of the promontory, along the stone-wall
edge of a disused vineyard, and then down through woods and tall
macchia to a house on the south-western edge of the village of
Viticcio. The entire distance is not much more than 2·5km. but it is
rough, adventurous path-finding; fortunately there is a café-bar in
Viticcio at the end of the walk.

EXCURSION D:
ROUND PORTOFERRAIO BAY TO BAGNAIA

Route	Follow the main road (Route Exit A) for 3km. to Bivio Boni (Boni road junction) where you turn left for Roman Villa (6km.) and Bagnaia (12·2km.) Optional excursions can be made to Nisporto (15km.), Nisportino (18·5km.), and/or Volterraio Fortress (7·5km.); the latter involves a $1/_2$ hour arduous climb (see below).
Roman Villa	Always open: no admission charge.
Restaurants	There is a café-trattoria open during the season at Magazzini, a restaurant open to the public at the Villa Ottone hotel, and two pensions at Bagnaia.

Although the distances involved in this excursion are not great, it takes in the site of the Roman villa at Le Grotte, at which some time may be spent, and also the ruined Pisan Church of Santo Stefano. And if it is also intended to undertake the steep and quite difficult climb on foot up to the imposing Volterraio Fortress, a full day should be allowed.

From the Bivio Boni the right-angle turning to the left gives on to a long, straight stretch of road between trees for about 2km. This runs through the district called San Giovanni; to the left is the flat land bordering on the bay and a coastline originally given up to salt pans. One avenue to the left leads to the San Giovanni medicinal bathing establishment (p. 64) which profits by the special mud deposits left by the salt pans.

To the right are wooded foothills leading up to the modest mountain range which occupies the central section of Elba. Among these foothills (second road to the right) is the *Casa del Duca* (House of the Duke) where Cosimo I de'Medici is reported to have stayed, watching the progress of the builders of his new walled city. The house is now private property and not open to visitors; it has evidently been much modified if not rebuilt since Cosimo's days. But from the knoll in front of it, there is a good view of the Portoferraio harbour and headland. Assuming that isolated houses were not likely to exist so near to the shore in the sixteenth century, when the danger of Moorish corsairs was at its height, it seems possible that the Casa del Duca may indicate the site of the medieval town of Feraia, shown on the early German map of Elba (see History, p. 108).

After the straight stretch, the road climbs in sharp curves to the top of the promontory called Punto delle Grotte. The word 'grotta' means 'cave' or 'den', and this promontory is so called after the surviving underground rooms of the enormous Roman villa which occupied the whole of its upper levels. An open gateway on the left side of the road gives access to the area; cars can either be parked here or driven down a track along the east side of the villa to a point nearer the end of the promontory.

Roman Villa

The villa, which has only been superficially excavated in modern times, is believed to have been built at the very beginning of the Christian era, possibly during the reign of the Emperor Augustus. Its sheer size and commanding situation, looking across the bay to the capital of the island, then called Fabricia, has suggested that it may have been the official residence of the local governor, but no inscription or other evidence has been found to confirm this. The Roman altar to Hercules, found at Seccheto on the south coast and preserved in the town-hall at Portoferraio, bears the name of Publius Acilius Attianus, known to have been Prefect of the Praetorian Guard under the Emperor Hadrian. If the altar was indeed commissioned by someone on the island and not intended for shipment to the mainland, a dignitary of such prominence may well have lived at Le Grotte.

Moving across the site from the main road, the visitor first enters a large open space probably given up to ornamental gardens. Further north the wall-foundations surround what was an almost Olympic-sized swimming pool crossed by a pipe of masonry which is believed to have conducted steam or hot water to warm the pool. The pool was surrounded by ornamental arcades. Beyond the pool to the north again, was a large hall, 58 feet by 36 feet, facing out on to the bay. On the east and west sides of the pool and the hall, the living-quarters of the owners of the villa are believed to have been situated, separated by a dividing wall from the servants' quarters and the storage rooms. But much of this analysis of the building is guess work; the site still awaits a modern excavation, although it has undoubtedly been ransacked during past centuries by 'treasure-seekers'. Staircases lead down from the uppermost level to rooms carved out of the hillside, some of which are accessible. The lower slopes of the promontory are wooded and precipitous: the whole area is a fine place for picnickers.

After Le Grotte the road continues round a series of sharp curves for a distance of 3km. to a junction; the main highway leads on to Porto

Azzurro, but the road followed on this excursion turns off to the left towards Magazzini and Bagnaia.

After about 3km. just before the turn off to Magazzini, the road takes a sharp, virtually right-angled turning to the left, towards the coastline. At this corner a country road leads off inland to the right; a not very obvious sign says it is the turning for Santo Stefano, and the corner is also marked by a bus-stop, a house offering rooms to let, and a group of six refuse bins. If you follow this country road for approximately 1km., you will see the church of Santo Stefano standing on the top of a high knoll to the left of the road; from a distance it looks like a barn with a red-tiled roof. Before reaching the knoll the fork uphill to the left, sign-posted 'Santo Stefano' leads to a small German summer colony and a corner where you can park a car and proceed up to the church on foot.

Church of Santo Stefano

The building has been re-roofed fairly recently but its fabric dates from the twelfth century, probably from 1160 when the Pisans were actively working the granite quarries of Monte Capanne. In spite of its simplicity of plan, this is the most ornate of the little romanesque churches which the Pisans left in Elba; it has a blind apse with two lancet windows on the sides. There is blind arcading on the west facade, and two small side doorways; that on the south side has a grotesque carving on the lintel. Other examples of the period in Elba are the roofless and abandoned churches of San Giovanni on the slopes of Monte Perone, and of San Lorenzo on the slopes below Marciana Alta.

Returning from Santo Stefano to the main road, the fishing village of **Magazzini** is reached by taking a short side-road to the left (sign-posted) down to the shore. It is a small group of houses round a shallow harbour protected by a breakwater. West of the harbour a narrow, gravelly public beach extends for about 1·5km along the district known as Schioparello. There is a café-trattoria here, open only during the season. Back again on the main road this swings right to a junction with a rough country road which heads inland towards the *Volterraio fortress* and the mountains (see optional extension below).

From this junction the main road swings left again to the eastern shore of Portoferraio Bay, following the coastline along the top of a steep slope down to the sea. It passes the Villa Ottone (hotel with private beach), rounds the Punto Pina, and enters the deep cove on which **Bagnaia,** another fishing village, is situated. Shortly before the village a side road to the right leads off to the San Michele Residence, a large and much advertised modern block of residential apartments erected in the foothills of the eastern mountain range. Bagnaia is a small-scale resort with a pebble-and-sand beach and two pensions (see p. 44). It is at present the end of the main road from Portoferraio.

Nisporto and Nisportino

After Bagnaia the road becomes a roughly metalled track, full of pot-holes and ruts. It is however negotiable by cars and gives access to Nisporto and Nisportino, two recently developed camping resorts along the rugged and hitherto inaccessible coastline which the Piombino ferries pass on their port side en route for Portoferraio. **Nisporto,** 2·5km. from Bagnaia, is a favourite spot for aqualung fishermen. **Nisportino,** 6·5km. from Bagnaia, can only be reached by a detour away from the coast. The road zig-zags up to the pass between Monte Strega (1,390 feet) and Monte Serra (1,371 feet); almost at the summit of the pass a side road to the left, leads sharply back downhill to the little rock-bound bay and campsite of Nisportino. The road over the pass goes on to Rio nell'Elba on the eastern slopes of the range (see Porto Azzurro excursions, p. 191). This extension of the Bagnaia excursion might seem pointless, but for those who are prepared to entrust their cars (or their legs) to a rugged road, it is an opportunity to see something of the scenery and wild life of one of the most unexplored parts of Elba.

Volterraio Fortress

The road towards Volterraio leaves the main road at a sharp bend between Magazzini and Bagnaia (see above). Although the surface of this sideroad looks unpromising, it is found to be quite passable for cars. It should be followed uphill for about 1·5km. as far as a group of small buildings on the left of the road. Immediately after them the road curves left towards an open grassy plateau where cars can be parked. From here the visitor should look slightly to his right for a footpath leading directly up to the fortress. Its early stretch is easily seen but it is so steep higher up that hands as well as feet must be used; care should be taken to avoid clutching at the tempting bright green tussocks of spiny broom which can inflict as much punishment as gorse or cactus. The climb takes about half an hour, and should only be undertaken by the able-bodied who are prepared to tackle a very steep scramble.

The fortress of Volterraio is one of the most venerable and dramatic surviving monuments of Elba. Perched on a precipitous mountain top, it can be seen on clear days from many miles away.

So far as is known, the fortress was constructed by the Pisans in the thirteenth century at a time when the possession of Elba was being disputed between the Pisan Republic and the rising power of Genoa; Pisan records say that Vanni di Gherardo Rau was sent to Elba in 1284 to begin the work. But some historians believe there was an earlier stronghold on the same site, either constructed by the Pisans in the eleventh century when their Republic was strengthening Elba's defences against the Saracen sea-raiders from North Africa, or a much more ancient structure dating from the days of the Etruscans. The only evidence in support of this last theory is the etymology of the name, which resembles that of the Etruscan city Volterra on the mainland and may come from the Etruscan *ful-tur*, meaning 'high fort'. Whatever its origins, Volterraio was never stormed or taken by siege during the recorded history of the island, and was always one of the few safe refuges against invaders from the sea. Although the fortress is now in ruins, much damaged by weather and the tunnelling of 'treasure-seekers', it is still possible to distinguish an outer rampart, a sentries' walk along the battlements, vaulted chambers, a square tower, and a flight of steps which once led to a drawbridge. Fragments of pottery have been found both within and without the walls, dating from all periods between the thirteenth and sixteenth centuries.

After returning to the grassy plateau below – and the descent must be negotiated even more carefully than the climb – the road may be followed uphill past the flank of Volterraio, through a cutting, and up to the summit of a pass called, for no obvious reason, *Le Panche* (The Benches). This is an excellent spot for picnicking, with a magnificent view and footpaths leading both north and south away from the road along the high contours. The road itself descends on the other side of the range to the main road connecting Porto Azzurro with Rio Marina.

EXCURSION E: MONTE ORELLO, COLLE RECISO AND MARMI

Route

Follow the main road (Route Exit A) for 3km. to Bivio Boni (Boni road-junction), here turning left on to the road to Porto Azzurro, from which you take the secondary road through the mountains described below (total distance 26km.). The secondary road is rough but negotiable by a small car except perhaps in very wet weather. However, as the stretch of secondary road through the mountains is only 13km. long and there are bus-stops at either end, an energetic walker could arrange his times to suit the bus schedules and do this stretch on foot. (For information about buses, see p.37).

Restaurants

There is an osteria rather of the 'lorry-drivers' café' type, on the main road just beyond the point where you turn off on to the secondary road. At Procchio there is the *La Lucciola* restaurant, as well as those belonging to hotels.

This excursion takes the visitor off the more frequented roads round Portoferraio and along one of the secondary roads through the heart of the countryside which are normally used only by the Elbans themselves.

After turning left at the Bivio Boni follow the main road for Porto Azzurro, passing the Punta delle Grotte and the turn-off to Magazzini and Bagnaia. Approximately 1km. along the Porto Azzurro road after passing this turn-off, the main road turns a right-angle corner to the left. At this corner, if you carry straight on instead of turning left, you enter the secondary road, or lane, leading uphill into the mountains. (Beyond the crucial corner, there is a conspicuous *osteria,* or eating-house, on the right side of the main road; it is a signal that you have missed the turning.)

The lane zig-zags uphill across the lower slopes of Monte Orello (1,225 feet) which rises to the left. Care should be taken on the bends, as this lane is used by lorries from the stone-quarry of Colle Reciso, which come downhill at a break-neck speed. Across the fields to the right of the lane there are pleasant views towards the Bay of Portoferraio.

About 3·75km. up the lane, you arrive at the busy stone-quarry of *Colle Reciso,* with two roads coming uphill on the right and another going off to the left towards the plain of Lacona on the south coast. Ignore all these and, keeping the quarry workings on your left, continue past them into a lane which follows a level course parallel with the contours of Monte Moncione (923 feet) on the left. A rusty notice informs you that this area is a military reserve but this no longer seems to be valid. The lane leads westwards, gradually climbing as it approaches the shoulder of Monte Barbatoio (1,200 feet). The countryside is clothed with the tall *macchia* interspersed with evergreen oaks, which is characteristic of this part of Elba. During the abortive French attempt to occupy Elba in 1799 (see History, p. 116), these hills were the scene of the final guerrilla fighting in which the Elbans, under Spanish leadership, drove the French forces of General Montserrat back on Portoferraio and forced them to surrender.

Beyond Monte Barbatoio, the lane zig-zags round the head-waters of the Valle di San Martino, the valley in which Napoleon's villa is situated. Then it curves sharply left round the upper slopes of Monte San Martino (1,072 feet), and begins the descent of the Serra di Literno (Literno Pass), at a point about 4km. beyond the Colle Reciso quarries. A well-marked bridle-path joins the road from the left, just after it begins the descent; this leads south to join the main motoring road across the south of the island at the point where it crosses the pass of Monte Tambone, at the so-called 'Monument' (see p. 201). Walkers can also find a bridle-track leaving the right side of the road at its highest point which will bring them down into the valley by a more direct and steeper route than that followed by the road, which descends round many curves and several hairpin bends into the lowland plain which divides the central sector of Elba from the western mountain massif.

Both road and bridle-track converge to join the main motor-road between Marina di Campo and Procchio, at a point opposite the small hamlet of **Marmi**. There is a bus-stop here where the walker may catch a bus back to Portoferraio via Procchio. He may, however, prefer to turn right and walk along the road to Procchio – a distance of 1·25km. – where he may also be lucky enough to catch one of the buses coming through from the west of the island.

The motorist also turns right to **Procchio**, an important junction in the Elban road network and the central point of the 'fashionable' north coast resorts. It has a long curved expanse of sandy beach stretching from Punta Agnone, outside Procchio itself, to Monte Pinello to the north-east, this beach also being available to the neighbouring family resort of Campo all'Aia.

The road back from Procchio to Portoferraio swings along the northern slopes of the central block of hills, climbing to a height of

468 feet above the Golfo della Biodola (Biodola Bay), before crossing a pass and descending a long hill down to Portoferraio.

ROUTE I: PORTOFERRAIO TO PORTO AZZURRO

Route	Leave Portoferraio by the main road for Porto Azzurro (Route Exit 0), turning left, after 3km. at the Bivio Boni (Boni road-junction) and then continuing on to Porto Azzurro (14·5km.).
Restaurants	There is a very plain *osteria* (roadside cafe) just before the 5th kilometre stone, and $^1/_2$km. further on there is the Hotel Acquabona just above the road on the right.

The road connecting Elba's two main harbours runs through the lowlands between the metalliferous mountains of the island's eastern range and the more rounded and lower hills of the central section. It links two parts of the island which were politically and administratively divided for so many centuries that they acquired and still keep a different atmosphere and distinguishable types of people. The towns, like Porto Azzurro, in the south-east of Elba were dominated from the beginning of the seventeenth century by the Spanish government of Naples and the succeeding Spanish-Bourbon 'Kingdom of the Two Sicilies'. Their inhabitants sometimes seem to have a calmer and more contemplative approach to life than the brisk Tuscan population of Portoferraio.

After turning left at the Boni road-junction, the road runs straight and level across the coastal plain of San Giovanni along the shore of Portoferraio Bay, and then zig-zags up the side of Le Grotte promontory. At this point it turns inland, passing first the junction with the road going off left to Magazzini and Bagnaia and then the secondary road going off uphill to the right to Monte Orello and Colle Reciso. Climbing gently round a series of bends it reaches its highest point (166 feet) at Acquabona, with the hotel of that name to the right and the nine-hole golf course attached to the hotel on the left. Just before the 6th km. stone, a stony track off to the left is the start of the climb up to Monte Castello (p. 197). As it begins the descent of Valdarna Valley towards the south-east, the road passes the junction

(10·3km. from Portoferraio) with the newly constructed highway going off to the right to Lacona and Marina di Campo. On the left are the foothills of the spectacular eastern mountain range; ahead and slightly to the right is a distant view of the hill-town of Capoliveri perched on the shoulder of the south-eastern promontory of Monte Calamita.

As the road comes down to the level of the coastal plain, it passes the junction with the road up to Capoliveri on the right, and swings leftwards along the shore of a shallow estuary called Mola. Two elaborately picturesque motels are built up the steep slope on the left of the road which finally turns sharply round a headland with a miniature lighthouse and descends into the bay of Porto Azzurro.

PORTO AZZURRO

Population	2,952
Buses	Buses stop and turn round in main square on sea-front. (For information about bus timetables see p. 37).
Taxis	There is no taxi-rank in Porto Azzurro but cars with or without drivers may be hired from Caporali, Piazza Matteotti (95078); Franco Capuano, Viale Italia; Benito Forti (95236).
Hotels and Pensions	See p. 44.
Restaurants	See p. 58.
Information	Ufficio Turistico Arrighi, Banchina IV Novembre, tel. 95000, 95150.
	Agenzia TO.RE.MAR.,Banchina IV Novembre, tel. 95004.
Central Post office	Via Roma.
Telephone Exchange	Calata Matteotti 15.
Market Day	Saturday
Entertainment	See p. 69.
Festivals	September 8th: Nativity of Virgin Mary: September 8th–15th: Pilgrimages to the Madonna of Monserrato.
Beaches	The nearest beaches are Spiaggia di Barbarossa (p. 188), Spiaggia di Reale (p. 188), and Naregno across bay on east side of Capoliveri promontory (p. 189).

The name *Porto Azzurro* (meaning Blue Port) is a consequence of the Italian passion for euphemism. The original fishing village at the water's edge was called Longone; when the Spaniards built their fortress on the headland dominating the harbour, they called the entire complex *Porto Longone*, in obvious rivalry with Portoferraio. After the unification of Italy the fortress was converted into a gaol, and 'a visit to Portolongone', like 'a stay on Dartmoor', acquired a double-meaning. So when the Elban authorities started a tourist industry, they decided to relieve the little town and harbour of this unfortunate association and gave them the somewhat banal name of Porto Azzurro, while the fortress-prison retained the title of Porto Longone. Unfortunately this attempt at distinction seems to have failed: recently the Italian press has taken to referring to 'convicts at Porto Azzurro'.

The small town can easily be explored on foot although it is possible to take a car up the steep hill to the outer ramparts of the fortress. The main life of the town revolves round the harbour which is usually full of yachts, fishing-boats and ferries; there is a direct ferry service once a day between Porto Azzurro and Piombino on the mainland. A piazza on the water-front offers limited space for parking cars; behind it the older part of the town climbs uphill in a maze of narrow streets and alleys. Hidden behind the buildings at the left-hand end of the main piazza, as you stand with your back to the harbour, is the parish church, dedicated to San Giacomo, with an adjoining eighteenth-century oratory built by one of the Spanish governors, Don Diego de Alarçon, who died in 1730 and is buried there. From the right-hand end of the piazza a steep lane winds up to the outer ramparts of the old fort.

Porto Longone Fortress

These outer ramparts form a sort of public promenade, open at all hours, but the public is only allowed as far as the entrance to the inner ring of fortifications, within which the modern prison has been constructed. Opening into the vault of the gatehouse is a small shop where paintings and handicraft objects produced by the prisoners are on sale.

The construction of the fort was begun in 1603 when the Spanish Viceroy of Naples decided to annex Piombino and win a footing in Elba to offset the De'Medici stronghold of Portoferraio on the north coast. The moment was propitious because the last descendant in the direct line of the Appiani, who had been hereditary Lords of Piombino and Elba for more than two centuries, had just died. An expedition, led by Captain Joseph de Pons y Leon, landed on the pretext that the harbour offered a refuge for pirates and began to construct a fortress to protect it; the ground plan was copied from contemporary Spanish fortifications in the Low Countries. Forty-three years later Porto Longone was captured by a French expedition despatched by Cardinal Mazarin during his efforts to expel the Spaniards from the Italian peninsula. But the French only held it for four years during which they strengthened the defences and built the outer ramparts. They were then besieged and eventually forced to surrender by a Spanish expedition led by Don John of Austria, victor of the Battle of Lepanto. In 1708 the fortress successfully withstood a siege by an Austrian expedition; in 1799 it was the base from which the first attempt by French revolutionary forces to capture Elba was defeated. Spanish control of Porto Longone ended only when Napoleon annexed Elba, along with the rest of Tuscany, in 1802. In 1814, when the Emperor was confined by the Allies to his 'principality of Elba', he decided to make the fortress one of his *chateaux* on the island and spent 9,400 francs (about £2,000) on modernising it. But he only resided there for eight days in September 1814, when his mistress, Countess Marie Walewska, had sailed from the harbour in stormy weather, and he was waiting anxiously for news of her safety (see History, p. 123).

EXCURSIONS FROM PORTO AZZURRO

EXCURSION 1A: SANCTUARY OF MONSERRATO

Route	Follow the main road for Cavo and continue for 1 km. A badly signposted track off to the left reaches the Sanctuary which is about 1·5 km. from the main road. Cars can be taken along this track which is well marked and level as far as the entrance to the wooded gorge; here it is advisable to park and continue up the final ascent on foot.
Opening Hours	There are no regular hours for admission to the sanctuary. On application at the farmhouse on the left of the track near the entrance to the gorge, someone will open the church (small gratuity expected).
Beaches	Spiaggia Barbarossa and Spiaggia Reale are both adjacent to this route.

The first Spanish governor of Porto Longone, Joseph de Pons y Leon, was born in Barcelona and had a particular devotion to the 'Black Virgin of Montserrat', not far from his native city. In Elba, exploring the neighbourhood of his fortress, he discovered a mountain valley which reminded him of Montserrat, and decided to build a sanctuary there enshrining a copy of the painting of the Virgin at the Spanish shrine. The little church he constructed for the *Madonna di Monserrato,* as the Elbans spell it, is situated on a crag in a deep narrowing gorge shaded with trees and often full of the song of nightingales, which climbs up into the limestone rocks of the eastern mountain range. Except during the week following September 8th, the Festival of the Nativity of the Virgin, when there are public pilgrimages to the shrine, it is a lonely and enchanting place.

The main road out of Porto Azzurro towards Cavo leaves the seafront just to the west of the harbour piazza and runs inland through the more modern parts of the town. On the outskirt it bends to the right at a fork where the left-hand road leads into the privately owned Valle di Botro, and follows the hillside roughly parallel with the coast. Across a dip to the right you can see the fortress-prison. Just 1km. from Porto Azzurro, a track leads off through the fields on the left side of the road towards the sanctuary: it is marked by an inconspicuous signpost which can easily be missed. A landmark warning you of your approach to the turning is the decrepit and otherwise uninteresting *Church of San Cerbone,* seen on the left overlooking the main road.

The field track is rough and rutted but negotiable by cars. It runs at right angles away from the main road towards the mountains passing a well overshadowed by a large palm tree; the Spaniards are said to have planted date-palms wherever they made a well. After 1·25km., the track swings to the left past an attractive villa of eighteenth-century Spanish architecture, and its terraced and walled garden, and reaches a small farmhouse where the key to the sanctuary is kept. It is advisable to leave the car by the roadside at this point and proceed on foot.

Sanctuary of Monserrato

Beyond the farm the path crosses a shallow stream and winds uphill; the sanctuary, dwarfed by the limestone slopes and pinnacles that form its background, becomes visible perched on a steep knoll at the head of the gorge. The path itself becomes a flight of rocky steps which wind upwards until they reach the side of the sanctuary and the little thatched terrace in front of it, from which you can look back down the gorge. The sanctuary itself is a small church, with several living-rooms built into its walls. A broken aqueduct behind shows how the incumbent originally obtained his water-supply from the mountain slopes; today a stand-pipe with a tap provides very welcome and drinkable water for the pilgrim.

The interior of the church is desolate except when it has been decorated for a festival; the votive offerings which it used to contain have been removed to one of the rooms, and are not shown. The replica-painting of the 'Black Madonna' still hangs above the altar behind a screen which can be raised on request by the guardian.

Beaches

The excursion to the Sanctuary of Monserrato can take in either or both of Porto Azzurro's two bathing beaches. That nearest to the town is called *Barbarossa Beach* (Spiaggia di Barbarossa), so named after the notorious North African corsair who carried out a devastating raid on this part of Elba in 1534. The beach lies in an inlet separated from Porto Azzurro harbour by the promontory, Punta dello Stendardo, on which the Porto Longone fortress is built. It can be reached by taking a signposted right turn off the main road, just opposite the above-mentioned Church of San Cerbone (p 187) at a point 1km. inland from the harbour-front, and a few hundred yards *before* the left-hand turning to the Sanctuary is reached. The track leads straight down to the sea, stopping outside a camping site behind the beach which is spacious and sandy.

The other beach, *Spiaggia di Reale,* is a little further along the coast and slightly more difficult to find. To reach it, look for another right turn off the main road to Rio, about 1km. beyond the track to Barbarossa, and after the main road itself has swung northward round a bend to the left. This track leading off to the right goes to a new villa development on the rocky promontory called Capo d'Arco (or Punta delle Cannelle), but a few hundred yards down it another track, forking off to the right, leads down the valley of the Fosso Reale to the beach. Alternatively, a second turning to the right off the track to Capo d'Arco brings you to a strange, rather uncanny landscape called *Le Terre Nere* (The Black Lands) at the northern end of the Reale beach. These are disused mine-workings and from the track above them, you look down on a lagoon behind the beach coloured a vivid green by the metallic deposits, and known as the *Laghetto delle Terrenere*. Subsidiary tracks lead down to the shore and the beach which is sandy. Care should be taken with children in this area, to see that they do not fall into the sinister waters of the lagoon or stray into the disused mine-tunnels which are not properly closed off.

EXCURSION IB: NAREGNO AND FORT FOCARDO

Route	Follow the main road to Portoferraio as far as the Capoliveri turn-off (1·8km.). Instead of climbing the hill, take the first turning off to the left to Naregno (3·8km.).
Restaurants	There are several hotels and pensions with restaurants behind the beach.

After the second left-hand turn the road follows the shoreline of the Mola inlet and then climbs over the rising ground called Capo della Tavola. Here it is joined by another road coming down from Capoliveri and passes the large and modern International Hotel before dipping downhill again to Naregno.

Naregno has an extensive sandy beach and a pleasant view across the bay to Porto Azzurro and the prison-fortress. It is a small seaside resort of comparatively recent date. At the far end of the beach a footpath leads through pine trees to Fort Focardo ($^1/_2$km.).

Fort Focardo is a subsidiary bulwark of the Spanish defences of the harbour, looking across at the ramparts of Porto Longone. It was built in 1678 and its name is a misspelt abbreviation of the name of the Spanish governor who constructed it, Don Ferdinando Gioacchino Foscardo di Roquentes y Zuniga. The fort is now used by the Italian coastguard and is not open to visitors, but through its gateway may be seen an inscription commemorating Don Foscardo.

For those who wish to extend this short excursion, a steep lane goes uphill from Fort Focardo to Capoliveri (p. 194) from where it may be possible to catch a bus back to Porto Azzurro.

EXCURSION IC: RIO NELL'ELBA, RIO MARINA, AND CAVO

Route	Follow the main road out of Porto Azzurro to Cavo (19·5km.). The well-surfaced and engineered motor-road, which is also a bus route, comes to a dead-end at Cavo. Optional diversions are to Rio nell'Elba (12km.) and Ortano (15km.) where there is a bathing-beach. From Rio nell'Elba to Cavo there is also a rough country road through the mountains via Grassera (approx. 9km.).

Iron-mines The iron-ore mines are open to visitors on Saturdays only. Permits to visit may be obtained either from the Ente Valorizzazione Elba in Portoferraio (p. 59) or from the offices of the mining company, Italsider, in Rio Marina. Italsider's offices, situated in a narrow street opening off to the left from Rio Marina's main piazza (opposite the municipal gardens), must be applied to in any case to obtain services of an authorized guide. The guide expects a gratuity and a small sum is also payable towards a benefit fund for retired miners.

Museum A small geological museum may be visited on the third floor of Rio Marina's town-hall (Palazzo Communale) in Via Principe Amedeo. It is open every day except public holidays from 9.00 to 12.30 and from 14.30 to 19.00

Mineral specimens Shops selling mineral specimens and semi-precious gem-stones are to be found in the piazza of Rio nell'Elba and in Rio Marina.

Restaurants There are two restaurants at Rio Marina, several hotel-restaurants at Cavo, and cafés at Rio nell'Elba and Ortano beach.

This excursion explores the north-eastern section of Elba and the mining area (which is much less disfiguring than might have been expected). The main road turns off to the left from the sea-front and climbs first north-east and then due north along the backbone of Elba's eastern block. As you travel northwards towards Cavo the main peaks rising to the left of the road are Monte Castello (1,268 feet), Cima del Monte (1,677 feet), Monte Strega (1,378 feet), Monte Serra (1,371 feet) and Torre del Giove (1,144 feet). Although their heights are not impressive in cold print and are greatly exceeded by the granite peaks of Elba's western sector, these mountains climb to their summits from sea-level in a distance of only about 1km. – a fact which makes their appearance much more striking than their vital statistics would suggest.

To the right of the road, during its first stretch between Porto Azzurro and Rio, lies the rising ground of Monte Arco (904 feet) with Capo d'Arco beyond it. Much of this area is highly cultivated and has not so far been developed for tourism.

Just before Rio, the road forks, the main road turning right and downhill towards the coast at Rio Marina, the left fork climbing up to Rio, or Rio nell'Elba as it is more properly called, clustering on the mountainside at a height of 383 feet above sea-level.

Rio nell'Elba

Its name derives from the Latin word *rivus* meaning 'stream', and the town is still renowned for its spring of pure water which is said locally to flow more abundantly in summer than in winter. Rio disputes with Marciana the title of being the oldest town in Elba; its history may be as old as the iron-mining industry which still employs many of its inhabitants. The people of Rio, the 'Riesi' as other Elbans call them, are tough and independent; their town has, by comparison with others in the island, a somewhat bleak aspect recalling small Yorkshire mining communities. But the central piazza is full of robust life and the Riesi are genial and helpful with visitors. On the piazza is a shop specializing in the mineral curiosities of the region; such shops are to be found elsewhere in Elba but that in Rio is nearest to the minefields where most of them are found. The *church* in Rio is an ancient one, but has so often been restored that little of the original building survives. It was fortified by the Pisans as a refuge for the townsfolk against sea-raiders, but the fortifications seem to have been demolished in the eighteenth century by the Spanish governor of Porto Longone after the Riesi had given support to the Austrian invaders of the island.

Detour via Grassera

A narrow street leading out of the lower end of the piazza joins the country road to Cavo. Ask for *la strada per la chiesa di Santa Caterina* (the road to the church of St Catherine). It follows a fairly level course along the hillside above the cemetery. The church of Santa Caterina is to be seen above the road on the left and is of no particular interest, but a little further on, 1·25km. from Rio, there are the interesting remains of the village of **Grassera** (or Grassula), one of Elba's 'lost cities', which was wiped out by sea-raiders during the sixteenth century (see History, p. 106). The remains of the inhabited area are to the left of the road; to the right are the ruins of the *Church of San Quirico*.

The road then passes between Monte Serra on the left and, to the right, the hill known as *Torre del Giove* with the ruins of an ancient *fort* on the top. The fort was built by the Appiano family in 1459 to protect the iron-mines, and was originally called the *Torre del Giogo* (or 'Tower of the Pass') but the name seems to have been subsequently corrupted to *Giove*, which means 'Jove'; there are in fact no Roman remains here. After the pass, the road winds westwards between the hills as far as the lower slopes of Monte Grosso (1,093 feet) with a signalling station on its summit looking down on the sea to the west of this promontory: it then doubles back eastwards and descends a long slope down to the main road at Cavo. The area through which it has passed is one of the most remote and inaccessible parts of Elba; the road surface is rough and rutted, but quite passable if taken slowly.

Those who cannot spare the time for this detour may leave Rio by the main road out of the piazza and return to the fork at the bottom of the hill. Then, turning to the left, they follow the hill down to the sea at Rio Marina, a cheerful and busy little port looking across the Piombino channel to the mainland, and the headquarters of the Elban mining industry.

Rio Marina

As a town Rio Marina does not date back much beyond the eighteenth century; earlier than that it was not safe to live in open villages beside the water's edge. But its little mole-protected harbour may be older; and on the sea-front there is also an octagonal watch-tower now surmounted by a clock-tower, which may go back to the Pisan period of Elban history when early warning of the presence of sea-raiders was essential. The cliff-path which goes up behind the tower offers a pleasant walk of about 1·5km. overlooking the rocky coastline; the path goes as far as a tiny inlet called Il Porticciolo where it is just possible to scramble down to the sea.

In Rio Marina's modern town-hall (Palazzo Communale), in Via Principe Amedeo, there is a small *mineral museum* on the third floor, where specimens of the various crystals and natural metal compounds to be found in Elba are on display (see p. 190 for opening hours). The town hall may be seen to the left as the main road enters the principal piazza. Further down the hill to the right of the main road a shop sells polished specimens, and ornaments and costume jewellery made from them; it also sells bags of roughly polished semi-precious stones for do-it-yourself jewellers.

The company, *Italsider,* which leases Elba's iron-mines from the Italian State, has its offices in Rio Marina, and application may be made there for permits to see the iron-mines which are open to visitors on Saturdays only (see p. 190 for details). The mines shown are open-cast − large arena-shaped scoops terraced out of the mountainside. Keen geologists may take hammers and trowels and are allowed to look for the 'fool's gold' or pyrites which are scattered throughout the workings.

As you leave the town at its northern end to follow the main road along the coast, an iron jetty, from which the ore-tankers carrying the output to the mainland are loaded, can be seen. The output of the mines under their present programme, which lasts until 1980, is 400,000 tons of ore a year; about 470 miners are employed.

From Rio Marina to Cavo, a distance of 7·7km., the road sticks fairly closely to the coastline to avoid the mine-workings of Monte Calendozio on the left. The mining operations can be glimpsed occasionally from the road but they are not obtrusive.

Cavo, at the end of the main road, is a rather old-fashioned residential resort spread out along an eastward-facing sea-front. The road then passes a second and much smaller inlet called Cala dell' Alga (Seaweed Cove), and ends among the private villas of Capo Castello. A secondary road to the left gives access to the shingle of another wide bay between Capo Castello and Capo Vita, the northernmost point of Elba which is rounded by steamers making for Portoferraio. (Some of the ferry-services from Piombino make an intermediate stop at Cavo.)

There are the remains of a second Elban Roman villa at Cavo but they are on private property and are not normally open to the public. A Roman water-tank, believed to have provided the water-supply for this villa, has been found on the slopes of Monte Lentisco (610 feet), the hill behind the town. A track leads up the slopes of Monte Lentisco from the secondary road which runs parallel to the Cavo sea-front, and ends at a small *chapel* from which there are panoramas of both the east and west sides of Capo Vita. The small islet which can be seen due north of Capo Castello is called *Isola dei Topi* (Rat Island).

Returning from Cavo towards Porto Azzurro, an optional detour may be made to the brand-new and highly developed seaside resort of **Ortano**. The road to it turns off from the eastern side of the main road as it climbs the hill out of Rio Marina towards the junction with the road to Rio nell'Elba. There is a fine sandy beach at Ortano, and various facilities such as a hotel and restaurant, bathing huts and water-ski-ing.

EXCURSION 1D: CAPOLIVERI AND MONTE CALAMITA

Route   Follow the main road from Porto Azzurro to
                   Portoferraio as far as a signposted junction (1·4km.). The
                   road off to the left climbs up to Capoliveri (3·5km.)
                   round two hairpin bends. From Capoliveri the road
                   continues down the western side of the peninsula round
                   M. Calamita but is closed to the public on the eastern
                   side.

Restaurants   In the town of Capoliveri there are three *trattorie*, 'F.
                   Corbelli', 'Da Marina', and 'Da Leda'. At Morcone there
                   is 'La Pisana'; at Punta Morcone, 'Ristorante Bistro'; at
                   Pareti 'Il Cavaluccio'.

This excursion takes you into the southern fluke of Elba's 'fishtail',
the mountain promontory dominated by *Monte Calamita* ('Mount
Lodestone') (1,342 feet), which contains so much of the magnetic iron
oxide known as magnetite that it is believed to affect the compass
needles of passing ships. Parts of the peninsula are mined by Italsider
which has here a few underground workings as well as the
commoner opencast excavations.

Capoliveri

Capoliveri belongs to the select group of Elban towns which date at
least from the Roman occupation of the island. Its name derives from
the Latin words *caput liberum*, meaning a 'free person'; it is believed
to have been a recognized sanctuary for debtors and other persons
wanted by the law. Provided they could reach the town they were
entitled to live freely within its precincts. Whether this theory is true
or not, the people of Capoliveri have always had a reputation for
stubborn independence; they resented the Spanish rule in this part of
Elba and later tried to withold the payment of taxes to Napoleon. The
Spaniards pulled down the walls of the city after it had been the
headquarters of Austrian invaders in the eighteenth century (p. 114);
Napoleon overcame Capoliveri's reluctance to pay taxes by
threatening to billet troops in the town.

There is limited parking space in the main piazza; if there is no
room, take the road to the left out of the piazza to the south side of the
town where more parking space is available. Although Capoliveri
offers no special historic monuments, a walk round its ancient streets
is worth while. They owe their cramped ground plan to the city walls
which used to enclose them before the Spanish authorities pulled

them down (see History p. 114). The original parish church stood outside the walls and has now vanished; it may have been Pisan in origin. The present church, in the heart of the town, has no records earlier than the eighteenth century owing to an odd happening when the Spanish forces resumed possession of Capoliveri after the defeat of Austrian invaders. The verger concealed himself and all the parish records in a tomb in the nave of the church. But the intolerable stench of his hiding-place forced him to emerge while Mass was being celebrated. He was seen by Spanish soldiers attending the service who searched the tomb for treasure; finding none they burnt the documents.

Excursions from Capoliveri

Walkers may make the ascent of **Monte Calamita** (about 2km.). The track, which climbs the northern shoulder of the mountain, starts from a road junction on the south side of the town where one fork goes downhill towards the shore and the other leads southwards across the slopes of the peninsula. On the left, at the point where the roads divide, there is a group of tenements, and the lane leading up the mountain begins between them. Where this lane, in its turn, forks, bear *right* and straight uphill, with a hedge on your right and the valley below you on your left. The lane, rough but passable for cars, comes to an end in front of a stone-mason's cottage. Passing round the left end of the house, walkers should pick up a field-path still leading directly uphill behind the buildings. In places this path is overgrown by *macchia* but its general line is easy to follow and also marked by a line of of electricity pylons. On the brow of the mountain, near the summit, is a military signal station out of bounds to the public, but the path veers left to meet a country road which has climbed the mountain from its southern flank. The upper slopes are forested on the eastern side and offer welcome shade on a hot day.

Motorists may take the roughly surfaced but quite passable road which, leaving the fork on the south side of Capoliveri, zig-zags round the peninsula high above the shoreline. It is open to traffic as far as Punta dei Ripalti at the southern tip (about 10km.), and then turns inland to follow a track up to the summit of Monte Calamita (about 3km.). The road runs at an average 550 feet above the sea along the west coast, zig-zagging inland wherever it crosses a water-course. On the shore below may be seen the houses and beaches of Morcone and Pareti; across Stella Bay lies the wooded mass of Cape Stella. South of Pareti is a secluded bay called Cala dell'Innamorata ('Sweetheart's Cove') where a fisher-girl is said to have drowned herself after seeing Saracen pirates carrying off her lover to slavery. Still further to the south two small offshore islets are called Isole Gemelli ('Twin Islands'). On a clear day you can see out to the south-west the flattened profile of Pianosa, where a penal farm-colony is located, and further away to the south the conical shape of Montecristo.

This road and its verges are reputed to be 'Tom Tiddler's Ground' for mineralogists and rock-hunters; pieces of the semi-precious hardstone, malachite, are to be found in the road metal along with other rare pebbles. Motorists are advised to be careful where they park their cars and especially to be wary of the numerous blind corners. Lorries from the mine-workings tear along at high speed and often cut corners. As it rounds the southern end of the peninsula, the road bends more and more frequently as it winds through disused mine-workings; side roads leading down to the shore are closed to the public. At a group of farm buildings called *Fattorie Ripalte* the main road is barred to public traffic and it is not possible to drive round to the eastern flank of the peninsula. But at this point a passable track leads off to the left and, after climbing the slopes of Monte Torricelle (1,105 feet), swings left to end in the woods below the summit of Monte Calamita.

To visit the shore from Capoliveri, take a clearly marked road on the south side of the town going downhill. When it divides, the left-hand fork leads to the bathing beaches of **Pareti** and **Morcone**. From Pareti a track leads over Punta Pareti into the next bay, *Cala dell'Innamorata.*

The right-hand fork leads to the local sanctuary of the *Madonna delle Grazie,* about 100 metres inland from a tiny beach. The domed sanctuary, built on the plan of a Latin cross, is architecturally more sophisticated than most of Elba's local shrines. The date of its foundation is unknown but it was being administered by Augustinian Fathers in 1773. If you are lucky enough to find the guardian on the premises, he may admit you to the interior where there is a fine painted ceiling and, above the altar, a painting of the Madonna and Child attributed to the School of Raphael. According to local legend the picture was found with several others floating in the sea after Turks, who had captured the ship in which they were being transported, had thrown them overboard. Presumably as good Moslems they objected to depiction of the human form. While the other pictures had been ruined by the salt water, that of the Virgin remained intact; and the Elban fishermen who had salvaged it planned to take it to the Mola inlet beside Porto Azzurro. But a squall drove them into this little cove, and when they attempted to carry the picture up to Capoliveri, they found themselves rooted to the spot where the sanctuary now stands. The festival of the Immaculate Conception is celebrated with pilgrimages to this shrine on December 8th.

EXCURSION 1E: MONTE CASTELLO AND CIMA DEL MONTE

Route

This excursion is primarily for walkers and hill-climbers although motorists can follow most of the route provided they don't mind rough going. It has been listed under Porto Azzurro because the mountains belong to that part of Elba, but it can be tackled equally easily from Portoferraio. Assuming a start from Porto Azzurro, follow the main road back towards Portoferraio, as far as kilometre-stone No. 6 (the numbering is from Portoferraio). About 100 metres beyond this stone, and 5·4km. from Porto Azzurro, a loose-metalled road turns sharply off to the right; it is not signposted and is rather unobtrusive but is to be found just before the boundary of the Acquabona golf course.

Follow this country road in a gradually climbing curve towards the eastern mountain range; at the point at which it appears to be barred by a farm gateway it actually swings to the left through a small cutting before resuming its generally eastward course uphill. After approximately 2·5km. the track swings right into a U-bend and opens out into what looks like a sand quarry on the brow of a hill. From here there is an extensive view to the south and a side track leading off downhill. For those who have come this far by car, this makes a convenient place to park the vehicle and proceed on foot for the last short stretch of mountain walking.

The track curves uphill to the left out of this open space and resumes its course along the western slopes of *Monte Castello*, with tremendous views towards Portoferraio Bay. As a track, it ends on a broad grassy saddle between Monte Castello and the next peak, *Cima del Monte* (Crest of the Mountain). Before the saddle is reached, a stone stile over the wall along the right of the track gives access to a short and very steep scramble up to the top of Monte Castello. The mountain drops precipitously on its eastern side and great care should be exercised. From this summit (at 1,268 feet), there is a wide panorama, taking in Capoliveri and Monte Calamita beyond it to the south, the Botro Valley and Porto Azzurro beyond it to the south-east, and an iron cross planted on a rocky shoulder called Monte Mar di Capanna. To the east and partly hidden by the limestone crags is the gorge containing the Sanctuary of Monserrato.

This gorge can, however, be seen more effectively by crossing the saddle where the road ends and making a short climb to a shelf on the north flank of Monte Castello from which you can look right down on the Sanctuary.

On the northern side of the saddle a well marked footpath climbs up to the highest peak in the chain, *Cima del Monte* (1,677 feet), with an equally generous panorama both to east and west. Maps show the footpath continuing north along the chain till it joins the road up from Magazzini past the Volterraio fortress. In fact it now appears to be blocked by a television relay station.

ROUTE 2: PORTO AZZURRO TO MARINA DI CAMPO

Route

Leaving Porto Azzurro by the main road for Portoferraio, turn off left on to the new south-coast road at a clearly sign-posted junction (5·1km.). After swinging south to the coastline and following it along low wooded cliffs the road descends into the Plain of Lacona and reaches another junction (about 9km.). The two diverging roads join up again at the far side of the plain but that which forks left is better for motorists. It turns south as far as the beginning of the Stella promontory and then west again behind the sand dunes and beaches of the shoreline. At the far side of the plain where the beaches end, the two roads join up and begin the ascent to the pass between Monte Tambone to the left and Monte San Martino to the right, reaching the summit (850 feet) at 'Il Monumento' (about 16km.). A long

winding descent reaches a junction with the main road
between Marina di Campo and Procchio (about 20km.).
Turn left to enter Marina di Campo (21km.) where there
is a one-way traffic system.

(*Note*: Although this excellent road has been in existence
for several years, it has not yet been recognized by
official Italian surveys except as a track and the second
part of it is not always shown on maps sold to tourists.
For the same reason it has not been accurately measured
for map-making purposes between Lacona and Marina
di Campo; the distances given above are approximate, as
measured by the writer.)

Restaurants　　During the high season, one or two wayside cafés cater
for bathers on the Lacona beaches, and for passing
traffic.

This route gives access to the three main bays into which the south
coast of Elba is divided: between the Capoliveri peninsula and the
wooded promontory called Capo Stella is *Golfo di Stella* (Stella Bay)
with two main sandy beaches named respectively Lido and
Margidore; between Capo Stella and the next and much more
mountainous promontory, Capo di Fonza, is *Golfo di Lacona* (Lacona
Bay) with one continuous sandy beach and a shingly extension at its
western end; after the road has climbed up the slopes of Monte
Tambone it descends again to the sandy beaches and harbour of
Marina di Campo on *Golfo di Campo* (Campo Bay).

The **Lido beach** may be reached from the first stretch of this route
which follows the main road from Porto Azzurro to Portoferraio.
After passing the junction with the Capoliveri road and 3·2km. from
Porto Azzurro, a lane off to the left leads down to the beach 1·6km.
from the main road. It is passable for cars which can be parked in a
field just before the beach.

The south-coast road begins at a signposted junction 5·1km. along
the main road from Porto Azzurro. It skirts round some wooded
rising ground swinging south and reaching the coast at Capo Pini, a
small promontory dividing Golfo di Stella into two sections. Cars may
park off the road at the neck of this promontory and footpaths lead
down from it to small pebbly beaches, which are screened by private
properties between the road and the shore. Access to Margidore beach
in the western half of the bay is not possible from here.

After following the road over some rising ground and past several private roads which turn off from it, you come down into the wide coastal plain of **Lacona** (formerly spelt l'Acona). Although it ranks as one of the island's resorts and although houses, shops and hotels are scattered along the roads crossing the plain, there is no recognizable village of Lacona – only a stretch of low-lying agricultural land bounded by sand dunes and the beach to the south, and by the hills of Elba's central section to the north. Immediately on entering the plain you come to a road junction. Both diverging roads cross the plain and join up again on the far side, but the recommended route to the left turns south to the neck of Capo Stella and then west again parallel with the Lacona beach.

At the point where it turns to follow the beach, a short track leading off to the left, past a café, gives public access to **Margidore beach** on Golfo di Stella. But visitors who have been misled by local maps into thinking they can follow tracks along Capo di Stella itself are disappointed. The whole of this large, wooded tongue of land is private property awaiting development by speculators. Entry is blocked by a normally locked gateway and although this may sometimes be found open for the convenience of workmen, it is liable to be closed and locked again without warning.

The main road runs for just over 1km. parallel with the shore. Several turnings off to the left lead down to the fine sandy beach and the camping sites behind it. A large proportion of the beach is divided into 'private sections' during the high season with owners charging small fees for use of the changing and toilet facilities. At the western end of the beach the road turns right and rejoins the other branch from the junction which has crossed the plain further inland.

This secondary road gives access to the *Sanctuary of the Madonna dell'Acona*. To reach the sanctuary turn back along the inland road from its western junction with the main road for a distance of about $^1/_2$km. Just after the road has crossed a watercourse over a culvert, a footpath leads off to the left towards the sanctuary, already clearly visible on its knoll. About 100 metres further along the inland road, a lane off to the left makes it possible to bring a car close to the sanctuary. The sanctuary church is nondescript and usually locked (except on its annual festival of August 5th), but its site – a rocky knoll at the foot of the climb up to Monte Barbatoio and Colle Reciso (see p. 181) – is more interesting. It is said to have been the site of *Meloa,* one of the places recorded as inhabited during the Roman period of Elba. There is little reliable documentation for this identification but Meloa is described in early records as a 'castle', and the present sanctuary has evidently been constructed out of the ruins of something larger and more substantial, perhaps one of the early Pisan fortresses, all of which seem to have been built on eminences overlooking the shore but some distance inland.

The Caubbio and other watercourses crossing the plain of Lacona have offered archaeologists several sites where prehistoric stone implements have been found (see Archaeology, p. 131).

From the western fringe of the plain the main road begins a finely engineered ascent up to the mountain-pass between Lacona and Campo, the low-lying valley dividing western Elba from the central block. In three kilometres it climbs from 30 feet to 850 feet above sea-level along the flank of Monte Tambone (1,225 feet) which lies to the left. At the top of the pass there is room beside the road for cars to park while their passengers picnic or admire the views. On a mound a few metres to the right of the road there is an enigmatic concrete block described on the maps as 'Il Monumento' ('The Monument'). It shows signs of having borne an inscription which is no longer legible. Some Elbans will admit, rather reluctantly, that the monument was erected by the French forces after they had captured Elba from the German occupying force in 1944 – an episode that was dishonoured by the indisciplined behaviour of the French African troops towards the civil population (see History, p. 130). The monument originally bore a metal plate recording the names of French soldiers killed in the operation but this was subsequently transferred to a small French war cemetery near the shore of Golfo di Campo.

Walks from 'Il Monumento'

This pass over the heights which link Monte San Martino, in the central block, with Monte Fonza overlooking the south coast can be the starting point of several pleasant walks through the *macchia* which clothes these hills.

(1) From the north side of the road, just east of the Monument, a good bridle-path leads north for about 2km. to connect with the country road through the mountains of the central block described on p. 182. From there the walker can either go east towards Colle Reciso and Monte Orello or westwards downhill towards the main road which links Marina di Campo with Procchio.

(2) From the south side of the main road, opposite the Monument, a footpath leads due south directly towards the summit of Monte Tambone (1,242 feet). Immediately after leaving the road it crosses the east flank of an eminence known locally as Monte Cocchero, although this name does not appear on the maps. At its summit, reached after a steep scramble, there is a small natural rocky arena with two or three standing stones which may have been erected by human hand. Excavations here have found artefacts ascribed to the 'Sub-Apennine Culture' which was the last of prehistoric peoples to inhabit Elba (see History p. 96 and Archaeology p. 131). Unfortunately the site seems also to have been fortified by the German garrison defending Elba against the French landing force and some of the entrenchments are obviously of that date. From the summit of Monte Tambone the path continues eastwards and then south-eastwards to the top of Monte Fonza (965 feet) which gives its name to the promontory. Between Monte Tambone and Monte Fonza the path crosses a better-marked bridle-track, which crosses the promontory from east to west and was one of the links between the two bays before the new road was constructed.

(3) Capo Fonza is one of the remoter areas of Elba which offer opportunities to the exploratory walker. Apart from the tracks crossing its heights, other paths follow much of its rocky coastline.

The main road leaves 'Il Monumento' to zig-zag downhill into the lowlands of Campo, a wide vale running from north to south. It is flat enough in its southern stretch to allow room for Elba's only airport – a single runway for light aircraft only – which is passed on the right of the road. Just past the airstrip, a road off to the left approaches Marina di Campo by a detour which gives access to the beaches and the line of hotels built behind them. The main road, followed in this route, continues to a junction with the road connecting Marina di Campo with Procchio. Turning left you enter the town down the main street, Via Roma.

MARINA DI CAMPO

Population	4.050
Buses	Main stop in town centre;connections with Procchio, Porto Azzurro, and, via the road along the west coast, Marciana and Marciana Marina. See p. 37 for information about bus timetables.
Car hire	Galgani, Via Roma, tel. 97139.
Boat hire and water-ski-ing	c/o Bar 'Da Mario', tel. 97015; Servizio Turistico Spinetti, tel. 97190; and inquire at the La Foce bathing-beach.
Yacht repairs etc.	Cantiere Nautico, tel. 97402.
Hotels and pensions	See p. 44.
Restaurants	See p. 58.
Information	Tourist office of C.I.P.A.T. Via Roma 86, tel. 97414.
Central post office	Via Marconi, tel. 97014.
Public telephones	Via Roma, tel.97021/2.
Market day	Wednesday.
Feast Day	August 7th, in honour of patron saint, S. Gaetano.
Beaches	Marina di Campo (sand); Cavoli (sand p. 209); Seccheto (sand and rocks p. 209); Fetovaia (sand, p. 210).

Marina di Campo, the centre of the Campo commune, is a cheerful, busy little town and Elba's third port, after Portoferraio and Porto Azzurro. Its harbour, protected by breakwaters, is suitable for fishing-boats and yachts of small tonnage, with provisioning and watering facilities and a five-ton crane; it is also the Elban terminus for a ferry service to the penal colony on the island of Pianosa. (Special permits from the Ministry of Justice are required for landing on Pianosa.) To the north of the harbour, along the promenade front, which faces east, and for about 1km. beyond, there are excellent sandy beaches, some of them public and some reserved for bathing establishments which charge a small fee for the use of facilities. South of the harbour the town ends in the narrow streets of the fishing village which was its original nucleus, with a watch-tower erected, like so many others in Elba, to give warning of and refuge from sea-raiders.

Apart from the tower, the town contains no historic buildings earlier than the eighteenth century. A house behind the harbour-front exhibits a plaque recalling that Napoleon slept there during his first tour of the island, 'In this modest abode, then owned by Thomas Degrosori, during a tour of his new realm, Napoleon the Great received hospitality on May 20th, 1814.' But Marina di Campo, thanks to its fine beach, was one of the first Elban resorts to be discovered by Italian holiday-makers and the comfortable nineteenth-century residences behind its promenade bear witness to its early popularity. With international tourism now ranking as Elba's main industry, it is now well provided with hotels and pensions, and most recently with a number of developments of bungalows, blocks of apartments, and villas which have begun to spring up in the countryside behind the town.

Because Marina di Campo is a junction for three main streams of traffic – from Proccio to the north, from Lacona and Porto Azzurro to the east, and from the resorts and villages along the road round the west coast – the municipal authorities have organized a one-way traffic system which channels vehicles through the narrow streets without overburdening them. The main stream, entering the town from the north and east, follows Via Roma, the street through the modern centre past the town-hall; traffic from the west enters this street at right-angles and turns right along it towards the harbour; a parallel road along the promenade and the sea-front carries eastbound traffic out on to the main road at the eastern end of the town.

Marina di Campo is a good centre for excursions both to the southern and eastern slopes of the Monte Capanne massif, including the two ancient hill-towns of San Piero and Sant'Ilario which look out from them, and also to the small resorts along the southern and western shoreline of Monte Capanne and the mountain valleys which lie behind them.

EXCURSIONS FROM MARINA DI CAMPO

EXCURSION 2A: SANT'ILARIO, MONTE PERONE, AND SAN PIERO

Route Leave Marina di Campo by the main road towards Procchio, passing the Elban air-strip to the right. At 2·4km. either of two turnings to the left lead into the township of La Pila. (The second is almost opposite the public entrance to the air-strip.) Follow the main street of La Pila uphill and round a sharp sign-posted bend where it becomes the road to Sant'Ilario (5·7km.) On leaving Sant'Ilario turn left in 1·3km. and then take the first right-hand fork into San Piero (8km. from Marina di Campo, 1km. from the left turn). Returning to the main road from San Piero, turn right and continue downhill to a junction with the main road along the west coast (4km. from San Piero). Turn left and re-enter Marina di Campo (3·1km. from left turn). Total distance 15·1km.

Restaurants In Sant'Ilario, Ristorante 'La Cava'; in San Piero, Trattoria 'La Rosa', and Trattoria 'Da Dina'.

After climbing through a succession of hairpin bends (*tornanti*) from La Pila, the road circles the outside of Sant'Ilario along the line of former fortifications and enters a tree-shaded external piazza at the western end of the town where it is possible to park. The little town should be explored on foot.

Sant'Ilario

Sant'Ilario in Campo, at 672 feet above sea-level, is believed to date from the Lombard occupation of Elba in the sixth century A.D.. It was fortified either by the Pisans when they took control of Elba in the twelfth century or by the family of the Appiani who became hereditary lords of the island in the fourteenth century. The fortifications may have been demolished in the eighteenth century by the Spanish governor of Porto Longone; he had defeated an attempt by the Austrian forces of the Emperor Charles III to capture Elba, and is known to have taken reprisals of this sort against several Elban townships who had given support to the Austrians. Today the only surviving fortifications are to be seen round the eastern end of the church which seems, as elsewhere in the island, to have served also as a castle keep. The church itself, which fills the eastern end of the oval town-plan, was so heavily restored by an energetic nineteenth-century arch-priest as to lack any intrinsic interest. Its western facade faces a small central piazza with a labyrinth of picturesque and spotlessly clean streets and alleys opening off it.

Walk from Sant'Ilario

From the piazza and car park outside the town, three lanes lead off from the north-western corner. Take the central one which runs due north, passing the town cemetery away to the left, and after about 2km. becomes a simple bridle-track. It continues generally northward across the lower slopes of Monte Perone, climbing from the 600 foot contour to a maximum of about 1,000 feet. After crossing two spurs, with the Redinoce stream descending between them, the track swings north-west to enter a country road which descends through the woods from the village of Poggio to the Golfo di Procchio. Turn left on to this road and round a bend you reach the sanctuary of the *Madonna del Buonconsiglio* (Our Lady of Good Counsel) at about 4km. from Sant'Ilario. It is of no particular historical importance but is one of the many Elban shrines which are the goals of annual pilgrimages.

Detour to Church and Tower of San Giovanni

Leaving Sant'Ilario by the main road out of the piazza towards San Piero, diverge from it at a signposted road junction (1·3km. from Sant'Ilario) and take the road uphill to the right. About 1km. from the turn off, and on the left of the road, are the ruins of the romanesque *Church of San Giovanni*.

The church was built in the romanesque style by the Pisans in the twelfth century. It is constructed of granite from the local quarries and is perhaps the oldest of its period in Elba. It was in use until the last century but is now roofless and abandoned like most of the other romanesque churches in Elba, the reason for their neglect probably being their isolation. But this was not always an uninhabited spot; concealed among the *macchia* vegetation on the slope immediately below the church precinct are the foundations of several substantial buildings. This is a quiet and attractive spot for a picnic; there is plenty of shade and green turf beside the ruins.

About 300 metres beyond the church and round a bend in the road is the *Torre (Tower) di San Giovanni,* a short distance to the right.

The tower, is one of the most impressive monuments of Elba's medieval past. It is a typical four-sided watch-tower of the Pisan period, and if the locality was at one time inhabited, it may have formed part of the defences, though it can never have housed a garrison of more than five or six men. Springing from the summit of a huge boulder, it dominates the whole wild landscape. Its doorway, on the northern side, is more than two metres above ground level and must have been reached by a retractable ladder. Archaeologists believe the tower may date from the earliest period of the Pisan presence in Elba. From its top a sentry could see not only the whole of Campo bay but also, on clear days, as far as Pianosa to the south. It may have been one of the defences erected against the first of the great Saracen sea-raiders, known to the Italians as 'Musetto'.

Beyond the tower follow the road upwards through wooded country as far as the main ridge behind Monte Perone. At a point about 11·8km. from Marina di Campo where a green lane, suitable for cars, leads off to the right to the end of the spur, there are fine panoramic views.

Back on the main excursion route, after leaving Sant'Ilario by the main road out of the piazza, turn left after 1·3km. and then take the first right-hand fork into the town of San Piero in Campo. If there is no room to park in the main piazza, follow a sign-posted route to the *Belvedere,* a viewpoint at the south end of the town where there is usually parking space in the adjoining streets.

San Piero in Campo

San Piero in Campo, 735 feet above sea-level, is often regarded as the 'twin' of Sant'Ilario, but it is larger – the ground plan has spread beyond the line of its original fortifications – and has a different atmosphere. It is probably also older. It stands on the site of a Roman colony known to have existed in the time of Octavius, who became the Emperor Augustus in 27 B.C., and to have been called *Glaucus,* the name of a sea-deity.

The existing *Parish Church,* dedicated to St Nicholas, is reputedly built on the foundations of a temple of Glaucus, although no visible traces of the older structure remain. It does contain the remains of some fourteenth or fifteenth-century frescoes, including *St Michael weighing the souls of the dead, St. Sebastian,* and the figures of an angel and a saint.

The Roman colony is thought to have been destroyed by the Lombard invaders in the sixth century A.D., but the site continued to be inhabited and had acquired its present name before the Pisans took control in the twelfth century. The Pisans built a church on the level spur at the south end of the town, now called the *Belvedere,* and dedicated it to *St Peter and St Paul,* giving it two naves, one for each saint. The fabric of that church, overlaid and encrusted with more modern additions, survives, and the twin-nave structure can be seen reflected in its western facade.

The *fortifications* of San Piero are believed to have been contributed by the family of the Appiani, hereditary lords of Elba, in the fourteenth or fifteenth centuries; fragments of them survive along the south side of the town.

The hill slopes between San Piero and Sant'Ilario and the course of the stream, the Bovalico, which flows down between them are reputed to be a good hunting-ground for mineralogists. Local guides report finds of beryl, garnet, tourmaline, feldspar, quartz, and other crystalline rocks (see Geology, p. 80).

Walk from San Piero

A number of footpaths and bridle-tracks lead westwards from San Piero across the lower slopes of the Monte Capanne massif towards the Vallebuia valley which runs southward to the coast at Seccheto. Unfortunately they are interconnected, making a network with its higher strands running up as hunters' tracks into the mountains, while others dive steeply downwards to the coastal road and Seccheto village itself. However if the walker presses forward through fairly rough country on a level course along the contours, he should be able to reach a hamlet in the Vallebuia valley called *La Cavallina* (about 4km. from San Piero). From here he can turn left for a short walk down to the sea at Seccheto, or walk further up the valley to the right.

The best access to the westbound bridle-path is from the southern end of San Piero where a short road leads to the gates of the town cemetery. Just at the point where this road leaves the built-up area of the town, a path leaves it on the right-hand side and, running up between the houses, then swings westwards across country. It first enters the valley of the Stabbiati watercourse, and here the track for Vallebuia branches sharply off to the left across the stream instead of following its eastern bank uphill. The track then swings round a large wooded shoulder climbing to a height of about 1,000 feet before slanting gradually downhill towards La Cavallina and Seccheto.

EXCURSION 2B: CAVOLI, SECCHETO, FETOVAIA AND POMONTE

Route	Take the signposted turning to the right out of Marina di Campo's main street, Via Roma, and follow the road past the turning-off to San Piero and along the coast. The first village reached is that of Cavoli (5·5km.), the second is Seccheto (6·1km.), the third is Fetovaia (8·1km.), and the fourth is Pomonte (11·8km.)
Restaurants	At Cavoli, Trattoria 'Batignani'; at Fetovaia, Trattoria 'Spinetti' and Ristorante 'Pino Solitaria'.

Cavoli is a small seaside resort with a good sandy beach which has become increasingly popular since the road circuit of western Elba was completed.

Seccheto, reached after crossing a blunt promontory, overlooks a small sandy beach flanked by rocky outcrops. The little town is the nearest approach to a 'centre' of the ancient granite-quarrying industry of Elba which goes back, beyond the Pisans, to the Roman period of the island. The quarries themselves are widely scattered across the hillsides and up the long valley of the Vallebuia watercourse which comes down to the sea at Seccheto. In one of them there survives an inscribed pillar probably cut by the masons who built Pisa cathedral, though some authorities attribute it to the Romans who used Elban granite for the Pantheon in Rome. Somewhere on the hillside above Cavoli and Seccheto, awaiting rediscovery, there is said to be a granite block carved with the bas-relief of a ship. It is described by eighteenth-century writers and is reported to have been found again in 1915 by quarrymen who said, 'it was so beautiful, no one wanted to destroy it.'

Walk from Seccheto

A sharp and steep turning to the right off the main road, just after it has crossed the second of two watercourses that come down to the sea at Seccheto, gives access to the Vallebuia valley. The road, which is narrow but passable for motor traffic, first follows the west bank of the stream and then crosses to the other side at a steep dip. About 1·5km. from the turn-off, it reaches the hamlet called *La Cavallina* and the junction with a bridle-track coming in from the direction of

San Piero in Campo, referred to on p. 208. The guest-house, 'Dell'Amicizia', beside the road serves meals and refreshments. Beyond La Cavallina the road passes on the left the access road to one of Elba's better wine-bottling establishments which can be seen across the valley. Although the *cantine* is primarily a wholesale establishment, concerned with collecting, grading, and bottling the produce of the local growers, there is a small retail shop on the premises offering a wide and interesting selection of Elban wines (see p. 144), some of them in special souvenir flasks, together with an agreeable side line in honey collected from a row of hives on the premises. About 1km. beyond La Cavallina, the road forks into two tracks, both of which eventually peter out in vineyards. But the left-hand fork gives access to a footpath − for walkers only − which climbs through the *macchia* and across a beautiful hanging-valley to the craggy ridge which connects Monte Capanne (3,311 feet) with an outlying spur called Monte Cenno.

The beginning of the footpath is not easy to find. It leaves the right-hand side of the track opposite a small lay-by about 200 metres from the fork, crossing upwards over what looks like a patch of exposed rock. Walkers will know they have overshot this point if they follow the track to where they see on the right a one-storey building with a terra-cotta mask plastered into its facade and the painted inscription, 'Ovile Fr. Baciotti' (Sheepfold of the Brothers Baciotti).

The path zig-zags uphill, passing three vineyards and reaching a flat granite outcrop which it crosses diagonally. Veering gradually to the left, it crosses another outcrop and then levels off along the flank of the hill. It swings across a boggy slope, past an abandoned orchard in the head-waters of the hanging-valley, and then turns more or less directly uphill towards the sky line ridge between Monte Cenno and the central massif. This stretch is well marked and easy to follow. It emerges on the top of the ridge at a point marked on some local maps as *Le Mure* (The Walls) in apparent reference to the massive outcrops which project from the turf. From the ridge which to the right leads upwards towards Monte Capanne, there is a view eastwards across the next valley towards Pomonte. Following the ridge to the left you can reach the summit of Monte Cenno with a view towards Fetovaia.

Fetovaia

The last of Elba's south coast resorts is Fetovaia, an attractive cove protected on its west side by a long, narrow spit of land, Punta di Fetovaia. There is an excellent sandy beach open to the public, with bathing huts and an adjoining pizzeria. The village has two hotels and a lodging-house (p. 44).

Pomonte

Beyond Fetovaia the coastline and the road curve northwards to Pomonte, lying on the boundary between the communes of Campo and Marciana. Just before reaching it, you can look down from the road on a rocky shoal known as *Scoglio di Ogliera*. At the time of writing there was still visible on the rocks the wreck of a small coastal steamer. Local sources said it hit the rocks while its entire crew was watching on television the fight between Mohammed Ali and Joe Frazier; the men all scrambled ashore and ran down the road to Pomonte to watch the end of the fight on the television of a small bar before reporting their shipwreck.

Pomonte is built on the site of a Roman settlement; its name is a corruption of *post montem*, the Latin phrase for 'beyond the mountain'. The old township was destroyed in 1533 by the Turkish fleet commanded by Barbarossa and there was nothing but a small and isolated fishing hamlet here until the new coast road gave better access. Although it has no beach – the foreshore is rocky – it is now a considerable village built along a horse-shoe curved street which connects at both ends with the coast road. The long valley of the Barione, which comes down from the mountains behind it, is extensively cultivated for vines.

Walks from Pomonte

From the bridge over the stream at the landward end of the village a good bridle-path, for walkers only, goes up the valley above the southern bank of the stream for about 1·5km. as far as some pleasant woodland. Here it crosses the stream and appears to peter out among the vineyards on the other bank, though some local maps suggest it should continue into the mountains at the head of the valley.

From the northern sector of the village street (opposite the house numbered 25) an inconspicuous bridle-path zig-zags up the steep and rocky side of Colle San Bartolomeo (1,664 feet), to join a fine mountain track which goes northwards along the contours at a level of about 1,000 feet and was Pomonte's main connection with the outside world before the coastal road was built. It ends at the Sanctuary of the Madonna del Monte above Marciana. More details will be given of this track under Route 3 on p. 219.

ROUTE 3: MARINA DI CAMPO TO MARCIANA MARINA

Route
The first stretch of this route, from Marina di Campo to Cavoli (5·5km.), Seccheto (6·1km.), Fetovaia (8·1km.) and Pomonte (11·8km.), has already been described as an excursion from Marina di Campo (p.209).From Pomonte the coast road continues north through Chiessi (12·6km.) and Colle d'Orano (18km.) to the turn-off to Zanca and Sant'Andrea (19·7km.). The main road bears first eastwards and then southwards, climbing round a series of bends to reach Marciana Alta (25·7km.). About ¹/₂km. beyond Marciana a turn-off to the left, sign-posted, leads downhill to Marciana Marina (34·5km.).

Alternative Route
It is also possible to reach Marciana Alta and Marciana Marina more quickly and directly by taking the route described as an excursion on p. 205, leaving Marina di Campo for Sant'Ilario (5·7km.), going from Sant'Ilario to the turn-off of the new motor road across Monte Perone (7km.), following the mountain road up to the pass and on to Poggio (15·8km.). You can then either continue along the road to Marciana Alta (18·9km.), or turn downhill from Poggio directly to Marciana Marina (20·2km.)

Restaurants
At Chiessi, 'Aurora' and 'L'Ulivo'; at S. Andrea, 'Da Anna' and 'Il Gabbiano'; at Marciana Alta, 'Il Castagno'; at Poggio (village 3·1km. from Marciana), 'Monte Perone', 'Publius', and 'Il Boschetto'; at Marciana Marina, 'Da Sauro', 'La Fiaccola', 'Marinella', pizzeria 'Da Zorba', pizzeria 'Il Gallinaccio'.

Excursions
Because many visitors may be staying in the hotels in Marciana Marina, excursions from Marciana Alta are described in the section on Marciana Marina (p. 217) as starting from that resort. They can also, of course, be followed with equal ease from Marciana Alta.

For description of route as far as Pomonte see p. 209–11. From Pomonte the coast road continues northwards above formidable cliffs and screes. Inland a number of valleys, almost always terraced as vineyards, lead up to the peak of *Il Troppolo*, (2,434 feet), the westernmost of the group round Monte Capanne.

Chiessi

The fishing village of Chiessi, 1·8km. north of Pomonte, has no beach worth mentioning but is a favourite base for skin-divers and spear-fishers. The clear and steeply-shelving waters all along this coast are said to be ideal for this sport. About $\frac{1}{2}$km. from the shoreline of Chiessi and at a depth of 160 feet, divers found a few years ago a deposit of some 5,000 amphoras, or earthenware jars, some containing wine and others the remains of salted and pickled foodstuffs, all of them dating back to the first century A.D.. The deposit marked the site of at least one Roman shipwreck, more probably of several. The danger of this coastline to early shipping is indicated by the fact that fragments of medieval pottery were also found in the same area. The site has been visited by acquisitive divers so often since its discovery that nothing now remains on the sea floor but broken potsherds. Inland, about 1km. up the valley of the Gneccarina, the stream which reaches the sea at Chiessi, a deposit of bronze axe-heads was found beneath a slab of sandstone; they are now on exhibition in the Archaeological Museum at Marciana and are dated to the eighth century B.C.

Beyond Chiessi the road runs due north along the clifftop past a rock where Napoleon is said to have sat gazing nostalgically towards his birthplace, the island of Corsica, a legend which probably owes more to Italian sentiment than historical fact. However Corsica is certainly visible from here in clear weather. After curving away from the cliffs to cross two valleys, the road passes through the village of *Colle d'Orano* (18km. from Marina di Campo) and its two adjacent hamlets, *Il Mortaio* and *La Guardia*. The names of the latter, meaning 'The Mortar' and 'The Guard-post,' suggest an attempt to protect this part of the coast from sea-borne invasion, probably in the eighteenth century. From La Guardia, a steep but practicable track descends to the lighthouse on Punta Pulveraia and shingle beach known as Patresi-Mare.

Sant'Andrea
This secluded but cheerful little resort is reached by turning to the left off the main route 2·8km. beyond Colle d'Orano. The side road leading to it passes through the hamlet of *La Zanca* and then twists steeply downhill to the seaside village of Sant'Andrea. It has about 50 metres of sandy beach flanked by rocks. Although it is somewhat cut off from the rest of Elba by the steep descent, its popularity as a resort is indicated by the comparative abundance of small hotels and pensions.

The main route swings eastwards, climbing steadily, until a sharp bend to the right turns it southwards towards the ancient hilltown of Marciana.

MARCIANA ALTA

Marciana Alta, ('High Marciana'), as it is sometimes now called to distinguish it from Marciana Marina on the coast below, is 1,125 feet above sea-level, overlooking the deep wooded valley of a stream called Uviale di Marciana. Imaginative eighteenth century historians ascribed its foundation to 'Greek colonists' at the dawn of history. It was certainly one of the Roman settlements on the island and has a good claim to be the oldest, continuously inhabited place in Elba. Its name appears in the earliest medieval records; it coined its own money in the thirteenth century; the Pisans not only fortified it in the twelfth century but probably also built the first structure of the formidable fortress at the upper end of the town. After the fall of the Pisan city-state at the end of the fourteenth century, the family of the Appiani, who became hereditary lords of Piombino and Elba, made Marciana their island capital and probably enlarged the fortress. The town can thus claim considerable seniority over Portoferraio. Indeed, long after the de'Medici family had created their Tuscan enclave on Portoferraio bay and the Spaniards had established themselves at Porto Longone, the people of Marciana remained obstinately loyal to the Appiani and their legal heirs who inherited the lordship after the family had died out. There is still a *Casa degli Appiani* ('Home of the Appiani') in the town, a modest early fifteenth century habitation which is in private hands and not open to visitors; local sources say sadly that its painted walls and ceilings have now been white-washed over. In 1553 Marciana, in spite of its altitude and distance from the sea, was among the Elban towns sacked by the Turks. It may have been then that it lost most of the fortifications which constricted its town plan and have left its steeply sloping maze of narrow streets inaccessible to motor-traffic. The 2,200 inhabitants make their living mainly from vineyards on the neighbouring hillsides and from flocks of sheep and goats pastured on the uplands. They are a reserved and dignified people who accept the presence of tourists and foreign visitors without appearing to notice them.

The main road skirts the lowest side of the town, outside the line of its former fortifications. From the road a broad, ramplike approach to the main gate provides limited parking space as well as room for an outdoor café. This ramp is called *Piazza Umberto,* and it flanks a surviving stretch of the old city wall which, like that overlooking the old Portoferraio harbour, has been converted into houses and shops. (If there is no parking space left on the ramp, cars may be left along the verge of the main road below.) At the top of the ramp the gateway through the wall is called '*Porta Medicea*', although the de' Medici family had very little to do with Marciana. Inside the gateway, on the left, the *Parish Church,* dedicated to St Catherine, contains the family chapel of the Appiani. From the little triangular piazza within the gateway the town scrambles uphill through alleys and up frequent flights of steps to the fortress at its highest point.

Fortress
If you want to avoid the climb on foot, the fortress is also accessible by road. A sharp, virtually hairpin turn-off to the right, just before the main road reaches Piazza Umberto, leads to the signposted '*Strada Archaeologica*' which detours away from the town only to return to it at a higher level. It terminates just above the fortress where a parking-lot is provided. The fortress itself is today only an empty shell within its outer walls and is usually closed. But barred iron gates permit you to look into the space within the bastioned walls.

Archaeological Museum
In a street just below the fortress is the Archaeological Museum (Antiquario Communale), open to the public from May 1st to September 30th. The opening hours are from 10.00 to 12.30 and from 16.00 to 19.30 except on Wednesdays, when it is closed. During May and again in September the museum custodian has in the past shown himself to be extremely casual about observing this timetable. Complaints should be made to E.V.E. in Portoferraio if visitors have trouble over this. The museum has a valuable and well laid-out display of relics of Elba's prehistoric and Roman past. Unfortunately the explanatory labels on the cases and the guide sold at the entrance are only in Italian.

Leaving Marciana by the turn-off to the left just beyond the town, follow the downhill road through the chestnut forests towards Marciana Marina. After an initial straight stretch the road zig-zags through a series of hairpin bends. On the left, after the fourth such bend, an inconspicuous but signposted lane leads down to the ruined romanesque **Church of San Lorenzo.** (Cars are best left parked on the verge of the main road.) This roofless church, its interior overgrown with weeds, is one more example of Elba's Pisan period; the little building is contemporary with the cathedrals of Pisa and Lucca.

The main road, after one more hairpin bend beyond the lane to San Lorenzo, joins another road coming downhill from Poggio, another hilltown neighbouring on Marciana Alta, and then descends directly into Marciana Marina.

MARCIANA MARINA

Population	1,846
Buses	Main stop in town centre; connections with Portoferraio (via Proccio), Marciana Alta and Poggio. See p. 37 for information about bus timetables etc.
Car hire	Adriani Amerigo, tel. 99335; Giovanni Olivari, tel. 99127; Giovanni Taglioni, tel. 99364; Bibi Mazzei, Via XX Settembre.
Hotels and pensions	See p. 44.
Restaurants	See p. 58.
Information	Agenzia Immobiliare G. Venci, Piazza della Vittoria 18, tel. 99279.
Central post office	Via Principe Amedeo, tel. 99074.
Market day	April 1st to Sept. 30th, Sundays; October 1st to March 31st, Wednesdays.
Feast day	12th August, in honour of Santa Chiara.

This pleasant and unpretentious seaside resort, well supplied with hotels and pensions and much favoured by English-speaking visitors to Elba, stretches along an open northward-facing bay with a long shingle beach. A broad promenade runs along the sea-front behind the beach and terminates to the west near a late medieval watch-tower known locally as the *Torre Saracena* ('Saracen Tower'), although it was constructed, perhaps in the fifteenth century, as a defence *against* the Saracens. The watch-tower stands at the landward end of a long breakwater protecting the harbour from western gales and providing moorings for a variety of yachts and small boats. The eastern end of the promenade, and a secondary road which runs parallel with the sea-front a few blocks inland, both connect with the main road which runs along the north coast of Elba, through Procchio, to Portoferraio (see Route 4 p. 225).

EXCURSIONS FROM MARCIANA MARINA

EXCURSION 3A: SANCTUARY OF THE MADONNA DEL MONTE AND MONTE CAPANNE

Route

Follow main road from Marciana Marina to Marciana Alta (8·8km.) and then take the signposted turn-off to Strada Archaeologica on the left of the road immediately after leaving Piazza Umberto in direction of Colle d'Orano. Shortly before reaching the castle, at the end of the Strada Archaeologica, a signpost on the right side of road indicates the footpath to the *Santuario della Madonna del Monte*. (A steep footway leads up through the town to the same point.) From here the climb must be made on foot up a cobbled track. Beyond the Sanctuary the track continues round the head of the gorge on the right and ends on the ridge of weather-worn boulders which has been visible on the right during the climb. The climb from the road to the Sanctuary can be done in half an hour, but most people will prefer to take longer and enjoy the scenery.

Restaurants

There are no restaurants above Marciana Alta and Poggio, but rustic tables and benches have been set up in the grove round the Sanctuary for the convenience of pilgrims and picnickers. There is a small bar with telephone in the Hermitage, adjoining the Sanctuary.

After the first steep stretch through woodland, the first of twelve roadside shrines is reached. These are spaced out at regular intervals along the track, and not until the twelfth is reached does the Sanctuary become visible ahead in a grove of trees.

The Sanctuary of the Madonna del Monte ('Madonna of the Mountain') is reputed to be one of the oldest religious centres in Elba; it has so often been piously enlarged or restored that it is difficult to date the original structure, but local antiquarians insist that it is 'at least as old' as the ruined church of San Giovanni on the slopes of

Sant'Ilario which dates back to the eleventh century. The cult of the Madonna del Monte is now focussed on a painting said to have been found 'miraculously' by a shepherd on the side of a hillside boulder. But the painting on the stone does not date back earlier than the fifteenth century, at which time it was incorporated into the shrine by the enlargement of an existing building. Prehistoric remains have been found in the vicinity, and the numinous atmosphere of the place is such that it is easy to believe the earliest Christian shrine may have been founded on the remains of some pagan place of worship. The sanctuary church stands some 2,000 feet above sea level on a spur of Monte Giove (2,779 feet), the northernmost peak of the Monte Capanne complex. (*Giove* is the Italian form of Jove or Jupiter.) It looks across a wooded gorge towards another spur, crested with a long ridge of fantastically weathered boulders. Beside the church and on the verge of the gorge is the Hermitage, formerly occupied by monks and now by the custodians of the Sanctuary.

It was here that Napoleon in 1814 had his brief rendez-vous with his Polish mistress, the countess Marie Walewska (see History, p. 122). The Emperor and his attendant staff officers stayed in the Hermitage while a tent was erected for the Countess. The church is the goal of a popular pilgrimage on August 15th, the Feast of the Assumption; there are also minor pilgrimages on Easter Monday and during the first three days of May. Apart from its legendary picture of the Madonna, the church also contains a fascinating collection of votive offerings which are now housed in the sacristy. There are two inscriptions here recalling different episodes in Elban history. On the façade of the church is commemorated the victory of Elban peasants over the French revolutionary militia force which attempted unsuccessfully to take over the island in 1799 (see History, p. 116). On the Hermitage there is a grandiloquent memorial of Napoleon's stay here; translated it reads, 'Napoleon I, with empires conquered and kings made his vassals, overcome at last not by force of arms but by the Ruthenian frosts, dwelt in this Hermitage transformed for him into a Palace from August 23rd to September 5th, 1814; and having re-tempered his immortal genius, from here on February 24th, 1815, he launched himself to capture anew the admiration of the world.'

At the chancel end of the church, a seventeenth-century devotee constructed an elegant 'grotto', consisting of a semicircle of masonry arches within which three grotesque stone masks funnelled the water of a local spring into a channel from which pilgrims could refresh themselves. Only one of the masks now functions, but the water that pours from its mouth is among the freshest and most delicious in Elba.

The track which runs between the sanctuary church and the Hermitage continues round the head of the gorge and on to the neighbouring ridge with its extraordinary assortment of weather-sculptured granite boulders. Some of them have been given names: the 'Eagle', resembling the head of a bird of prey, is easily recognizable. There is also the 'Man' and, inevitably, another 'Napoleon's Seat' from which the nostalgic emperor is supposed to have gazed westwards to Corsica.

Walks from the Madonna del Monte Sanctuary
The climb to the Madonna del Monte sanctuary is also the starting-point for a number of walks through the magnificent scenery of the Monte Capanne massif.

Walk from Sanctuary to Pomonte
Along the left side of the track between the Sanctuary and the rocks on the ridge beyond runs a stretch of wire fencing. If you turn off the track to the left at the point where the fencing ends, you can find without much difficulty the beginning of the bridle-path which used to be the only route between Marciana and Pomonte on the west coast (see p. 211). It runs along the brow of the mountains, following the contours between 2,000 feet and 2,250 feet. After rounding the slopes of *Monte Giove,* it crosses the upper reaches of two torrents – the Castagnola and the Pente di Caiello. Then it swings round another buttress of *Monte Capanne* – *Il Troppolo* (2,435 feet) – and across the rocky slopes of the Gneccarina Valley. Finally it zig-zags down a long ridge called *La Terra* to descend the steep south-western slopes of *Monte San Bartolommeo* into the village street of *Pomonte.* (about 9km.) By careful timing it should be possible to catch one of the few buses which link Pomonte with Marciana and Marciana Marina. There are also subsidiary tracks which diverge down to the coast-road at points north of Pomonte. One of them leaves the main track on the slopes of Il Troppolo and reaches the main road just north of Chiessi; another descends directly into Chiessi from the ridge called La Terra.

Walk to the Shrine of San Cerbone
This charming and easy walk takes you at a comparatively low altitude, just over 1,500 feet, into the great semicircle of peaks which

look down on Marciana. The distance is only 9·5km. there and back, and the going is good along a smooth and well-marked track which diverges from the left side of the cobbled way up to the sanctuary of the Madonna del Monte. Its start is about 10 metres above the second of the wayside shrines, and it follows a fairly level course, sometimes through chestnut woods and sometimes across the open hillside, crossing several mountain streams including the Uviale di Capepe and the Pedalla. After passing beneath the line of cable-cars which runs up to the summit of Monte Capanne, you finally reach the humble and austere little shrine of San Cerbone in a wooded glade. The saint was the bishop of Populonia who fled to Elba from the invading Lombards and died in his hermitage in these woods (see History, p. 101). The site of the shrine was disputed between Marciana and the neighbouring village of Poggio, with the consequence that the surviving building, erected in 1421 by Jacobo II di Appiano, was constructed exactly on the boundary between them, the doorway in Marciana territory and the altar in that of Poggio. Some ancient graves, possibly dating back to the religious community founded by San Cerbone, have been found near the shrine. The saint himself, thanks to the cover afforded by a miraculous storm, was buried on the mainland in his proper diocese under the very noses of the Lombards. From the shrine a footpath leads downhill to the main road between Marciana and Poggio, but walkers may prefer to return to the track up to the Sanctuary of the Madonna del Monte.

Note Large-scale maps show other footpaths leaving the Sanctuary track higher up and making the same mountain circuit at a higher level. The writers found the beginning of one such path leaving the track on the left immediately below the fourth wayside shrine. It was very rough and, instead of following the level course suggested by the maps, climbed uphill first through woodland and then across the open slopes, slanting upwards until it reached the col between the peak called *La Stretta* and the neighbouring *Monte di Cote*. They did not follow it further but its general line suggested that it might eventually run south-west in the direction of Pomonte or Seccheto. There was no trace of the path alleged by the maps to cross the upper slopes of Monte Capanne towards the Valle della Rivera.

Walk across the Ordicole Gorge towards the coast road

Another bridle-path leaves the track to the Sanctuary of the Madonna del Monte on the right, as you are going uphill, between the fifth and sixth of the wayside shrines. It curves round the head of the gorge of the Ordicole torrent and then climbs up to the boulder-strewn ridge on the far side. From the ridge it swings westwards, descending from a height of 1,732 feet to a point some 400 feet lower where it crosses the ravine of another torrent called Marconi. Just beyond this ravine the track divides, its right-hand branch descending steeply to the main road opposite the *Zanca* turn-off while the left-hand branch continues westwards, dropping more gradually to the main road at *Il Mortaio*. The distance from the Sanctuary track to Il Mortaio is approximately 5km.

EXCURSION 3B: MONTE CAPANNE (BY CABLE-CAR), POGGIO AND MONTE PERONE

Route Take the road uphill from Marciana Marina to Marciana Alta, turning *right* when you reach the road which links the latter with Poggio. A short distance from the junction, this road makes a wide bend to the left where it crosses the valley of the Pedalta watercourse. In the angle of the bend there is a derelict building and a patch of waste ground used as a car-park by those wishing to take the cable-cars (which operate only in good weather) to the summit of Monte Capanne. From the edge of the car-park a short, easy path leads uphill through the trees and across the stream for about 100 metres to the cable-car terminal. (Tel. 99920 to inquire about operation of cars and weather conditions at summit.) It is also possible to walk to the summit from Poggio (p. 223). For Poggio, follow main road to right from car-park. In Poggio, turn snarply left off main road and left again at the next fork to enter a small parking-space in the piazza at the lower end of the village.

For Monte Perone return to the main road and follow it eastwards in a steady ascent to the watershed. The return to Marciana Marina can be made from Poggio where a road leads downhill to join up with that coming down from Marciana Alta.

Restaurants At cable-car terminal, bar where snacks are available and also open-air picnic tables; at Poggio, Ristorante 'Monte Perone', Ristorante 'Publius', and Ristorante 'Il Boschetto'.

Monte Capanne

Monte Capanne (3,308 feet) is Elba's highest mountain, and the easiest and quickest way to its summit is by the *cabinovia,* or cable-cars, which are carried directly up its slope along a line of unsightly pylons. The cars themselves are of the simplest variety — open metal cradles each holding two standing adults – and the ascent takes approximately fifteen minutes. The cars are operated only during the season, between mid-May and mid-September, and the service is liable to be suspended in cloudy or windy weather. Those making the ascent are advised to carry an extra sweater or other over-garment as there is often a sharp contrast in temperature between the terminal and the windy mountain-top. Strong-armed attendants are on hand to help passengers into the cars as they swing round the terminal platforms, or help them to dismount.

From the top terminal a short scramble up a well-marked footpath takes you up to the crest of Monte Capanne; the path is not fenced and a sharp eye should be kept on children as there are dangerous slopes just off it. From the summit on a clear day the view is outstanding. You can see not only the whole of Elba, the mainland coast to the east and Corsica to the west but, looking north and south, virtually the whole of the Tuscan Archipelago from a distant blue fleck which is Gorgona to the north, to Giglio and Giannutri to the south. Closer at hand are the subsidiary peaks of the granite massif, *La Tavola* and *Monte di Cote* to the west, *Monte Giove* to the north-west, *Monte Maolo* and *Monte Perone* to the east.

Fonte di Napoleone

The Fonte di Napoleone ('Napoleon's Spring') lies just off the main road between Marciana and Poggio. After leaving the *Cabinovia* car-park and turning right away from Marciana and towards Poggio, you round a spur into the next valley. Here at the apex of a bend to the right you come to the buildings of a small establishment where Elba's own mineral-water is bottled, the well-advertised Acqua di Napoleone. The Emperor is said to have discovered its virtues early in August 1814 when he was investigating the possibility of entertaining Marie Walewska at the Sanctuary of the Madonna del Monte. He had stopped his carriage to refresh himself at the natural spring and found that its water exercised a beneficial effect on a chronic bladder complaint from which he suffered. Subsequently he stocked barrels of the water at his various residences on the island and decided to start a commercial concern at the source. Modern visitors can sample the water from a wayside drinking-fountain if they have not already consumed its bottled version in hotels and restaurants.

Poggio

The substantial village of Poggio (the name means literally 'mountain-spur') lies about 1km. beyond the *Fonte di Napoleone,* (3·1km. from Marciana Alta). The main road runs through the upper part of the village, but there is little parking-space here and those wishing to visit Poggio should turn left downhill and left again into the little piazza at the lower end of the village. It is in some respects the 'twin' of Marciana Alta − another ancient hilltown with narrow streets and flights of steps huddled together in a defensive pattern originally dictated by an exterior wall. And while Marciana has its fortress-castle, Poggio clusters beneath the massive bastioned *Church of San Niccolò* which was fortified to serve as a refuge in times of trouble. Poggio does not claim the Roman ancestry boasted by Marciana, but the original church of San Niccolò is said to have been founded in the eighth century A.D., which gives the place a respectable antiquity. What makes Poggio different from Marciana is its atmosphere: the people are more outgoing and welcoming to visitors; there are three restaurants in and around the town, including one of high quality opening off the lower piazza, as well as a cheerful little bar. The householders are fond of decorating their doorways with geraniums and other pot-plants; the streets, narrow and winding as they are, have a livelier aspect than those of Marciana. Near the lower end of the village there is the *Church of San Difendente* dedicated in the sixteenth century. Although badly damaged by a tornado in 1958, it has now been restored and redecorated in the elegant style of its period, and is well worth seeing.

Walk from Poggio to summit of Monte Capanne

From Poggio runs the footpath to be followed by those who prefer to climb Monte Capanne on foot. Signs indicating the path are distributed about the village below the main road but the start of the climb may be found most easily from the main road itself at the upper level of Poggio. At the point where the stripes of a pedestrian-crossing are marked on the road, signs point uphill into a yard between the houses on the upper side of the road, and then up a flight of steps in the corner. The path then follows the watershed of a long shoulder of the mountain, marked on the maps as *Ferale*; it climbs steadily, directly across the contours, in a south-westerly direction towards the summit. The time quoted for the ascent on the Poggio signpost is $1^1/_2$

hours and the total map distance from the main road to the summit is slightly under 4km.

Walk from Poggio to the shrine of the Madonna del Buon Consiglio
Another and easier walk from Poggio begins from the road leading downhill towards Marciana Marina. Shortly after the first hairpin bend and immediately before the road crosses a watercourse, a bridle-path leads off to the right. It bends sharply away from the road and descends into the valley of the Nivera, crossing that stream by a bridge. It then swings north-east across the lower slopes of three wooded spurs before reaching the shrine of the *Madonna del Buon Consiglio* (approximate distance 4km.). From this point other tracks go downhill to the outskirts of Marciana Marina. Alternatively if a longer walk is planned, follow the main track past the shrine and you will eventually reach the fork where the country road from Sant' Illario (described on p. 206) comes in.

Monte Perone
The ridge of Monte Perone may be reached by following the Marciana – Poggio road eastwards beyond Poggio. It climbs steadily round a series of dramatic bends through the forest and up to the pass which has already been described in excursions from Marina di Campo on p. 207. Off to the left, when approaching from this direction runs the short green road, to the easternmost spur of *Monte Perone,* with spectacular views. The main road continues down the south-east side of the massif towards Sant'Ilario and Marina di Campo.

EXCURSION 3C: WEST COAST TOWARDS SANT'ANDREA

Route   From the car park at the western end of the Marciana
                             Marina sea front a rough road leads directly inland, then
                             west over a headland to Ripa Barata farm (2km.). From
                             here a footpath continues along the coastline for a further
                             4km..

While most of the excursions for visitors staying in Marciana Marina radiate from Marciana Alta and Poggio or the road between them, there is a stretch of comparatively unfrequented coastline to the west of the resort and it is possible to escape along it from the apparent dead-end at the western end of the town.

The rough road from the sea front crosses a somewhat rickety wooden bridge before winding uphill over a steep headland ending in two rocky promontories, Punta del Nasuto and Punta della Madonna. It descends on the far side of the headland and goes as far as a farm called Ripa Barata where it comes to a full stop. A sign asks motorists not to park at the extreme end of the road where it has been widened to enable cars to turn round.

From the farm a footpath follows the coastline, passing well above a cove called *La Caletta* and through the grounds of a lonely guesthouse, Pensione Andreina. After crossing two water-courses the path finally descends to the shore at a second cove alled *La Cala* and appears to peter out among some farm buildings (6km.). However, before the path crosses the first of the two water-courses after Pensione Andreina, another path diverges inland, running uphill. This has not been explored by the writers but appears from the map to connect with a track running across the hillside at a higher level and leading to the resort of *Sant'Andrea*.

ROUTE 4: MARCIANA MARINA TO PORTOFERRAIO

Route
Take the main road eastwards out of Marciana Marina along the coastline towards Procchio (7·4km.) At the Procchio road junction take the left-hand fork, passing Campo all'Aia and then climbing the hillside to the turn-off for Biodola Bay (11·7km.) (see Excursion C from Portoferraio, p. 175). After passing that point the road goes over a pass and begins the gradual descent to the Bivio road junction (16·9km.). Keeping straight on for another 3km. you reach Portoferraio and the mainland ferry pier (19·9km.).

Restaurants
At Procchio, Ristorante 'La Lucciola', Ristorant 'Lo Zodiaco', Pizzeria 'Terrazza Paolina', Ristorante 'Sette Bello'.

This route, which completes a clockwise circuit of the island, connects the main seaside resorts along the north coast of Elba. Its first stretch, from Marciana Marina to Procchio, although well engineered and surfaced is perhaps the only dull road in the island. Although it runs close to the seashore high hedges block the view and make a series of blind bends rather dangerous.

Having passed **Bagno,** a hamlet on the shore with a small private beach, the road makes a sharp bend inland to cross the valley of the Redinoce watercourse. Just before the stream is crossed, a track turning off to the right leads up the hillside to the *Chapel of Santa Rita* and then on to the shrine of the *Madonna del Buon Consiglio.* It passes a group of springs known as *Acqua Calda* (Warm Water). The main road returns to the coastline and shortly before it enters Procchio passes a small wooded island close inshore called *Isola Paolina.* On it the foundations of a Roman building, possibly a trading warehouse, were excavated. Roof-tiles, pottery lamps and utensils, all dating from the Augustan period, were discovered and are now in museums on the mainland. There is a small shingle beach on the shore almost opposite the island.

Procchio

Procchio is a substantial seaside resort and also an important junction of the island's road system. The road going off to the left from the junction, and which is followed in this Route, connects with Portoferraio. The road to the right crosses the island from north to south, passing the airstrip at La Pila and connecting with Marina di Campo. Procchio has given its name to the *Golfo di Procchio* (Procchio Bay) with a magnificent curving stretch of sandy beach, about 1km. in length, between two headlands – Punta Agnone to the west and Monte Pinello to the east. A subsidiary road off to the left as you come from Marciana Marina, just before you reach the main road junction, leads directly down to the beach, sections of which are reserved for the guests of various hotels. The modern town which has developed round the road-junction has shops, bars and restaurants and there are numerous hotels and restaurants (see p. 58).

Campo all'Aia

At the eastern end of the Golfo di Procchio, Campo all'Aia has grown up as a secondary resort with a modern development of small villas behind the beach. It has a distinctly family atmosphere and is a favourite for Italians with small children. Campo all'Aia is also of some interest to archaeologists. On the eroded slopes of Monte Pinello palaeolithic stone implements are reported to have been found, and on the beach itself Roman potsherds and the slag from primitive iron-smelting can occasionally be unearthed (see Archaeology, p. 131).

After leaving Procchio and Campo all'Aia, the road climbs up to a col behind Monte Pinello, called Colle Pecorino, and then runs fairly levelly along the contours of a *macchia*-clad hillside some 450 feet above the sea. Soon after passing a small roadside oratory on the right, you reach a track turning off to the left and running downhill to the western end of the Golfo di Biodola (p. 175), the Hermitage Hotel, and the little cove called Porticciolo. The main turning off to Biodola and Scaglieri is reached shortly afterwards. Almost opposite the turn-off a footpath leaving the main road on the right climbs to the summit of Monte Pericoli (1,088 feet), one of the modest hills of Elba's central sector.

After the Biodola turn-off the main road crosses a watershed and descends fairly rapidly into the Madonnina Valley which debouches into the Golfo di Portoferraio. The turn-off to the Villa San Martino (p. 170) is passed on the right, and soon afterwards the Bivio Boni (Boni road-junction) gives notice that you are in the suburbs of the island capital, Portoferraio.

GIGLIO

GETTING TO GIGLIO

Giglio, the main island in the southernmost group of the Tuscan Archipelago, falls within the administrative province of Grosseto; it is reached by ferry from Porto Santo Stefano, the main town on the Monte Argentario peninsula. But Monte Argentario itself is linked to the mainland only by three narrow isthmuses which enclose two salt-water lagoons; and on the neck of the central isthmus is the ancient town of Orbetello with its railway station in an unattractive industrial suburb on the mainland. A motor-road, which is also a bus route, runs from the mainland sector of Orbetello along the isthmus to Porto Santo Stefano.

Travellers to Giglio must therefore make Orbetello their first objective by road or by rail. The nearest convenient international airports are Rome and Pisa, the former being slightly nearer.

Road

The journey from Rome is 155km., going north on the Via Aurelia (National Route 1) along the Italian west coast as far as the Orbetello turn-off, and then another 13.2km. through Orbetello to Porto Santo Stefano. From Pisa, by the most direct route south, the distance to the Orbetello turn-off is 179km.

Rail

The rail journey from Rome to Orbetello takes from $1^1/_2$ to 2 hours in the faster trains, although it is important to note that not all the expresses travelling north along this route stop there.

A number of slower, local trains also leave the *Stazione Tiburtina* in Rome for Orbetello, stopping at many stations along the route. From Pisa the railway journey to Orbetello takes from 2 to $2^1/_2$ hours according to the train.

The distance between Orbetello station and the harbour-front at Porto Santo Stefano is covered by a local bus-service which meets the main trains and is alleged to make the journey in half an hour. Experience has shown, however, that the service is subject to long and unpredictable delays in transit: it is therefore safer to allow an hour for the trip either way, especially if you have a particular train or ferry to catch. Motorists should note that the road is narrow and has a number of blind corners, as well as a one-way system through the town of Orbetello; there is a large but sometimes crowded parking-lot on the harbour-front at Porto Santo Stefano.

Sea

Between Porto Santo Stefano and Giglio Porto, there are two car-carrying services, TO.RE.MAR. and Maregiglio. During the summer season – from June 28th to September 9th – there is also a hydrofoil service for pedestrians. The regular car ferries take approximately one hour for the passage between the mainland and the island; the hydrofoil takes about 25 minutes. Motorists who want to take their cars to Giglio are advised to book passages in advance as the space for vehicles on the ferries is strictly limited.

TO.RE.MAR. has its head office in Rome at Via del Tritone 87 (tels. 479358/476093/478806), where bookings can be made and the latest timetables consulted. The same facilities will be found in branch-offices as follows:

Livorno, Piazza Micheli 9 (tel. 28334/24113)
Piombino, Piazzale Premuda (tel. 32508/31100)
Elba, Portoferraio, Calata Italia (tel. 92022)
Elba, Porto Azzurro, Banchina IV Novembre (tel. 95004)
Elba, Rio Marina, Via Palestro 23 (tel. 962073)
Giglio, quayside (tel. 809349)
Porto Santo Stefano, Piazza IV Novembre (tel. 814615)

Maregiglio has its head office in Giglio on the harbour-front of Giglio Porto, just opposite the quay (tel. 809309/809238); it also has a branch office at Porto Santo Stefano in Piazza IV Novembre (tel. 812920).

Both lines run four services a day each during the high season between June 28th and September 8th, roughly alternating with each other. During the low seasons, April 1st to June 27th and September 10th to September 30th, there are three services a day by each line; during the winter months there are two services a day, by TO.RE.MAR., and two services a day by Maregiglio only up to October 31st.

The hydrofoil *Freccia del Giglio*, run by Giuseppe Rum of Giglio Porto, operates only between June 28th and September 9th; it makes the trip each way four times a day and five on Sundays, sometimes calling at the island of Giannutri *en route*.

During the high season, Maregiglio also runs the following motor-boat excursions from Giglio Porto: to Montecristo on Mondays and Wednesdays; to Giannutri on Tuesdays, Thursdays and Sundays; round the island of Giglio on Tuesdays, Thursdays and Sundays; along the coastline of Monte Argentario on Saturdays. Bookings should be made at the Maregiglio office in Giglio Porto (see above).

TRAVEL ON GIGLIO

Roads

The road system on Giglio is as limited as might be expected on so small an island. There are less than 13km. of asphalted motor road and about as much again of roughly metalled but passable tracks. Mule-tracks and footpaths make up the rest of the cross-country network, and access to many of the inlets along the coastline is by boat only. The highly coloured tourist map on sale at Giglio Porto indicates a much more extensive road-system optimistically described as 'under construction'. But the allocated funds ran out long ago, and there is no sign of any present attempt to complete it.

The main road (*strada provinciale*) connects Giglio Porto, the harbour-town on the east coast, with Giglio Castello, the ancient walled town on the crest of the island, and with Giglio Campese, the little seaside resort on the west coast; the distance from Giglio Porto to Giglio Castello is 6km., to Giglio Campese 8·5km. A branch of this road also leads off to Punta Arenella, a modern residential resort on the east coast, about two miles north of Giglio Porto. The narrowness of this road and its numerous bends as it zig-zags across the mountainsides demand special care from motorists.

Buses

Giglio Porto, Giglio Castello, and Giglio Campese are linked by a bus-service. There are about seven services a day – more in the high season – and a restricted service on Sundays and national holidays.

Taxis and car hire

A minibus taxi service meets incoming ferry-boats and charges from 5,000 lire upwards to transport visitors to their hotels. Its genial proprietor, Signor Ottaviano, who lives in Piazza Gloriosa, Giglio

Castello, will hire out self-drive cars (see under Elba, p. 38, for rates).

The only filling-station on Giglio is on the harbour-front at Porto. The so-called tourist map of the island can be purchased at a stationery and newspaper shop on the harbour-front, near the filling-station. A better and more accurate map of Giglio, to the scale 1:25,000 is issued and sold by the Istituto Geografico Militare, Firenze 50100 Viale Filippo Strozzi 14; the reference number is Folio 142 Section III.

HOTELS AND RESTAURANTS

For information about categories and prices see under Elba, (p. 42). Telephone numbers are given in brackets.

Giglio Porto and environs

HOTELS

Second Class   *Saraceno,* overlooking the sea from the headland between Giglio Porto and the next bay, Cala delle Cannelle, to the south. A modern and well equipped establishment constructed in and around the scanty remains of Giglio's only Roman structure, a villa. The hotel provides both rooms with baths and small self-contained suites (809234).

Castello Monticello, in a commanding position on the hillside about 1·5km. above the port and on the bus-route connecting with Castello, a castellated Victorian villa which has been extensively modernized(809252).

Arenella, overlooking the Caletta, a secluded cove with small sandy beach, north of Giglio Porto, it is about 3km. by road from the harbour and 1km. from the nearest point on the bus route. It is a pleasant, modern establishment with wide terraces providing rooms with baths or showers, furnished apartments and a number of dependent small family bungalows (809340).

Third Class   *Da Ruggero,* on the road leading up to the headland between Giglio Porto and Cala delle Cannelle, a small hotel which also provides furnished apartments (809121).

Fourth Class   *La Pergola*, The oldest inn in Giglio, short on modernity but long on atmosphere, situated on the sea-front above the yacht anchorage, at the northern end of Porto harbour; excellent family restaurant (809365).

PENSIONS

1st Class   *Demo's Hotel*, large (31 rooms) establishment situated at the northern end of Porto harbour, recently renovated; all rooms with W.C. and view of sea (809235).

2nd Class   *Bahamas*, villa situated on hillside above Giglio Porto; rooms available with baths and W.C. Provides motor-boat with air compressor for clients interested in under-water fishing (809254).

Uncategorized   *Pardini's Hermitage*, villa situated above isolated rocky cove to south of Giglio Porto, only accessible by sea. Management meets ferries with own motor-boats (809034).

Giglio Campese and environs

HOTELS

Second Class   *Campese*, a big, modern and conventional hotel built right on the beach of Campese Bay; 40 rooms, 27 with bath or shower (809203).

Third Class   *La Lampara*, Small hotel overlooking Campese beach: 12 rooms all with baths or showers (809022).

Fourth Class   *Albergo Le Palme*, overlooking sea at northern end of Campese Bay; quiet with garden and terrace; some rooms with bath (809208).

Bungalows and camping sites

La Ginestra   a small 'tourist-village' of modern bungalows on the hillside above Giglio Porto, accessible from the main road. Each bungalow has hot and cold running water, refrigerator, and modern conveniences (809380).

Clary   another *villago turistico* of 26 bungalows, just off the main road between Castello and Campese, overlooking the Bay of Campese; each bungalow has one double bed, one double-decker sleeping berth, and one extra cot; hot and cold water, free cooking gas cylinder, kitchen with equipment and refrigerator etc. Minibus available for excursions (809213).

Free camping is not permitted on Giglio but there is a controlled camping site, *Baia del Sole* (tel. 809387), on the west side of the island, north of Campese Bay and accessible from the main road between Castello and Campese. It gives directly on to a stretch of rocky seashore from which it is possible to bathe; site facilities include water, electricity, sanitation, telephone, restaurant, food-shop, discotheque, and the recharging of compressed air cylinders for drivers.

Holiday lodgings are also provided in the private houses of many of the inhabitants of Giglio, some of whom offer self-contained apartments. A list of such accommodation may be obtained on application to the Azienda Autonoma Soggiorno e Turismo della 'Costa d'Argento', with its head office at Porto Santo Stefano, Corso Umberto 55A (tel. 814208), and its information office in Giglio Porto, Via Umberto I, 44 (tel. 809265).

Restaurants

Restaurants in Giglio generally offer unpretentious Italian menus with an emphasis on sea-food. Many of them are attached to the hotels already listed, and of these perhaps the most congenial is that of La Pergola with a long, vine-shaded terrace overlooking the harbour of Giglio Porto (and giving the hotel its name), and with several vaulted and gaily painted rooms for meals in cool or windy weather.

There are, however, a number of independent restaurants and *trattorie* of which perhaps the most highly recommended is 'Da Giovanni', situated just above the southern end of the beach at Giglio Campese. Others along the sea-front at Porto are the 'Cavaluccio Marina', with a reed-awning, near the ferry landing-stage, 'Da Meino' and 'Da Ruggero' in the same area, and 'Doria', slightly more expensive, further along the front towards the northern end of the harbour. At Campese, the 'American Bar' on the sea-front is in fact a restaurant.

In Giglio Castello, where there are no hotels, there are several *trattorie*. In the square, Piazza Gloriosa, outside the walls of the old town, 'Da Angiolino' serves good, unpretentious food at a reasonable price, and there is also 'Da Ede' with much the same appearance and reputation.

PRACTICAL INFORMATION

For most categories of information see the relevant sections under Elba.

Tourist information
Information Office 48, Via Umberto I, Giglio Porto (tel. 809265).

Health and drinking water
The doctor and health officer for the Commune of Giglio lives in Porto; his telephone number is 809289. There is a first aid post at Giglio Castello in Via Circonvallazione (tel. 809293). The pharmacy is in Giglio Porto; it is run by Signor Pieri in Via Oreglia.

It is inadvisable to drink ordinary tap-water in Giglio unless it has been boiled or otherwise sterilized. Bottled mineral-water, which can be tasteless and still (*non-frizzante*) makes a safe substitute.

Bank
Cassa di Risparmio di Firenze, 14 Via Oneglia, Giglio Porto.

Shopping and Souvenirs
There is a grocery, stationer and one souvenir shop situated along the harbour front of Giglio Porto. There are also shops along the Via Provinciale.

Dancing
The Hotel Campese at Giglio Campese has music for dancing.

Holidays and Feast days
The two local holidays are September 22nd, the feast day of the patron saint, St Mamilian, and November 18th, anniversary of the victorious repulse of the last raid by Tunisian pirates at the end of the eighteenth century.

Post Office
Via Oneglia, Giglio Porto.

GEOGRAPHY

Giglio, the second largest island in the Tuscan Archipelago, lies 14·5km. west of the Monte Argentario peninsula and just north of Latitude 42. The island is the summit of a submerged mountain of granite, a granite streaked with bands of quartz which is different in type from that of the western end of Elba and probably an older formation. The island is approximately 8·8km. long from Punta del Morto in the north to Punta del Capel Rosso in the south; it is 4·9km. across from east to west at the point where the Franco promontory on the west coast gives it greatest width. Its general structure is that of a steep-sided, hump-backed ridge, running north and south, its highest point being Poggio della Pagana (1,618 feet), interestingly named after the heathen female spirit which is traditionally a threat to newborn babies in the archipelago. Round most of the coastline the sides of the ridge plunge so abruptly into the sea that they are broken only by rocky little coves where water-courses have furrowed the cliffs. There are a few sandy beaches however, notably a long one at Campese where the rocky Punta del Faraglione shelters the shoreline, and in the Caletta and the Cala delle Cannelle, the two coves north and south of Giglio Porto. The climate is noted as being particularly mild; there is no record of the temperature ever having reached freezing-point in winter or having climbed above 77°F (25°C.) in summer.

There are now three inhabited centres on the island. Until the nineteenth century, there was only one, Giglio Castello, the ancient walled village huddled round a fortress near the apex of the ridge as far away as possible from the sea and the sea-raiders who periodically descended on the island from North Africa. Giglio Porto, the obvious point of access from the mainland, was developed during the nineteenth century, its miniature harbour being protected by two elbow-shaped moles. Today it is the business and shopping centre of the island with a bank, a post office and a church. The third centre, Campese on the west coast, only grew up when Italian and foreign holiday-makers discovered the island and were attracted towards its beach and its afternoon sunlight which is screened off from the eastern coastline by the ridge of mountains.

From Giglio the two other southernmost islands of the archipelago are normally visible, **Giannutri** about 20km. to the south-east, and **Montecristo** 51·2km. to the west. Giannutri is a low-lying, eastward-facing crescent of land, about 2·4km. long, which used to be privately owned by one family, but now has a group of week-end cottages, mainly owned by Italians interested in underwater fishing, along its rocky coastline. Because for much of its history it was unpopulated, it preserves the ruins of a large Imperial Roman villa probably erected by the family of the Domitii Aenobarbi which owned Monte Argentario, Giglio and Giannutri in the first century A.D. During summer there is a regular ferry-service to Giannutri from Porto Santo Stefano. Montecristo is a rugged cluster of granite peaks, about 3·2km. from east to west and 4km. from north to south. The principal peak, *Monte della Fortezza*, reaches the impressive height of 2,096 feet. The island is difficult of access as the coastline is rocky and precipitous, and covered with dense *macchia* vegetation. It is uninhabited and strictly preserved as a nature reserve. Although summer excursions to Montecristo are run from Giglio, permission to stay there must be obtained from the Italian Government's office of state property (see p. 28).

FAUNA AND FLORA

The wild life of Giglio is limited to a few rabbits, and migratory birds, including grey partridges and woodcock. The only snake seen on the island is the non-venomous *Coluber viridiflavus*. Trees are comparatively scarce; those growing in the more sheltered areas include olives, chestnuts, figs, umbrella pines, evergreen oaks, and arbutus. The non-cultivated mountain slopes are covered with a low-growing version of the Mediterranean *macchia* which includes several varieties of rockrose (*cistus*), buckthorn, lentisk, and tree-heather. When this *macchia* becomes dried out towards the end of summer, it is a serious fire-hazard.

HISTORY

Giglio was already an island in that remote epoch when Elba was still part of a promontory attached to the mainland; consequently it was not accessible to those nomadic hunters of the Palaeolithic Age who have left their relics in Elba. But the polished and sophisticated stone implements of Neolithic seafarers have been found in Giglio, which may have been their first landfall in the Tuscan Archipelago.

Apart from such archaeological indications, nothing is known of the island's early history. It is presumed that it was visited and perhaps settled by the Ilvates, that Ligurian people which is thought to have left its name to Elba. The Etruscans left their mark on the neighbouring mainland – at Orbetello and Monte Argentario – and may therefore have come to Giglio. The island's Roman name, *Aegilium*, is obviously Greek in derivation and is likely to have been bestowed by early Greek sea-farers: it appears to mean 'Goat Island' or, conceivably, 'Island on which the sea breaks'. Its modern name is, of course, a corruption of *Aegilium* and has nothing to do with the Italian word *giglio*, meaning 'lily', although this flower has now become the stylized emblem of the island.

From Latin authors, we know that the Romans used both Giglio and Giannutri as places of enjoyment and refuge; their testimony is supported by the remains of Roman villas constructed on both islands. Little now survives of the Giglio villa, though some of its brickwork is to be found on the premises of the Hotel Saraceno; in the eighteenth century its ruins were more conspicuous, with columns and capitals still standing and a system of lead water-pipes. There was then a harbour-mole of Roman brickwork which has also been demolished. It seems likely that the inverted marble Corinthian capital, used as a holy water stoup in the church at Giglio Castello, may have come from this site. In the first century A.D., both Giglio and Giannutri, like Monte Argentario itself, belonged to the immensely wealthy Roman family of the Domitii Aenobarbi who probably built the villas. Literary evidence suggests there was more vegetation on Giglio in classical times; even as late as the fifth century A.D., the late-Roman poet, Rutilius Namazianus, describing his voyage to Rome from Gaul, wrote, 'From a distance I looked up at the wooded heights of Igilium'. It is interesting to note that by his time the island's name had already taken one step towards its present form.

Not long after Rutilius had passed Giglio in his ship, the fifth century Bishop of Palermo, Mamilianus, arrived by a circuitous route in the Tuscan Archipelago. He had been removed from his see in Sicily by the king of the invading Vandals, Genseric, and banished to North Africa. From there he escaped in a small boat, along with three monks, and fled first to Sardinia and then to Elba where he lived on the outskirts of what is now Marina di Campo. But on the southern horizon loomed the profile of Montecristo, an even lonelier refuge, and eventually he went there to settle in a cave high up on the mountain slopes and to gain the reputation of a wise and saintly hermit. He forecast that, when he died, a cloud would rise from the mountain top, and this was in due course spotted by the people of

Giglio who, for reasons of self-preservation, kept a good watch on the horizons. They hastened over to Montecristo and secured the body of the saint for their island, being protected by a storm from a party of Elbans who had sailed on the same pious errand. St Mamilian remained undisturbed in his tomb at Giglio Castello for six hundred years until the Pisans became the dominant power in the Tuscan islands and removed his bones to their city. But Giglio was permitted to retain his right arm which is still preserved there, encased in a silver reliquary and honoured on the Saint's feast day, September 22nd.

The first mention of Giglio after the dark ages of invasions and confusion comes in an agreement of about the year 800 between the Emperor Charlemagne and Pope Leo III to hand possession of the island over to the monks of the Abbey of Three Fountains, just outside Rome. But the monks, unable to defend their possession, offered it to the powerful medieval family of the Aldobrandeschi. Thereafter, in a series of dynastic transactions, it passed from one noble family to another and finally to the Commune of Perugia. In 1241 the people of Giglio were able to watch, in the channel between their island and the mainland, the sea-battle in which the Emperor Frederick II, nick-named *Stupor Mundi* (Wonder of the World), defeated a Genoese fleet; the Genoese, who supported Pope Gregory IX, were ferrying prelates and clergy to Rome to attend an ecumenical council which the Pope had convoked against the Emperor.

Throughout this period of changing overlordships the Gigliesi were in fact obliged to keep an anxious watch on the sea: they were constantly a prey to the Saracen pirates from North Africa and Sardinia who would sweep along the Italian coastline in search of slaves and booty. In 1448, when the island was occupied by Alfonso of Aragon, he found it so depopulated that he transferred to it fifty families from the Neapolitan area of his possessions. However, eleven years later he sold it to Pope Pius II, head of the Piccolomini family, and for the next hundred years it passed from one member of that family to another until one of them, the Duke of Amalfi, sold it to Eleanor of Toledo. This princess married Cosimo de'Medici and so, in 1558, Giglio became part of what was to be the Grand Duchy of Tuscany. But once again, it was in sad condition; in 1544 it had been raided by the notorious Saracen pirate, Khair-ed-Din, nick-named Barbarossa, who had carried off 700 of its inhabitants, probably more than half the population, into slavery.

Under the Grand Duchy, which undertook the defence of the archipelago against the corsairs, Giglio seems to have enjoyed peace and comparative prosperity. Ferdinand I, the third of the Tuscan grand dukes, built the massive watch-tower which still stands overlooking Campese Bay. And after the grand duchy had passed to the Lorraine dynasty, one of the Austrian grand dukes, Peter Leopold, enacted that all the land in Giglio should be divided up among its families who thus became peasant-proprietors. The only exception he made was the westward-jutting promontory, south of Campese where the Gigliesi had traditionally enjoyed the free right to cut wood and which was therefore called *Franco* or 'Common land'. Unfortunately, in comparatively modern times, through some mysterious transaction by the local administration, the land called *Franco* was sold to a wealthy newcomer to the island and has now become private property.

After it had been absorbed into the grand duchy, Giglio virtually ceased to have any history of its own. However, long after Europe had moved on to the era of revolutions and the advent of nation-states, Giglio did live through one episode which recalled its troubled past. Late in the autumn of 1799, ten years after the French revolution, a force of 2,000 Tunisian pirates made one more raid on the island and attacked Giglio Castello. They were beaten off – stopped in their tracks, according to local tradition, by the spiritual strength of St Mamilian's right arm which was brandished from the walls. The islanders' victory is still celebrated with a public holiday every November 18th.

ARCHAELOGY AND ARCHITECTURE

The archaeology of Giglio still awaits systematic investigation. The neolithic people who may have been its first settlers left traces of their presence in the form of arrow-heads, flint knives, bone needles and daggers, and bone sickles set with flints. Some bronze implements, dating from the late Bronze Age, have been found near Campese.

Both at Giglio and at Giannutri, skin-divers have found traces of a number of wrecked Roman cargo-vessels. The most productive was discovered in 1962 off the north-west coast of Giannutri in what appears to have been the anchorage off the Roman villa on that island; the cargo was pottery – mainly dishes and vases of Campanian ware – which was found still in its straw packing, and all that was salvaged is now in the possession of the Commune of Porto Santo Stefano.

A list of localities in which indications of other wrecks have been detected is as follows:

Giglio

Le Scole, offshore rocks near the promontory between Giglio Porto and Cala delle Cannelle; at a depth of 170 feet, pottery dating from the second and third centuries A.D.

Punta Arenella, north of Giglio Porto; at depths between 90 and 150 feet, amphoras of several periods.

Punta Capel Rosso, southernmost point of Giglio; large quantity of pottery fragments attributed to first century B.C. found at a depth of between 150 and 200 feet.

Punta Gabbianera: anchor-stocks and amphoras of various shapes and sizes, dating from second century B.C. to second century A.D.

Secche del Campese, in Campese Bay; presumed wreck identified at depth of approximately 100 feet but strong local currents have buried it beneath the sand; a few amphoras, attributed to second or first century B.C., recovered.

Giannutri

Cala Scirocco, on SE coast; at depth of 130 to 146 feet, Roman cargo-ship, its salvaged contents now in museum at Orbetello.

Punta Secca, at northern tip of island; wreck lying at depth of about 80 feet.

Cala dello Spalmatoio, on east side of island, wreck at 146 feet.

Roman Villa

The Roman Villa on Giannutri probably dates from the first century A.D., though parts of it may be earlier. Its ruins, which include the colonnade of the bath-house and walls constructed in the brickwork known as *opus reticulatum,* are the most extensive of any of this period in the Tuscan Archipelago. A similar villa on Giglio, just above the harbour of Giglio Porto, survived with conspicuous remains until the eighteenth century but has now been virtually obliterated apart from a few fragments of *opus reticulatum* on the premises of the Hotel Saraceno. The ruins, which presumably included the usual swimming pool and baths, were known to the islanders as *Bagni del Saraceno* (Saracen's Baths) but were of course Roman in origin.

The medieval period of the Tuscan islands is richly illustrated by the stronghold of Giglio Castello, perched on the humped backbone of the island at a height of 1,314 feet, and looking out on three sides over a precipitous drop to the sea. The township shelters behind high medieval walls, fortified with cylindrical and quadrilateral towers;

within there is a labyrinth of steep and winding alleys and flights of steps, sometimes passing through archways beneath the ancient granite-built houses. Unfortunately the two central points of the township, the *Parish Church of St Mamilian* and the *Fortress,* have both been extensively altered and modernized. Traces of fourteenth century masonry may be seen along the side of the church; within are the remains of two fourteenth-century frescoes, and an ivory Christ, attributed to the sixteenth-century sculptor, Giovanni da Bologna. The silver reliquary, containing the right arm of St Mamilian, has several votive offerings attached, including a number of Turkish coins presumably captured from pirates attacking the island. The fortress, at the highest point of the town, is now an Italian navy signal station and the public is not admitted; its gateway dates from the fourteenth century.

Within the entrance to the walled town, a mural tablet records the repulse of the last raid by North African pirates on Giglio. The Latin inscription may be translated, 'In memory of the people of Giglio, few in numbers and comparatively unarmed, who on the 18th of November, 1799, repulsed and put to flight two thousand Tunisians, the Communal Council one hundred years later decreed that the 18th of November should be a public holiday as a lasting memorial.'

Apart from the picturesque maze of medieval streets in Giglio Castello and the majestic watch-tower erected by Ferdinand I, Grand Duke of Tuscany, to protect Campese Bay, there are no architectural monuments of note in Giglio. Of specialized local interest are the numerous, small, stone-vaulted wine-presses scattered over the terraced hillsides. They are called *palmenti,* and contained troughs in which the grapes were trodden by the peasant-owners of the vineyards. Today most of them are in a ruinous condition and many are used as stables for donkeys; but in the more complete specimens you can still see the stone sill with a central runnel through which the grape-juice flowed into containers.

POPULATION AND ECONOMY

The latest figure for the native population of Giglio is 1,714, more than half of which lives in and around Giglio Porto. The island's traditional industries are agriculture — which means vine-growing — and fishing, but both of these are in decline, and the tourist industry has become its principal source of income. The steep rocky slopes of

Giglio have been extensively terraced for vines and during the early nineteenth century the wine produced from their grapes was an important export. But the vines were wiped out by the phylloxera epidemic in the 1860s and 1870s, and although the terraces were replanted by resistant stocks, they have suffered much from summer fires which periodically sweep across the hillsides and destroy the vegetation. The Giglio wine industry has also been hit by the fact that Italy as a whole produces more wine than it can consume or export; the tendency therefore is now to reduce output to that which can be consumed locally. Unlike Elba, Giglio has no important mineral resources although there was until recently a small pyrites mine near Campese which offered limited local employment. The modest island fishing fleet is based on Giglio Porto.

GOVERNMENT AND ADMINISTRATION

The island forms a single Commune, with the official seat of the Mayor and Council in Giglio Castello.

Giglio is included in the Italian administrative province of Grosseto, and up-to-date information about its hotels and their tariffs may be obtained from the tourist organization of that province – the *Ente Provinciale per il Turismo di Grosseto* – its address being Viale Monterosa 206, Grosseto (tel. 22534). A delegate of the provincial council lives on the island.

The only Italian police force normally operating on the island is the *Carabinieri* who have an office on the harbour-front at Giglio Porto.

RELIGION

Like other Italians, the people of Giglio are officially Roman Catholic, and their island is too small to accommodate places of worship for other denominations. There are only two Roman Catholic churches in the island, a modern edifice in Giglio Porto and a much older one, though altered and restored, in Giglio Castello.

THE PEOPLE, LANGUAGE AND CUSTOMS

The people of Giglio are clean, vigorous and friendly; they speak an Italian which has much less of the Tuscan aspirated 'c' than that spoken in Elba. Since the island has been until recently mainly an Italian holiday resort, it may be more difficult to find English-speakers among the staff of its hotels and shops. But some there are, and no doubt the number of local linguists will increase as more foreign tourists find their way to the island.

Like the people of Elba, the Gigliesi are of mixed descent. Neapolitan families were transplanted to the island in the fifteenth century, and it seems possible that at least some of the corsairs who raided Giglio may have settled there: one of the island surnames is Rum which seems to derive from the Turkish *Roum,* meaning Roman or European.

The only local custom observed by the authors is the engaging habit, typical of a very small community, of everybody on the island referring to each other by their Christian names, prefixed by the respectful *Signor* or *Signora*; thus the Provincial Delegate was known universally as Signor Giuliano, and the taxi-driver as Signor Ottaviano.

WINE

The wine made on Giglio is virtually all white, and ranges from a rough and sometimes even cloudy *vino sciolto* (carafe wine) to a superior bottled product called *Ansonaco.* This is said to be related to the Elban *Procanico* but has a character all its own. It is amber in colour, dry and elegant in flavour, and has a fairly high alcoholic content which is not surprising considering the amount of sunlight that falls on the slopes where its grapes are grown. It has enough authority to be drunk as an aperitif, but also goes excellently with highly seasoned sea-food.

ROUTES

The minuscule dimensions of Giglio make it possible for a motorist to see all parts of the island accessible by road within half a day; the visitor without a car can explore the same roads by bus within the day. But it cannot be emphasized too strongly that this 'quick tour' – from Giglio Porto up to Giglio Castello and then down the west slope to Campese – does not in any way convey the flavour of the island. There are two reasons for this: on the one hand, the asphalted road system is confined to the northern half of the island while the southern half can only be penetrated by rough tracks and footpaths; on the other hand, much of the coastline of Giglio is only accessible by boat. Many Italians, who go there regularly for their holidays,

Punta del Fenaio

Antico Faro

Punta del Faraglione

CAMPESE

GIGLIO CASTELLO

La Caletta
Punta Arenella
Punta del Lazzaretto
Punta Gabbianara

GIGLIO PORTO

Poggio d. Chiusa

Poggio della Pagana

Cala delle Cannelle

Monte Casteluccio

Poggio Terneti

Giglio Diagram of Excursions & Walks

—— Roads
—— Bridle tracks
--- Footpaths

Punta del Capel Rosso

N

0   500m   1km

insist that it is primarily a place for 'mucking about in boats' rather than for exploring on foot. With an inflatable rubber dinghy and a small outboard motor, you can go off for the day to one of the enchanting rocky coves which are otherwise inaccessible, and pass the day there bathing or sun-bathing and skin-diving in the incomparably clear water. Small yachts, of course, give the same liberty but require moorings either at Giglio Porto or in the Cala delle Cannelle.

EXCURSIONS FROM GIGLIO PORTO

1: To Cala delle Cannelle (1 km.)

This short walk takes you over the headland to the south of Giglio Porto and into the next bay where there is a sandy beach, a small marina, and (at the time of writing) a still unfinished development of miniature seaside apartments.

Follow the main road uphill out of Giglio Porto and just after its first bend to the right take the first turning to the left – a track signposted *Le Cannelle* which is also passable for cars. After crossing the neck of the headland, it follows an easy slope down to the area behind the beach.

2: To La Caletta and Punta Arenella (3·5 km.)

This excursion, which can be done either by car or on foot, takes you north of Giglio to the only other sandy beach on the east side of the island.

Follow the main road up the hill as far as the Castello Monticello hotel, easily recognizable by its castellated façade and commanding position. Turn right off the mainroad just below the hotel; the fork is about 1·5 km. from Giglio Porto. You then follow a road which pursues a fairly level course across the hillside above the Punta Gabbianara and the Punta del Lazzaretto; immediately below the road on the right can be seen the large private villa which is a conversion of the old *Lazzaretto*, or quarantine hospital, set in extensive and well-kept grounds. As the road begins to run downhill, it passes also on the right the Hotel Arenella and its dependencies; then a sharp turn to the right leads steeply downwards, past several private villas, to the small beach in the cove called La Caletta; the promontory at its southern end is the Punta Arenella.

3: To the lighthouse on Punta del Fenaio (7·2 km.)

This lighthouse is situated on the northernmost point of Giglio; part of the way to it can be done by car or bus, but the final stretch is a rough mule-track which can only be followed on foot. (If taking the bus, ask for *Il bivio dell'Antico Faro*.)

Take the main road up out of Giglio Porto as far as the Old Lighthouse (*Antico Faro*), a massive building partly in ruins with the tower projecting from its roof. Just below it, at a distance of about 3·5 km. from Giglio Porto, an unmade road leads off the main road to the right; this can be followed for some distance by car but it is advisable to park beside it before reaching the end so as to be able to turn and also to leave passage for other cars. This road passes the fenced grounds of the Old Lighthouse and eventually comes to a dead-end, with a mule-track leading out of it towards the headland. On clear days there are magnificent views of the Italian coastline to the north-east, the islands of Pianosa and even Elba to the north, and, after you have emerged on the final slope down to the modern lighthouse, of Montecristo to the west.

EXCURSIONS FROM GIGLIO CASTELLO

4: To Campese Bay (6·5 km. from Castello; 8 km. from Porto)

Since Campese is one of the three termini of the island's asphalted road system, it can of course be reached by car as easily from Giglio Porto as from Giglio Castello; but since there is a bus-route to it from Castello, we have listed it here.

For those following the main road twisting downhill from Castello, the road to Campese turns off to the left soon after the fourth bend; it zig-zags down the north-western slopes and enters the cluster of houses that line Campese Bay just above a little promontory crowned with the fine cylindrical *tower* erected towards the end of the sixteenth century by the Archduke Ferdinand I of Tuscany, fourth son of Cosimo de' Medici. The tower, which rises from a rectangular, fortified base, was intended as a decisive answer to the raids by Tunisian pirates; today it is private property and not open to visitors. But its exterior is impressive and lends distinction to what is otherwise a pleasant but unpretentious little seaside resort. Campese Bay faces north, with the tower and its promontory sheltering an inlet for small craft at its eastern end, and with the cliffs of Punta del Faraglione swinging round to a detached pillar of rock at the western end of the curve. Between the tower and the cliffs, there is almost 1 km. of fine sandy beach, making Campese the best place in Giglio for families with small children.

For determined walkers, there is also a footpath down to Campese from Castello, leaving the main road just below the walls of the old town. Unexplored by the writers, the map shows it as following a more direct but much steeper route down to the bay than that taken by the road.

5: To Punta del Capel Rosso by the western road (8 km.)

This excursion to the southernmost point of Giglio begins from the piazza outside the main gate of Giglio Castello, a square sloping gently upwards from west to east which is used as car-park and bus-stop. From its upper right-hand corner, a road leads south between modern buildings to give access to the southern part of Giglio. For 1 km. its surface is asphalted for the convenience of carts and lorries transporting rubbish to the island's tip; it runs almost due south across the western slopes below a height called *Poggio della Chiusa* (1,572 feet). Visitors making this excursion should turn off to the right along an unsurfaced but roughly metalled road which swings first west and then south again round the slopes of Giglio's highest peak, *Poggio della Pagana* (1,618 feet); it is quite passable for cars. It swings steadily downhill round the spurs of the central ridge on the left and above the terraced vineyards dropping to the sea-shore on the right and comes to a full stop at a point about 5 km. from Giglio Castello in a valley called Bredice. (Although the local map shows several footpaths or mule-tracks leading down from this road to the shore, these have been virtually obliterated by disuse or vineyard terracing and should not be attempted except by those prepared for a very rough scramble.) At the end of the road cars should be turned and parked; the rest of the journey is on foot along a rough but practicable path which winds in and out of the torrent valleys in a south-easterly direction, and then turns due south to the lighthouse above the point.

6: To Poggio della Pagana and by mountain-path to Punta del Capel Rosso (about 8 km.)

This excursion, which is offered only to those who enjoy rough walking, also begins from the road which leads south out of the piazza of Giglio Castello. Follow the asphalted road past the turning taken in Excursion 5 to the point at which it crosses a saddle between Poggio della Chiusa and Poggio della Pagana. Here it splits into three; the lefthand (and asphalted) fork goes only to the far-from-salubrious and most unsightly tip on the slope above Cala delle Cannelle; the central fork leads obliquely downhill; the righthand fork is to be followed. It starts as an unsurfaced road going slightly uphill to a small quarry on the eastward slope of Poggio della Pagana; just before the quarry is reached, a footpath branches off to the left and carries on southwards across the eastern slopes of the central ridge. Those wishing to climb Poggio della Pagana should leave both path and road and follow the general line of the spur leading up to the summit from the east side. From the summit (1,618 feet) there is on clear days a fine panorama which embraces most of the island, a wide section of the mainland coast and the neighbouring islands; in good conditions you can see as far as Elba to the north and Corsica to the west. Those following the footpath south will find that its general line is indicated by poles carrying a telephone-line to the lighthouse at Punta del Capel Rosso. After passing on the right both Poggio della Pagana and the next peak (called *Monte Casteluccio,* 1,547 feet) it crosses a pass to the west side of the ridge and the western slopes of the southernmost peak, *Poggio Ternete* (1,261 feet). Within sight of Punta del Capel Rosso, the path turns downhill towards it, joining further down with the path followed in Excursion 5.

SELECTED BIBLIOGRAPHY

IN ENGLISH

Vernon Bartlett, *A Book about Elba* (Chatto & Windus, 1965). Now in paperback.

Major-General Sir Neil Campbell, *Napoleon at Fontainebleau and Elba* (John Murray, 1869).

Robert Christophe, *Napoleon on Elba* (Macdonald, 1964), translated from *Napoléon, Empéreur de l'Ile d'Elba* (Librairie Arthème Fayard, 1959).

Sir Richard Colt Hoare, Bt, *A Classical Tour through Italy and Sicily (districts not described by Eustace)* (Mawman, 1818), containing the first English description of Elba.

A.S. Mackenzie-Grieve, *Aspects of Elba and the other islands of the Tuscan Archipelago* (Jonathan Cape, 1964).

Polunin and Huxley, *Flowers of the Mediterranean* (Chatto & Windus, 1965).

IN ITALIAN

Ente per la Valorizzazione dell'Isola d'Elba, *Questa è l'Elba* (Portoferraio, 1972).

Vincenzo Mellini, *Memorie Storiche dell'Isola d'Elba* (Giusti, Livorno, 1890).

Giuseppe Ninchi, *Storia dell'Isola d'Elba* (Broglia, Portoferraio, 1815).

Luigi de Pasquali, *Storia dell'Elba dalle Origini ai Tempi Nostri* (Stefanoni, Lecco, 1973).

Michelangelo Zecchini, *L'Elba dei Tempi Mitici* (Pacini, Pisa, 1970), with appendix on the exhibits in the Antiquarium at Marciana.

L'Archeologia nell'Arcipelago Toscano (Pacini, Pisa, 1971).

INDEX

Accommodation, 32, 42–56, 59; (Giiglio) 231–3
Acquabona, 71, 183
Acqua Calda, Springs, 226
Acquaviva, 173; Promontory, 135
Agriculture, 140; (Giglio) 241
Air Travel, 34
Allied Poweers, 118, 121, 123
Amiens, Peace of, 117
Appiano Family, Lords of Piombino and Elba, 104–5, 107–11, 113, 117, 132, 133, 185, 191, 205, 208, 214–15, 220
Archaeology, 99, 131–7, 202; (Giglio) 239–41
Aristotle, 97–8
Aroodje, 106
Arrighi, Monsignor, 157–8
Austria and the Austrians, 112–14, 128, 161, 171, 186, 194, 205, 239

Baciocchi, Elisa, 118, 120, 165
Bagnaia, 176, 178, **179**, 181, 183
Bagno, **226**
Banks, 65–6; (Giglio), 234
Barbarossa see Aroodje and Khair-ed-Din
Barbarossa Beach, 70, 72, 136, 184, 186, **188**
Barbatoio, Mt., 182, 200
Beaches, 30, 70
Bello, Mt., 115, 173–4
Bellucci, Giovanni Battista, 108, 155
Bertrand, Count, 118, 124, 158, 161, 164, 171
Biodola Bay, 30, 32, 37, 69, 70, 77, 174, **175**, 182, 225, 227
Bivio Boni, 65, 69, 154, 170, 174–6, 181, 183, 227
Boating, 70; (Giglio) 245

Bonaparte, Letizia, 122, 125, 168
Bonaparte, Mathilde, 160, 171
Bonaparte, Napoleon, 28, 31, 73, 115, 117–28, 157–68, 170–2, 186, 194, 203, 213, 218–19
Borghese, Paolina, 120–2, 124–5, 166–8, 170–1
Borgia Family, 105
Botro Valley, 198
Buoncompagni Family, 113–14, 118
Buses, 37–8, 60; (Giglio) 230

Cala delle Cannelle, 235, 240, **245**, 248
Cala dell'Innamorata, 196
Calamita, Mt., 30, 32, 70, 77, 81, 137, 184, **194–7**, 198
Cala Scirocco, 240
Cala della Spalmatoio, 240
Calendozio, Mt., 193
Caletta, 235, **245**
Cambronne, Marshal, 120, 124, 161, 164
Camerini, Architect, 108, 155–6
Campbell, Sir Neil, 123–4, 164, 172
Campiglia Marittima, 37–6 232–3
Campo, 78, 112, 116, 134, 137, 141, 143, 199, 201, 202, 207, 211
Campo all'Aia, 70–1, 132, 135, 182, 225, **226–7**
Capanne, Mt., 29, 32, 78–81, 83, 86, 97, 100–1, 140, 174, 178, 204, 208, 210, 212, **217–24**
Capo d'Arco, 137, 188, 190
Capo Bianco, 70, 131, 135, 154, 173
Capo Castello, Roman Villa, 134, 193
Capo d'Enfola, 81, 135, 140, 154, **173–4**
Capo di Fonza, 199, 202

Capoliveri, 37, 69, 73, 77, 81–2, 100, 103–4, 107, 109, 113–14, 116, 128, 134, 137–8, 142, 184, 189, **194–7**, 198–9
Capo Pero, 136
Capo Pini, 199
Capo Poro, 137
Capo S. Andrea, 103, 136
Capo della Tavola, 189
Capo Vite, 136, 193
Capraia, 28, 41
Car Hire, 38–9; (Giglio) 230
Casa del Duca, 108, 131, 176
Castello, Mt., 183, 190, **197–8**
Castiglione, 132, 172
Caubbio, 134, 201
Cavalline, La, 208–10
Cavo, 30, 35, 37, 69–70, 77, 100, 133–4, 136–7, 186–7, **189–93**
Cavoli, 69–70, 78, 80, 203, **209–11**, 212
Cellini, Benvenuto, 109, 115, 161
Cenno, Mt., 210
Cerbone, St, 101, 132, 220
Charles, Archduke, 113–14
Charles V, Emperor, 105, 107–8, 110, 155
Chiessi, 133, 135–6, **212–13**, 219
Cima del Monte, **190, 197–8**
Cinemas, 69
C.I.T., 34, 39
Classical Period, 97–100
Climate, 30, 60–2; (Giglio) 235
Clothes, 62–3
Cocchero, Mt., 134
Colle d'Orano, 212–13, 217
Colle Reciso, 97, **181–3**, 200, 201
Corbella Island, 137
Corsairs, 102, 105, 112, 155, 239, 241–2
Corsica, 28–9, 78, 96, 102, 105, 109, 129, 213, 219, 222, 248
Cote, Mt., 220, 222
Customs and Folklore, 143–4; (Giglio) 243

Dalesme, General, 118–19
Dancing see Night Life
Dark Ages, 100–2
de Fisson, Lieut.-Col., 117
de Gregorio, Marquis of Squillace, 116–17
de l'Herault, Pons, 120, 164
Demidoff, Prince Anatole, 160, 162, 171
Dentice, Brigadier, 116
de Pons, Captain Joseph, 111, 156–7
Dragut, 109
Drinking Water, 32, 65; (Giglio) 234

Economy, 139–40; (Giglio) 241
E.N.I.T., 34, 36–7, 42, 59
Etruscans, 99, 180, 237; Remains, 99, 131–2
E.V.E., 39, 42, 59, 139, 151, 159, 189, 192, 215

Fabricia, 100, 108, 157, 177
Faleria, 100, 134
Fauna, 84–6; (Giglio) 236
Feast Days, 72–3; (Giglio) 234
Feraia, 107–9, 151, 155, 176
Fetovaia, 37, 70, 78, 137, 203, **209–11**, 212
Flora see Vegetation
Focardo, Fort, 113–14, **189**
Fontainebleau, Treaty of, 118, 120, 123, 157, 165, 171
Fonte de Napoleone, **222**
Fonte del Prete, 80
Fonza, Mt., 201–2
Food, 144
Forno, **174**, 175
Fosse del Pino, 134
Fosso della Madonna, 108
France and the French, 106, 109, 112–13, 115–18, 124, 182, 186
Franco promontory, 235, 239

Galenzana, 137
Gemelli Islands, 137, 196

Genoa and the Genoese, 36, 103–6, 109, 111; 180, 238

Geography, 28–30, 77–9; (Giglio) 235

Geology, 29, 79–83

Ghiaie Beach, Le, 70–1, 81, 154, 173

Giannutri, 28, 96, 222, 230, **235–6**, 237, 239; Roman Villa, **240**

Giglio, 28, 33, 96, 101, 222, **228–48**; map, 244

Giglio Campese, 230, 235, 239, 240, 242–3, **246–7**

Giglio Castello, 230, 235, 238, **240–1**, 243, 246–7

Giglio Porto, 229–30, 235, 240–3, 245–6

Giogo Fort, 109–10, 114

Giove, Mt., 132–3, 190–1, 218–19, 222

Gneccarina Valley, 133, 213, 219

Golf, 71

Gorgona, 28, 41, 222

Government and Administration, 141; (Giglio) 242

Granite Quarries, 100, 134, 178, 209

Grassera, 106, 133, 189, **191**

Great Britain, 115–17

Greeks, 98–9, 154; Remains, 132, 134

Gregory XI, Pope, 79, 104

Grosseto, 28, 36, 228

Grosso, Mt., 82, 137, 192

Grotta d'Oggi, 80

Grotta Reale, 135

Grotte, Le, Roman Villa, 131, 135, **176–7**; Promontory, 135, 176, 181, 183

Guardia, La, 213

Guided Tours, 38, 60

Health, 63–4; (Giglio) 234

History, 96–130; (Giglio) 236–9

Hotels *see* Accommodation

Hugo, Victor, 159, 168

Iron Mines, 29, 77, 81, 98–100, 102–4, 111, 115, 120, 129, 132–3, 138–9, 151, 190–4

Italy, Unification of, 118, 128–9, 161, 185

John, Don, of Austria, 112, 186

Khair-ed-Din, 106–7, 109, 211, 238

Lacona, 30, 32, 69–70, 78, 114, 134, 181, 184, 198–9, **200**, 201, 204

Language, 142; (Giglio) 242

Lentisco, Mt., 134, 193

Leopold, Grand Duke of Tuscany, 115, 161, 166

Lido Beach, 69–70, 112, **199**

Literno Pass, 182

Livorno, 28, 35–6, 41, 104, 109, 115, 117–18, 125; 141

Lombards, 101, 132, 205, 208, 220

London, Treaty of, 110

Louis XVIII of France, 118, 120, 123, 124

Luceri, 103, 107

Madonna del Buonconsiglio, 81, 142, 206, **224**, 226

Madonna delle Grazie, 142, 196

Madonna di Lacona, 134, 200–1

Madonna di Monserrato, 31, 73, 113, 142, 184, **186–8**, 198

Madonna del Monte, 31, 73, 122, 132, 142, 211, **217–20**, 222

Madonna delle Neve, 142

Madonna Serrapinella, 142

Magazzini, 30, 86, 103, 176, **178**, 179, 181, 183, 198

Mamilian, St, 100–1, 237–9,

Maolo, Mt., 134, 222

Maps, 40, 149–50; (Giglio) 231

Mar di Capanna, Mt., 198

Marchand, Napoleon's valet, 118

Marciana (Alta), 30–1, 37, 73, 78, 83, 100, 103, 109–11, 113, 116, 122,

135–6, 138, 141–2, 178, 191, 211–12, **214–16**, 217, 220–4; Fortress, **215**; Museum, 131, 133, 213, **215**

Marciana Marina, 32, 37, 41, 73, 123, 133, 141, 203, 212, 214, **216–17**, 219, 221, 224–6

Margidore Beach, 70, 199–200

Marie-Louise, Empress, 120, 122, 124, 163, 166, 172

Marina di Campo, 30, 32, 37, 41, 69–71, 73, 78, 101, 140, 182, 184, 199, 201–2, **203–4**, 205, 207, 209, 212–13, 224, 237

Marmi, **181–3**

Mary Tudor, Queen of England, 110

Massa Marittima, 101

Mazarin, Cardinal, 112, 186

Medical Services see Health

Medici, de', Cosimo I, Grand Duke of Tuscany, 31, 106–10, 115, 129, 131, 138, 151, 155, 157, 161, 176, 238, 246

Meloria, Battle of, 103–4

Middle Ages, 102–4

Minerals, 68, 80–3, 191–2, 196, 208

Mola Bay, 136, 184, 189, 197

Moncione, Mt., **181–3**

Money Changing, 65–6

Montecristo, 28, 101, 104, 196, 230, **235–6**, 237–8, 246

Montserrat, General, 116–17, 182

'Monumento, Il', 182, 198, **201–2**

Morcone, 32, 69–70, 194, **196**; Promontory, 194

Mortaio, Il, 213, 221

Murat, Joachim and Caroline, 121, 124

Musetto, 102–3, 207

Napoleon III, Emperor, 128, 164

Naregno, 70, 113, 184, **189**

Night Life, 59, 69; (Giglio) 234

Nisportino, 176, **179**

Nisporto, 176, **179**

Ogliera Beach, 203

Orbetello, 228–9, 234

Ordicole Gorge, **220–1**

Orello, Mt., **181–3**, 201

Orsini Family, 105, 111

Ortano, 112, 189

Padulelle, Le, 115, 173

Palmaiola, 102, 112

Panche, Le, 180

Paolina Island, 132, 136, 226

Pareti, 37, 70, 137, 194, **196**

Patresi, 136, 213

Pericoli, Mt., 227

Perone, Mt., 85, 103, 134, 178, **205–8**, 212, 221–4

Petrol, 37, 40

Philip II, Emperor, 110

Philip V of Spain, 113–14

Pianosa, 28, 41, 79, 96, 104, 123, 125, 196, 209, 246

Pila, La, 140, 205, 226

Pinel, Governor, 113–14

Pinello, Mt., 182, 226–7

Piombino, 28, 34–6, 41, 99, 104–5, 107–12, 114–16, 118, 120, 130, 185, 193

Pisa and the Pisans, 34–6, 101–4,, 101–4, 110, 178, 180, 191–2, 205–9, 216, 228, 238

Pliny, 99

Poggio, 30, 32, 37, 83, 103, 132, 142, 206, 212, 216–17, 220, **221–4**

Poggio della Chiusa, 247–8

Poggio della Pagana, 235, **247–8**

Poggio Ternete, 248

Pomonte, 37–8, 81, 97, 100, 136, **209–11**, 212, 219

Poppe, Mt., 173

Population, 138; (Giglio) 241

Populonia, 99, 101, 132, 220

Porticciolo, 227

Porto Azzurro, 31–2, 37, 41, 65, 68–73, 77, 131, 135–8, 140–2, 171, 177, 179, 181, 183, **184–6**,

187–90, 193–4, 197–9, 203–4
Portoferraio, 28, 30–2, 35, 37–9, 41,
  59, 62, 64–6, 68–74, 77–8, 81, 98,
  100, 102, 104–5, 108–9, 112–18,
  121–2, 124, 128–32, 135, 138–41,
  143, **150–69**, 170, 172, 174, 177,
  179, 181–3, 185, 189–90, 193–4,
  197–9, 203, 214–17, 225–7
  Bay, **176–80**
  Falcon Fort, 108, 120, 129, 155,
    168
  Old City, 31, 151, **155–61**
  Palazzina dei Mulini, 31, 119, 120,
    124, 129, 159–60, **161–8**, 170–2
  Stella Fort, 108–9, 115, 120, 128,
    155, **161**
  Teatro dei Vigilanti, 125, 168
  Other Sites, 73, 109, 151–3, 156,
    168–60, 177
  Map, 152–3
Porto Longone, 68, 77, 111–14, 116,
  118, 120–1, 123, **184–5**, 186,
  188–9, 191, 205
Porto Santo Stefano, 28, 33, 228–9,
  236, 240
Postal Services, 73–4; (Giglio) 234
Pre-history, 96–7; (Giglio) 236;
  Remains, 131–5, 218, 227, 239
Procchio, 30, 32, 37, 69–70, 73, 78,
  117, 132, 170, 175, 181, **182**, 199,
  201–6, 216–17, 225, **226**
Profico, 134
Public Holidays, 72
Punta Agnone, 182, 226
Punta Arenella, 230, 240, 245
Punta del Capel Rosso, 235, 240,
  247–8
Punta del Cotoncello, 136
Punta del Faraglione, 235, 246
Punta del Fenaio, **246**
Punta Gabbianera, 240, 245
Punta del Lazzaretto, 245
Punta Le Tombe, 137
Punta della Madonna, 225
Punta dei Mangani, 137

Punta del Morto, 235
Punta del Nasuto, 225
Punta Perla, 137
Punta Polveraia, 136, 213
Punta dei Ripalti, 137, 195
Punta dello Stendardo, 188
Punto Pensiola, 174–5
Punto Pina, 179

Rail Travel, 35–6; (Giglio) 228
Ravelli, 171–2
Reale Beach, 70, 184, 186, 188–9
Religion, 141–2; (Giglio) 242
Restaurants, 58; (Giglio) 233–4
Riding, 72
Rio Marina, 30, 41, 68, 70–1, 73, 77,
  81, 133–7, 141, 151, **189–93**
  Mineral Museum, 192
Rio nell'Elba, 30, 68, 73, 77, 82, 99,
  103, 106, 109, 111, 113–14, 116,
  125, 129, 132–3, 137–8, 141, 143,
  179, **189–93**
Ripabianca, 137
Road Travel, 30–2, 36, 39–40, 148;
  (Giglio) 228, 230, 243
Romans, 99–100, 194, 207, 209, 214,
  237; Remains, 31, 99, 131–7, 157,
  159, 177, 193, 213, 226–7, 236–7,
  239–40
Rome, 28, 33, 35–6, 100, 104, 228

Sailing, 30, 71
San Bartolomeo, Mt., 211, 219
San Cerbone, Church, 187–8
San Cerbone, Hermitage, 132–3,
  219–20
San Francesco, Monastery, 120
San Giovanni, 115, 122, 131, 142,
  176, 183
San Giovanni in Campo, Church,
  103, 134, 178, **206–7**, 217
San Giuseppe, Cave, 133
San Lorenzo, Church, 103, 133, 178,
  216
Sanmarino, Architect, 108

San Martino, Valley, 131, 182; Mt., 198, 201; *see also* Villa San Martino

San Piero, 32, 37, 69, 80, 103, 113, 134, 143, 204, **205–8**, 209–10

San Quirico, Church, 133, 191

San Rocco, Church, 78, 151

Santa Caterina, Church, 191

Santa Lucia, Shrine, 73, 142–3

Sant'Andrea, 37, 78, 132, 136, 212, **213–14, 225**

Santa Rita, Chapel, 226

Sant'Ilario, 30, 32, 37, 80–1, 103, 113, 143, 204, **205–8**, 212, 218, 224

Santo Stefano, Church, 103, 176, **178**

Saracena, Torre, 133, 216

Saracens, 102, 104, 180, 196, 208, 216, 238; *see also* Corsairs

Sardinia, 78, 101–2, 237–8

Sardinian Sea, Battle of the, 99

Scaglieri, 70, **175**, 227

Schioparello, 73

Scole, Le, 240

Sea-fishing, 70–1, 140

Sea Travel, Excursions and Ferries, 35, 40–1, 60; (Giglio) 229

Secche del Campese, 240

Seccheto, 32, 68, 70, 78, 80, 100, 134, 159, 177, 203, 208, **209–11**, 212

Serra, Mt., 179, 190–1

Shooting, 72

Shopping, 66–8; (Giglio) 234

Skin-diving, 30, 70, 131, 213

Spain and the Spanish, 110–14, 186–7, 194–5

Spanish Succession, War of the, 113–14

Spartaia, 70

Spas, 64

Sport, 70–2

Stecchi Beach, 137

Stella Bay, 70, 78, 99, 137, 196, 199–200

Straccoligno, 70

Strega, Mt., 179, 190

Tambone, Mt., 182, 198, 201–2

Tavolla, La, Mt., 222

Taxis, 38; (Giglio) 234

Tennis, 71

Terme San Giovanni, 64–5

Terra, La, 219

Tipping, 68–9

Topi Island, 193

Torricelli, Mt., 196

Tourist Agencies, 59–60; (Giglio) 234

Travel Documents, 36–7

Troppolo, Il, 212, 219

Turkey and the Turks, 106, 109, 155

Tuscany, 28, 30, 79, 85, 99, 105, 110–11, 113–14, 116–17, 128, 143, 161–2, 186, 238

Valdarna Valley, 183

Vallebuia Valley, 108–9

Valles, Count, 113–14

Vegetation, 29, 78, 83–4; (Giglio) 236

Villa San Martino, 31, 71, 122, 166, **170–2**, 227

Virgil, 99

Viticcio, 32, **173–4**, 175

Volterraio, 31, 99, 103, 105, 107, 109, 132, 176, 178, **179–80**, 198

Walewska, Countess Marie, 122–3, 186, 218, 222

Walking, 31, 37, 63, 148–50

Waterloo, Battle of, 125, 128, 162, 166

Weights and Measures, 75–6

Wines, 66, 68, 140, 144–5, 210; (Giglio) 242–3

World War I, 128–9

World War II, 129–30, 139, 154, 159, 174, 201–2

Zanca, 212–13, 221; Promontory, 136